THE GREAT AWAKENING

Volume - II

A series of superbly informative and prophetic messages, downloaded and transcribed originally as newsletters by

Sister Thedra

These precious messages are reprinted herein.

Copyright © 2020 by Halls of Light, LLC

All rights reserved. This book or any portion thereof may not be reproduced or used in any manner whatsoever without the express written permission of the publisher except for the use of brief quotations in a book review.

ISBN: 978-1-7363418-4-1

CONTENTS

Mission Statement iv

A CALL TO ARMS 1

WONDERFUL NEWS 17

THE STAR MAKER 37

FROM JUDY IN SPIRIT 79

THE PLANES OF SPIRIT 125

PART I: THE CELESTIAL CITY IN THE SUN 161

PART II: THE PHILOSOPHY OF HEAVEN 171

PART III: THE SECOND COMING OF THE LORD 187

CLOSING NOTES 195

A TIME-TABLE OF CHANGES 231

Mission Statement

Give the truth to the world. Let it be received where it will. Many will read the messages. Some will accept the truth, others will read through curiosity, a few will ridicule. Yet to all is the truth given, and to all remains the power of choice.

The hope of the world in these times is in spiritualizing all forms of activity---promoting understanding through love and service. These must be the watchwords if the world is to come into lasting peace. We are trying to influence a world that is going astray and could cause undreamed of suffering. We are trying to overcome the thought of materialists and to bring a spiritual outlook into the earthly life. We need the help of all on earth who can think in spiritual terms. The great battle to be fought now is between the spiritual and the material, between idealism and carnalism. You can help by spreading the word---we are asking that you help because the battle may be long and the victory far away.

Halls of Light is not allied with any sect, denomination, political entity, organization, neither endorses nor opposes any cause. There are no dues for membership. Halls of Light is self-supporting through its own voluntary contributions. Halls of Light has but one purpose: to help through encouragement and understanding...

To contact the publishers or to obtain copies of our other books, please contact us at email: goldtown11@gmail.com

Esu Jesus Sananda

This reproduction is from an actual photograph taken on June 1st, 1961, in Chichen Itza, Yucatan, by one of thirty archaeologists working in the area at the time. Sananda appeared in visible, tangible body and permitted His photograph to be taken.

A CALL TO ARMS

These newsletters have always contained Sananda's words, just as it was given to Sister Thedra. In the last newsletter we printed transcripts of talks which Sister Thedra gave on Mt Shasta, and since then I have been thinking about this next newsletter and what it would contain Since the work has always been directed by Sananda, through Sister Thedra, I wanted only that it continued according to his wishes, not mine.

One night several months ago, I was awakened at about 2 a.m, and as I lay awake I found my thoughts focused on specific things which Sananda has said to us. As more and more of his words came into my thoughts, a picture began to emerge of the foundation which he has been trying to awaken with each of us.

He has given us the "Keys" time and time again, yet it is only through our own efforts that we use those keys to open the door to greater understanding. For over an hour this picture filled my thoughts until finally I got up and wrote down the outline.

The next day I began typing up this newsletter, yet I was not convinced that I wasn't just putting out my own interpretations. I remembered Sananda's words to Sister Thedra, saying: "*You are the needle... I am the thread which shall sew all this together. By nine own hand shall we continue that which hast been foreseen and recorded... So be it and Selah*". Wanting to be certain, I set it aside and asked Sister Thedra for conformation that it was compatible with her wishes and with the work as directed by Sananda.

Within a few days I received a call from a woman who is very trustworthy. She told me that Sister Thedra had come to her and ask her to take a letter, which she was to forward to me. As if to set any apprehension aside, it contained references to things which only Sister Thedra and I would understand, and also ad dressed specific questions I had silently asked of her only days before. The following is an excerpt from that letter:

"...How often my thoughts correlate the job-at-hand with both the serenity and the sometimes emotional chaos of our work and time together. Many times, while there, I wondered if my work was as effective as we thought at the time we placed our hands in the Father's and trusted His wisdom and compassion for our brothers and sisters on earth.

How often my mind consoles you as you travel on to new vistas, different thoughts and procedures. Please know that the blessings that are mine to give I send freely and with unconditional love in my heart of hearts. Know that I am ever with you, just as we were of one mind on earth as far as the plan for the over-all mission.

Now, as to my continues efforts in that regard... Please remember, that the promise my covenant with the Holy Father embraced while there, still encompasses my devotion to truth and light. A suitable channel for the combined effort of bringing the heavenly perspective and my earth perspective as Sister Thedra together, has not satisfactorily manifested.

Several false starts have been in progress, but please do not fret over this. All is in divine order, and the end times will proceed as planned by the Most High Father of all. Your efforts have continued the work which I began, just as you put forth the energy into distribution and personal support in my years on the physical...."

"...I am now occupied going about "my Father's business" on a different plane of existence, yet my ties with the earth and the transformation, which for so many years I gave my all to help facilitate, still keeps a portion of my consciousness. It is an honor to be so concerned for a corner of the Father's kingdom that one lowers ones vibration to communicate with ones brothers and sisters on lessor planes of life. Does not the Master do this daily? It is my heart's desire to continue to concentrate a portion of my attention and love toward my brothers and sisters of earth....

"...Know that I am with you always... I am only a thought away. Does not the Master Sananda himself do this? Can I, who served him *lo these many lifetimes on earth and elsewhere, do less? I ask you to contemplate this on my behalf and yours as well."...*

... "The work continues. Many around the earth flourish through the seeds which you and I planted and continue to sow in the hearts and minds of men. I assure you of this, as I envision it with the capability of higher perspective."

ALL THIS COMES FROM THE FATHER'S BOUNTY AND LOVE. I HOLD IT IN MY HEART OF HEARTS, AND SEND IT TO YOU WITH LOVE ETERNAL...

Over the years, we have all been given much in formation through the hand of Sister Thedra. During those years many great beings have given their time and their energy that we might begin to see the Truth of our existence, the greater reality and purpose of life itself.

They have tried to help us to understand the darkness and falsehoods which have clouded our lives and our perceptions, which has kept us from seeing the truth of life as it truly is. They have also tried to help us to understand the spiritual awakening process by helping us to see the spiritual nature of life itself.

We have often been told that they are giving us the truth a portion at a time, in order that we might understand it as we go along. After a while those pieces should begin to fit together, and we should begin to awaken to the "reality of what they are saying... to awaken to the greater purpose of our lives here on earth. This newsletter is an attempt to put some of those pieces together, to try and view the greater picture.

The outline was to begin at the beginning, the very "Source of life itself, and go outward into creation to our own lives here on earth. But the most important point was... that this is not about the words or information, it is about the TRUTH which the words are trying to awaken within each of us... to awaken our memory of where we came from, of why we are here, and where we are going.

- - -

THE SOURCE - THE FATHER - THE SON
THE CREATION - THE ORDER OF MAN
- OUR SOUL, OUR CONNECTION -
- THE DARKNESS & THE LIGHT -
- THE SIFTING & SORTING. -

- - -

The Source

To begin at the beginning we need only look to the Source of all Life...

But for one moment, just think of what it would be like if "Life" did not exist... never existed... ever! Not just you or me, or life here upon the earth, but if the very CAUSE of life itself had never existed! If Eternity held only the silent voice of darkness!

Just think about it...

But to our joy, "Life" does exist. It Always has and Always will, because there exists that mystery of mysteries, which is the "Source" of all life. Call it what we will, it is simply the "Source" from which all life comes forth. It is the very CAUSE behind the Light that stands apart from the dark void of eternity, and it sends forth the light of life, marking the center of all Eternity as "Here and Now". And since each one of us know "Life", then that which we feel and ARE at any given moment, is coming forth directly from that "Source" in that same instant. We cannot exist "outside" of life itself... and likewise we cannot exist outside of the "Source" of that life. We are ONE with it... we are that Light.

The light within a light bulb comes not from the bulb itself... but from the "Power" which flows through it from the massive generator which lights all bulbs. The "Source" is that unfathomable generator of Life itself, and we are like the bulbs that shine forth that light as Life itself. The thinner the wire (the connection) the dimmer he light... the greater the wire, the greater the light.

Our "connection" to the Source of all life is our Spirit. The more we awaken our Spirit, the more we strengthen that connection... and to strengthen that connection allows greater life, greater light, to flow through each of us. We see ourself as separate entities only because we have "forgotten" our Source, but when we put forth the effort to "reawaken" our spirit, we re-awaken our Oneness with all of life. That is the spiritual awakening process which is now going on here upon the earth... yet there is more to it than just Source and creation. The following is an excerpt from newsletter #56...

The Source - The Father

ccc This ye shall recognize as mine Order, for I come on behalf of my Order which is ONE with the ♪♪♪ and the ♛♛♛. For we, as the three, are ONE... One of mind, intent, and purpose, in the light of the One which ye call God. We call It "Father", Source of being, for in this Source we have our being; unto this Source of light we owe our life, our allegiance; on this Source we rely. We are of it and in It - It sustains us. This Source we call Solen Aum Solen. There is no greater name, no greater sound than this, for this be that which brings forth great reverberations throughout the cosmos.

(Note: We are told "Solen" means "Ensouled within"... within all that IS.)

The Father - The Son

From the thought of Solen Aum Solen was made lesser light (a being - the Father) yet of the same and only Source, for there is but one "Source" of life. From this thought (The Father) was made or created a being (The Son of the same Power and Substance as the thought set into motion. From this motion another thought created a likeness of the first being (now two Sons). These two Beings were also set into motion, which in endless ages took form, yet not dense bodies of flesh and bone.

Another period of creation came about by this breathing in out, in which these two took upon themself another change, wherein they became aware of themself as ONE, of One Source. This Source gave unto them free will, and as they became creatures of the will, they desired to create as the Source, in Light and Power.

The Son - Creation

Now, we have the two (Sons), as separate entities with free will... each empowered with the Power to create. One chose to create material substance (matter-worlds), the other to give of himself that other entities be sent forth even as he, in light body yet aware of the Source. This one, now aware of his being, his Source and Power, surrounded himself with many light beings (the Angelic Orders) with no will of their own, only to serve the Source of all light and energy. These creatures (Angels) were of light and energy, and the purpose of their creation was to serve the one which chose to give of himself that others might come forth as he..."

... "Now in this period these first two entities which emerged within the ALL, became two sperate entities. One was given the mind to create planets, systems of star patterns, and fashion the heavens about, which is called the firmament. The other was given the privilege/gift of overseer, the "Guardian Spirit"..."

Man

Now, within him (The Son) the desire to create like unto the source became manifest as a conscious entity which was called Man. This Man became, after aeons of countless changes, a creature prepared to take physical form, a dense body (of flesh). This became an age in which man was given free will, and a plan on or in which to work as he progressed...

Now, many of us have read that message previously, but did we perceive what they are saying? If we understand it correctly, we come to see that the Source is just that, the "Source"... the CAUSE of life itself... from which all life comes forth, and which sustains all life in each and every moment. It is the mystery of mysteries, unknowable and unfathomable. It is the Source of ALL, and it sustains All... yet it, in and of itself, is not the "creator" of the universe as we know it.

The Creator, as they refer to Him, is the Father for although He is ONE with the "Source" itself, He is an individual Spirit, the "Creator" who brought forth life as we know it.

And from the Father was created the "first born, the Son who, even like ourselves, went through "Ages" before taking form and again "another period" in which he became aware of himself as of One Source. It was he, this Creator Son, who 2000 years ago took on physical embodiment as Jesus, and who is now called Sananda... he was of the first born of the Father, yet he is also our Elder Brother, in that we are of the same Source.

The following excerpt will explain it further.

Excerpt from Newsletter 61

The "Source"

In the beginning, "Source" breathed forth a thought of pure light, (as a being) which we the Awakened Ones know as "Father". First the thought, second the stirring within the Father/Mother womb or Matrix.

The Father\Mother

These did not have bodies of dense matter, they were of pure light, yet with all the attributes of the ALL ,the "Source". They had the mind of their Source and also the endowment of the Source, such as Power to create buy thought.

The Son

From this step in creation, in timeless spaceless existence, was created by thought, one which went forth into the ethers (The Son) as a conscious Entity/Being. This one divided and became two, yet this one remained ONE of mind and spirit, yet two. This pair was endowed with the individual awareness of Self, and the power to create in the Fathers likeness. These are now known unto thee, mine beloved, as Sanat Kumara and Sananda. These are known as the "First Born" of the Father, yet there are none in mortal form which can tell this unspeakable story of The Beginning. Even the greatest of parables are not sufficient, therefore by one feeble step at a time ye awaken from thine deep sleep...

- end except -

From the previous messages we might understand that "*In the beginning, "Source" breathed forth a thought of pure light, which the Awakened Ones know as "Father".* Therefore from the "Source" came forth a being which is called "Father", a being which we refer to as God the Father, the Creator, possessing all of the attributes of the Source, yet personified as an individual spirit.

From the Father was created the "First Born" Sons... an "Order" of beings, who, even like ourselves, went through a period of development before coming to understand their Oneness with the "Source". And it was through this Creator Son that the entity called "Man" was brought forth.

As Man, we too are now going through our time of development, coming to understand our own Oneness with the Source... yet it was through him, the Creator Son, that the entity called "Man" was brought into manifestation... therefore he is called "*The Lord God*, for he is "Lord" of, and responsible for, that which he has brought forth. And although we ALL (The Father, The Son, and The Creation) know life because of the "Source" itself, yet it is the individual "spirits" which are The Father and The Son who seek to guide us in our development as Man, in our upward ascent.

I would also like to add here a few excerpts from. the book by William Dudley Pelley, entitled *The Golden Scripts*, which will shed further light on this. The following excerpts are from Chapter 91, and are given by the Christ Spirit:

20 When I speak then of the Father, I speak verily of one who ruleth the Host of all Thought Streams... a Spirit so aged that no man knoweth its antiquity.

21 This Spirit in power is beyond even my conceiving, even as I was temporarily beyond your conceiving whilst in mortal flesh.

22 This Spirit exiseth and endureth... older I say than any known to the host of those of whom I have? knowledge. He is not God as men conceive God (the Source itself), nevertheless He is so wise in His conceiving that His power transcendeth that of any spirit projected onto any plane of which we have wisdom.

23 When I say that I am Son of God and refer to the Father, invariably I refer to this Spirit, because with Him I am in touch and know no greater beyond Him.

24 I tell you beloved, I believe others to be beyond Him, but of them I have no knowledge and probably never will have knowledge, for they ever receding (in stature) as we approach them.

37 What I would tell you this hour is this: There is one God in respect that there is a Ruler of the planetary systems. This ruler, I say, is an old, old Spirit, older than any of us have a knowledge.

38 His comings and goings are marked by vast cataclysms, so that stars do perish and reassemble in His presence. Verily is He incarnate in the universe as ye do know the universe of sight and sound, yet doth He dwell in presence upon a far, far planet, greater in extent than your minds can encompass.

39 Behold I do go unto Him for instruction at intervals... a Living Entity who hath so great a power that for Him to speak is for creation to consummate.

49 ... for verily ye do have two rulers; He who was Jesus of Nazareth ruling you immediately, and He who ruleth over the Order of which Jesus of Nazareth is a member and in whose household He standeth well."...

Our Connection - Our Soul

So here we all are as "Man"... yet individual Souls seeking greater understanding of our Source. But for us to somehow envision the Source, we must first realize... that "Life" as it goes forth from the Source is without form... it is the very "Substance" of life in its purest essence... it is pure Light. And that Light goes forth unto all living beings, with unconditional love.

Since our Soul is a "living fragments of the Source itself, an individual ray of that Light, therefore it too is pure in its essence. It is not bound by any form, for it too is formless... it is pure light as consciousness... it is Spirit, having a common bond with all other Souls as Spirit. It is the individual fragment which gives us our identity, as an entity different from all others. And although each Soul comes forth pure, as pure Spirit, and ever remains So... it is also endowed with the gift of free will, by which it may thereafter choose its own course.

Now, if the Soul is pure Light then there can be no such thing as a "dark Soul" or an "evil Soul"... yet there are what are called "dark spirits" or "evil spirits", so how can this be? If all Souls are pure Light then what is the origin of evil or dark spirits?

All Souls are brought forth in the beginning as equal, pure in essence, yet each without distinction. A newly created Soul is much like a new born baby, having all the attributes of life, yet lacking in both self-identity and stamina. An infant acquires stamina in due course, and acquires a self-identity through confrontation with experience. In this same sense, a Soul must develop a sense of its own identity, and also comes to understand the nature of its free will, through experience.

The following is an excerpt from "Star Guests", by William Dudley Pelley:

...*"Know that in the beginning, my beloved, was no form... Intellect was, but man had no image of physical body. Always was he created spirit, by Spirit.*

Know ye that Intellect sought flesh for a purpose. Man had no evidence of "Self in spirit, meaning self as identity... Spirit had no identity as such. Only after long experiences on planes of flesh doth spirit feel itself. This identification cometh through the trial and error of life as mortal being....

...*"Know therefore that man, as spirit, came into this earth-plane to incarnate for continued experience. Men were to know pair and pleasure through earthly senses, and thus gain to knowledge of themselves as separate entities"...*

- end excerpt -

So at some point after its inception, a Soul goes forth into creation and begins to take on embodiments in form, and it progresses upward according to its own development. And as it gains in self-expression it develops an "identity" all its own, a sense of "self", an individual "spirit" all its own, according to its own free will choices. When the "spirit" develops as an expression of its own Soul, it is guided by the Soul, and its nature is that of light, a reflection of the Source from which it came forth.

It expresses life in a positive way, with love and compassion for others, uplifting itself and in its own small way uplifting all others around it. As it goes through experiences in flesh it slowly grows towards maturity, towards "wholeness" within itself, towards the purpose of its own creation. Such a spirit becomes a "bright spirit", a reflection of the Source from which it came forth.

There is an excerpt in "Star Guests" which reads:

"Life was a simple and straight forward proposition to those children of the early days of humanity. But even in the simplest organizations of life there are those who strive to follow what little light they have, and there are those who choose to close their eyes to the light and choose to dwell in darkness"... "Not even Infinite Spirit can explain why this choice is made in the beginning..."

- end excerpt -

The Light within our Soul seeks ever to guide our spirits, for it is the "silent voice' of our conscience which keeps us on an upward course. But when a spirit closes its eyes to the light, and no longer integrates the Soul into its expression, then it no longer expresses the light of its Source. It identifies only with "self", therefore it no longer perceives its Oneness with all others.

It begins to identify only certain peoples or certain beliefs, and often feels justified in mis-treating or even killing others because of "self-centered" beliefs. It lives in darkness, for without the guiding light of the Soul it no longer perceives the difference. Such spirits often wreak havoc and suffering on others through indifference, bigotry, hatred, crime, greed, exploitation, terrorism, war, etc. Some try to justify such cruelty by invoking the name of God... yet there is no Light within their actions or their thinking... they have become "dark Spirits", for they no longer express the light and purpose behind their own creation. They have separated themselves from the light within their own Soul.

But in most, when the sense of separation becomes too great it begins to feel like a "lost soul"... it cry out to God for help, and searches within... and therein finds the light within its own Soul... and it is guided by the Soul back towards unity, for the separation was only in our own thinking. It learns the greatest or all lessons, and once again embraces light and return to its upward accent.

The following is an excerpt from Sananda:

... *"That is why we have ambassadors of Heaven that deal directly; "directly", with the living Soul... and there are ways and means that we have that we quicken, or can I put it another way, attach the spirit to the higher self (the Soul) to make communication. For there is such a thing as man (a spirit) going so low, sinking so low, that his Soul detaches itself. It doesn't have to be for eternity... shall we say it just rests, until that (spirit) which is so deep in the mire of degradation and evil that the Soul has let them go, again <u>seeks the light</u>, because the Soul is "light"...*

- end excerpt -

The Lighted Ones seek ever to guide such spirits back to the light, back towards unity, for they know that these have not yet learned the greatest of all lessons... that life and light are synonymous. Yet despite their love and efforts, there are some spirits who become so defiant, so devoid of light, that they come to believe that they are truly separate from all else. They become so identified with "self" that they come to believe the "self" to be the seat of all power, and willfully embrace the darkness for their own ends.

They seek only for power, and they reject the light of their own Soul, rejecting the "silent voice" of their own conscience, in willful disregard. Such spirits oppose the Light, for they oppose anything which would interfere with their quest for greater power, including the light of truth which would expose them for that which they have become. And since Love is the force which motivates Light, these spirits become "anti-Christ"; for in opposing the Light which he represents, they have become devoid of the Love which would make of all men brothers.

In William DudleyPelley's book "Star Guests" there is a phrase which I find very descriptive. He is told, *"These entities will simply program themselves right out of existence"*. A very suitable term, since these entities choose to go further and further from the Light, until they go backwards unto oblivion. Such too, is the power of free will... for such a spirit literally chooses its own extinction.

Another excerpt from "Star Guests" reads:

"Know that those who hate the Light are devolving backwards into everlasting namelessness... while those who love the light are evolving upward into everlasting transitions of glory, until they are One with the Godhead.

- end excerpt -

Now through all of this, the Soul remains ever untainted by either darkness or evil, for the Soul is created of the very "Substance" of the Source itself... it is Light. It is a living a fragment of the Source, wherein there is no darkness. It is only the spirit (the soul's developing "identity") which has created the separation, and therefore must learn the greatest of all lessons... that Life and Light are synonymous.

Those few spirits who choose to reject that Light are much like the young bud of a rose, becoming so enamored with itself that it willfully severs its connection with the bush upon which it grows... wherein it withers and dies for lack of sustenance... and the Soul simply returns to the Source.

Our Memory

We have all gone through many experiences, within many embodiments on various planes since our inception, yet we find that our memory of these experiences are not retained from one embodiment to the next. We find ourself within this embodiment with no memory of what has come before, yet we are told that our memory is intact, and will one day be restored. So if we do not retain the memory of previous embodiments, then where is our memory?

If the Soul is that which is eternal, then it is the one constant throughout all of the experience that you have ever had. The Soul has recorded the memory of every experience you have ever had, since its inception into creation (which for most of mankind on earth, was over 8 million years ago). We lose our memory with each embodiment because the Soul does not take embodiment - it is our "spirit", our developing "identity" which struggles with the lessons of flesh. And within each experience your free will choices add to the development of your "spirit", for the Soul seeks to guide it towards greater perfection, towards that unity and wholeness.

So when we say that we are seeking to become One with God, what are we saying? How do we really become "One with God"?

If the Soul is a living fragment of the Source, then "Oneness" is the process of becoming One with that which is of the Source... the fragment of the Source which we ARE... our own Soul. Our Soul is our Higher Self which seeks to guide our spirit towards perfection, towards unity and Oneness. It is through this experience that we finally come to understand our "free will"... for we must choose to return to that Oneness. And with the As always, we will guide humanity towards the higher road of the opportunities for the greater good for all. Both works have a powerful and common thread in the tapestry, by being master-minded by my beloved Jesus/Sananda. He is here beside me now, and I cannot tell you in words the glory of it all. When the Blessed Mother Mary cried "My Heart doth magnify the Lord", there is a proximity of my commitment to you and to our work there. So let it Be as it Is.

In Love and Light, Sister Thedra and Sananda... two within the Oneness.

- - -

Sister Thedra and Sananda:

We come in the face of humanity's self-perception of imminent catastrophe, as the world now prepares for the coming tide of transformation. From the race's perception of a world in economic and environmental collapse, there will rise a new nation of people, analogous to the Phoenix rising from the ashes of rebirth. And so continues the tide of humanity's transformation.

In the days to come, light from the sky will fill the hearts of people, likened unto the effect of the Star of Bethlehem and the Angel's appearance to the shepherds of old (*for clarification see "The White Star of The East", recorded by Sister Thedra*). The shepherds were compelled from the depths of their Souls and hindsight to share the glad tidings. Behold, a Messenger brings tidings of great joy!

And so we begin now a journal, which brings tidings of great joy. This "Journal in the making", is to be shared with humanity around the world. Those who resonate with the work of Sister Thedra and The Association of Sananda and Sanat Kumara, will leap for joy in their hearts on hearing the good news that I, Sananda, and my dedicated colleague Sister Thedra, are joined in one heart and mind to bring you the good news".

..."Let us proceed together then, to produce the work which Sister Thedra and I promised you all in the final days of Sister Thedra's life on earth. And so be it! It is time."

- end excerpts -

Since this was received after the newsletter went to the printer I have included it as a supplemental page insert. I thought you would all want to know that yes, Sister Thedra and Sananda fully intend to fulfill the promise which they gave us before her transition, that the work would indeed continue in greater measure.

WONDERFUL NEWS

After first hearing from Sister Thedra many months ago, I began putting this newsletter together. The message from Sister Thedra which begins this newsletter was recorded by a woman who had previously received instruction from Sananda and who is very trustworthy. As I was sitting at my computer completing the final corrections to this newsletter before sending it to the printer, I once again asked for final confirmation that it was in accordance with the will of both Sister Thedra and Sananda.

Within a few minutes the phone rang... it was the woman who had received the first message from Sister Thedra, and she was calling to tell me that Sister wanted to convey to me that "yes, it was in complete accord with both her wishes, and with the work as directed by Sananda". After this newsletter was sent to the printed and the ball was apparently rolling forward, both Sister Thedra and Sananda asked this same woman if she would be willing to continue the work. The following are excerpts from the communique which I received from her:

Note from the recorder: On the morning of Friday, January 27, at 3:30 a.m., I awoke and did a meditation which is my habit on awakening in the night. Sananda and Sister Thedra were very present. We talked, and they asked if I would consider taking on the assignment of Sister's work which she promised to the people who resonated with her work around the world before her transition.

I considered for awhile, and Sananda said, "Will you just try it?". Trying it left me free enough to not say yes or no, but just try it. Sananda asked me to get a pen and paper, and I saw a vision of pages of writing with Sananda sometimes talking, Sister Thedra sometimes talking, and sometimes they were both talking in the same paragraph.

The following are excerpts from those first pages

Sister Thedra speaking:

Ted, you were given instructions from me before I passed from that plane. We may now modify those as the situation with this messenger and your own life circumstances are taken into consideration. We have in mind a compilation of material which we generate from the dimension where my consciousness lives now and material I generated while living on earth, to be received by one who will receive it the way I did while on the earth. In that way the correlation and continuation of the teachings set forth in past years combine with the level humanity is within at this moment. The old/new teachings will outline the pitfalls as well as the opportunities for human choice present as time and evolution move ever onward. In the final union of our <u>Soul</u>, our <u>spirit</u> and our <u>will</u>, there is wholeness... there is Unity... and there is Oneness... and therein is our eternal unity within the Source itself.

The Creation of Souls

Now, although all Souls come forth as equal at the time of their creation, all souls did not come forth at the same time. If the Source of all life has ALWAYS BEEN, then life itself has always been... and "Life" insinuates that there are beings who know and express that life. So if life has previously expressed itself through other beings, then there must, of necessity, be a vast array of beings within a vast number of higher dimensions of life.

There is a quote in "Star Guests" by the Christ spirit which reads:

"25 ... We have spirits here with us upon the higher side, so powerful of knowledge, concept, and constructive emotionalism, that they do transcend even myself who am given the earth as my temporary ruling place. These Infinite Spirits, for I call them such, greater in power than any known to mortal men, have control of the universe as men know it. They are omnipotent and omnipresent in the world and in the universe, ruling it by Thought Projection, and enabling it to function"

- end excerpt -

In one of the previous messages we are also told of the Angelic Orders, who have their existence within higher dimensions... beings of infinite power and understanding. But our focus here is on those who, like ourselves, have previously evolved upward through physical forms, even as we are now doing.

Shortly before Sister Thedra's passing she began receiving the information for a book concerning the origin and development of "Men". Not just mankind as we know it here upon the earth, but what is called the "Order of Man", which had its beginning in the long distant past. Within the Order of Man, she was given specific symbols which represent various "Orders" within the Order of Man. These symbols represent the progression and standing of the various Souls within these Orders, and taken as a whole they paint a much greater picture of "Man" than we ever imagined.

The first and highest of these Orders ℯℯℯ are referred to as our "Elder Brothers, for although they are part of the "Order of Man" just as we of the earth are, these beings underwent their spiritual evolution and grew to maturity within a much earlier cycle than ours. Having gone through the same process that we are now going through, and having come to understand their Oneness with the Source, they are no longer bound within forms of flesh, and now have their existence within the higher dimensions of life. As our Elder Brothers they have watched-over and guided the progress of younger Souls, we younger brothers, throughout this cycle here upon the earth, and they now seek to assist us in our ascent, from the bondage of flesh into greater freedom within the higher dimensions of life, which is our inheritance as sons of God.

It is important that we come to understand these "Orders" if we are to understand the larger picture of who we are as "Man"... yet with limited space in this newsletter, we will leave that for another issue of the newsletter.

Light & Darkness

We have all read the words in "Genesis":

...And the earth was without form, and void and darkness was upon the face of the deep...

...And God said, Let there be Light, and there was Light." And God saw the Light, that it was good... and God divided the Light from the darkness.

Probably the most important thing we will ever come to understand is the difference between Light and darkness. If we seek to understand the Source of all Light, then we must first understand what light is... but before we can perceive light, we must understand the difference between darkness arid light. We use the words Light and Darkness, but do we really understand why they differ? Some people say, without thinking, "*It is all God... light and dark are just two sides of the same coin... its all just an expression of God*". But, are light and darkness then, both attributes of God?

If you Look around yourself, you see light coming from the Sun, from electric lights, from candles, from wherever... but you will notice that light, wherever we find it, always comes from a source... light is always created by a SOURCE. Light does not just exist... it always come directly from a SOURCE. Darkness on the other hand, has no Source... it has NO Source! It is simply the ABSENCE of Light... the void which exists when light is absent. Can darkness then, be an attribute of God? Can the ABSENCE of Light come from God? Since darkness cannot come from a lighted light bulb, then how can it come from the Source of all Light. If darkness can only exist when Light is absent, then darkness is NOT an attribute of God... it is the ABSENCE of God... for God IS Light.

But Light also signifies a "Source" of Power... and since darkness has no Source, it therefore has no "power" in and of itself. It is simply the void created by the absence of light. When you enter a dark room and you turn on a light, the darkness does not struggle with the light, for it has no power to directly appose light. Light always dispels darkness, for they cannot exist in the same space. Likewise, when the light of God, the Light behind all of life, is allowed to manifest within us, all darkness ceases to exist, for they cannot exist within the self-same space.

So who are the dark brothers and what is the dark force so often spoken about? They are those who use the life force, to enhance their own power, in willful disregard. The manifest the life force, yet they reject the light from which it comes forth. They are chose spirits in which the Light of God, is absent. They likewise reject their Oneness with all other beings, for in their delusion they seek only for greater power. And since darkness has no power in and of itself, they can only create the illusion of power, by keeping others in ignorance. Their determination to do this represents the dark force... for they perpetuate darkness to conceal the Light which would expose them for that which they are.

The Origin of Separation

If we look at our own records we see individuals throughout history who would destroy humanity for their own power and gain, with no Love in their hearts. And even though they were each but one man, they created the illusion of power, and the masses (blinded by darkness) followed them blindly to exploit, to conquer, or even to kill whole races of men. In our own nightly news broadcasts we see the masses still following these kind of men, and the bloodshed and carnage wrought by one people against another. Yet this is NOT the intended expression of Life as it comes from the Source... it is the manifestation of dark spirits, a manifestation wherein the Light is absent. But how is it that such dark spirits came to find expression here upon the earth in particular?

All of this, we are told, had its origin in the Lucifer rebellion... but if you are like me, then somehow it all seemed like something in mythology, something archaic, having no connection to the "reality" of our own lives and illusions. Yet we are told that this event forever altered the development of life throughout the Cosmos, but nowhere more than here upon the earth. Therefore, if we are to understand our own situation as man, then we must also understand the "dark brothers" and how they came to be here upon the earth.

The first separation between the "Creator" and the "Creation." seems to have occurred when Lucifer (*one of our Elder Brothers, if you will*) rebelled against the Father, the Creator Spirit from which he himself had come forth. He, Lucifer, was a High Son of God, who had within him the power of creation... yet he became puffed up on his own greatness. He gave unto the Father no credit, and gave unto himself credit for all that he was.

Excerpt from Script #10

... "For he had the power invested within him of God the Father to create even worlds, yea, to create and to populate them"....

... "He was of the Father born, and he had received his inheritance in full, yet he had the audacity to call himself "Father" of all that is and was. He used the Law for his own end, and gave no heed unto the warnings of the Father. And when he, which is called Lucifer, was given the ultimatum, he called together his followers and said unto them: "*Ye have seen my work... have I not created these things, have I not given unto these things life, and have I not been with you these days? If ye follow me I shall make of thee great a wondrous beings*"... And when they gazed upon his handiwork they fell down and did worship him. I say great was and is their sorrow, for unto this day do they pay the price"...

- end excerpt -

Does that sound familiar? It sounds very much like the voice that still drives our "world" today. That same voice still says:

"That "Jesus" stuff is not for you... you are intelligent! Listen to me and I will make you rich and powerful... vanity, greed, self-indulgence, exploitation... are all acceptable because that's just the way life is. Everybody does it?"

Such is still the voice of the dark ones... yet how is it that these dark ones come to be here upon the earth and not on other planets?

Excerpt from Script #10

..."*Now when the war in heaven was but begun, Prince Michael was the one which came forth as the defender of Truth and Justice. It was he which gave unto Lucifer the ultimatum which banished him into the world of darkness. Even then, when the earth was in a different part of the firmament, and before her axis was changed, she was a dark planet, for little light went out from her. Now when this was accomplished, that Lucifer was cast out of heaven to the dark planet earth, he set about to all manner of experiments*".

... "*I say unio thee my child, that unto this day does he make of mortals a plaything. I say he uses Life for his own gratification. He gives no thought of his Godhood which was endowed unto him, and he has been as one imprisoned upon and within the earth for a long period of time.*

Yet, I say he shall be removed forever, and the earth shall be freed from all his pollution, from all memory of him... So be it! He shall be bound in yet another place of darkness, and he shall take with him his legions which choose to follow him. For the earth shall have a new berth (within the firmaments) and a new birth, for she too shall be born again. She shall go through the baptism of fire, and she shall be purified unto the last atom. I say she shall be purified unto the last atom!"...

- end excerpt -

Of this same period, Sananda told Sister Thedra in an unpublished message from 1954:

"*... They were as the time of the experimentalists with the UN (the greater mind) in the sense that they were of the mind to improve upon the work of the creator*".

"The ones who were the scibes (the experimenters), the ones who accepted in the name of the false god scibe, were as ones who were cast down by their own hand, with Lucifer, to their laboratory earth"...

"Unto this day thy treal has been to return to thy Father's house. To many who call themselves "Adamics", it is told that they are the first of these to reach the earth. To this it was cast that they find their way as a carrier, or one who carts himself. There is no savior to cart him, he must be his own. To this we (of the Host) are coming to the earth as ones who have been watching for those who are ready of their own treal (will), to take the sice (imposter) as the sice and the King as the King. To you I have revealed the past. The present is thy heritage. Take thy crown and say "No more will I be a wayfarer of Lucifer. To the home of my Father I returneth..."

- end excerpt -

Keep in mind that there were spirits evolving here upon the earth before Lucifer and his followers arrived here. But since they were young spirits with little light of their own, they were easily influenced by the dark ones. This is referred to in a quote from "Star Guests":

..."It has been many ages since the spirits that have since become known as men, arrived upon this earth-plane, and engaged in creative mischief with the spirit particles developing here, and imbedded qualities into their composition that were never intended to disclose here...

- end excerpt -

I would also like to add here another excerpt from "Star Guests" which read:

..."And at the apex of them all stands a coterie of beings whom we might best describe as Super Angels, of such extraordinary capacity spiritually that they can manifest in any form desired for the accomplishment of their purpose. Lucifer was one of these, and well known is the story of how he used his transcendent powers wrongly. He *is still in existence as an entity, we tell you, but shorn of many of his destructive capacities. He is not loose promiscuously, as so many theologians believe and teach, but is gradually being bound tighter and tighter by the Christ Force, so that he is retrograding gradually into mon-entity"...*

- end excerpt -

This apparently was the event which befouled the natural evolution of the earth. This also was apparently the introduction of the "Dark Ones" into the evolution of the earth... who for many centuries have polluted our thoughts and thinking with a muddle of darkness, falsehoods and untruths... This darkness has also created separation within the populace, in differing beliefs, and in false gods, which are not the "Source", the "First Cause", yet the masses have been hoodwinked into accepting the darkness as the light. They have also created the mind within the masses to ridicule and belittle those who would speak the Truth or represent the light, even unto crucifixion.

But the end of this cycle upon the earth, the end of this age of darkness, is now here. Rays of light are now beginning to pierce the darkness, through the efforts of Sananda, the first born Son, and through his ambassadors of heaven, our Elder Brothers, who have NOT separated themselves from their Source. They are now calling unto each and every one of us to awaken to our true heritage, to our true origin. And those who hear and who choose to turn their attention and thoughts back unto the light will find that NOTHING which is of the dark can hold them back, for light and dark cannot exist within the self same space.

The Sorting

As this age of darkness draws to a close here upon the earth, there is a sifting and sorting process which is now taking place. There are spirits of many varying natures now upon the earth, yet each must now choose their own course, their next environment, be it light or dark. This has been described as "Separating the sheep from the goats"... the difference being, that sheep understand that the shepherd is there to guide them, thus they follow him to greener pastures... Goats on the other hand are defiant, and simply do as they please. Within the information received by Sister Thedra, mankind of earth has been described as being of four distinct natures.

... First are the ones of Light - These are the ones who have come to realize that life has a far greater purpose, and are searching within their own Souls for greater understanding. They are asking for greater light, and are choosing to listen to the voice of the Soul, to listen within their heart. These are no longer willing to accept the darkness or to follow blindly, but are seeking greater Light and are reaching for greater understanding,

... Second are the Sleepers - These are the people from around the world who are basically good people, yet they are asleep. They feel no urge to search for greater understanding, for they are still content within their dreams in flesh. They believe there is a God, yet they are content with false or limited concepts... believing that only the churches or the priesthood have the power to grant them entrance into heaven. They do not yet realize that they are already *ONE* with the Source itself. But the call is now going forth upon the "ethers" for the sleepers to awaken. We are told that when all is said and done that many of these will awaken to the final call, and will come forth seeking greater light. Yet those who choose to keep their fingers in their ears, who choose not to awaken, will pick up where they left off, yet in another place.

... Third are the Laggards - These are the one who have made little progress during their long sojourn here upon the earth. Throughout many embodiments in flesh they have heard none of what has been given for their upliftment. While others sought for what little light was available these "encased" themself within their own ignorance and unknowing, and didn't even want to hear it. These, we are told, will go into the next cycle according to their choosing, to take the course over again so to speak. Within another place and yet another time, they will begin again and once again they will be given the opportunity to go forward in their spiritual evolution.

... Last are the traitors - These we are told are the saddest of the lot, for they are the ones who have repeatedly betrayed themself unto the whole rest of their species. These are the ones who have repeatedly sold out their fellow man for their own power and wealth, for their own gain and glory. Time and time again they have exploited their brothers and sisters, for they care only for themselves. They are also the war mongers, the hate mongers, who have repeatedly come into embodiment time and time again to incite hatred and oppression towards their fellow man, to incite violence and bloodshed, one against the other.

In the book "*The White Star of The East*", we are told:

..."*While they shall awaken in the place prepared for them, they shall have their memory blanked from them and they shall have nothing! By their bare hands shall they scratch the soil for their substance (as primitive man). They shall have no memory of their previous existence, as tho they had none. These shall be the ones which have scoffed and put aside the many warnings sent forth from the realms of Light. These are the "traitors".*

- end excerpt -

In the book "Star Guests" there is also a quote which reads:

..."*If from the beginning you were one of those who had closed his eyes, it shouldn't be hard to understand that so many visits into fleshy form would be necessary to get a desire for Light into the heart that has become inured in darkness.*

Many times, a soul that has constantly chosen wrongly must go back to the earliest form of Man, and join his brothers who are not far removed in consciousness from early animal groups"...

- end excerpt -

Our Creation - Our Harvest

The Life Force, as it comes from the Source, is unqualified, and does not judge our actions. It goes forth with unconditional Love, and it sends forth that Love unto one and all alike. It sustains all alike, be they light or dark. Yet that which each of us "creates", becomes our own, OUR creation, OUR harvest. "*As ye sow, so do ye reap*". The Source sends the Life Force to each of us with unconditional Love... yet that which we BECOME is that which we ourselves have chosen.

For those who would choose light, the process then is turning our attention back towards our Source, of again becoming an expression of life as it was intended to be... ONE with the whole of creation. That is why the Elder Brothers are here this day, that with the closing of this cycle we might finally end our long and troubled sleep in flesh, that we might remember our Source, and the greater light and life which are our inheritance as Sons of that Source, as Sons of God. That is the spiritual awakening process.. that is the awakening. To re-awaken our spirit to our true origin, our Oneness with the Source of all life... the brotherhood of Man in the Fatherhood of God. We are the prodigal Son returning home...

The Laws

We have been told time and time again that all of life is governed by Laws, the greater Laws... the Law of Life. To abide by that Law brings life more abundantly... to transgress that Law brings destruction and death. Lucifer, we are told, understood the Law, yet he used it to his own ends... mankind, on the other hand, continually transgresses this Law because he is ignorant of it, therefore the earth is in the state we find it today.

Within the Scripts (the 73 booklets recorded by Sister Thedra) we are given much about the many facets of The Law, and they are repeated again and again. I have often heard it said that the Scripts are just too repetitious... but that is because we do not hear it the first time or even the tenth time, therefore we do not apply what is said. Despite what we have been told, we somehow believe that greater understanding will just be given to us, or that God will do it for us. But why should we expect help if we are not willing to put forth the effort? How can we say we have read the Scripts and still ask: *What are the Laws?*"

Sister Thedra once said: "*Many call themselves light workers... yet no matter what we might call ourselves we have no excuse in the world for dragging our feet... none! And for the past forty years I have asked many times: Oh God are they all dead out there... And He says: No, they've just got their fingers in their ears.*"

- - -

The majority of people on earth are not of a dark nature, yet few put forth any effort towards greater understanding. Yet even those who are truly searching for greater understanding read through reams of material, and they try to decide what is true and what is not, because we do not yet KNOW the truth. We have been given much information, yet we find that having the information is still not the same as Knowing.

Yet we are told: "*When you are made "whole" your memory will be restored - and when your memory is restored you will no longer "think"... you will KNOW, and you will KNOW that you know*".

Having spent more than 20 years around Sister Thedra, I always saw in her that Light that was unmistakable... it was the light of someone who KNEW, and who knew that they Knew. When someone would come to her for counseling, she would usually ask them: "*What do you know for sure?* They would usually say: "*Well, I believe (such and such)*, and would often repeat what they had read somewhere. She would let them go on until they were finished, and would reply: "*Yes, I have read that book too... but now tell me... What do you know for sure.*

She used to say: *Knowing is not an opinion or a belief, it is knowing what Is... it is letting go of "opinions" and seeking to know what IS... Don't just believe something, but seek to KNOW what IS.*

Notes

In the past, Sister Thedra would record the words as they were spoken to her, and I would send them out to all of you in these newsletters. She was tine "connection" through which they spoke to us, but the purpose was to awaken that connection within each of us. Thousands of pages have been given in the Scripts, in newsletters, books, and manuscripts, but we must put forth the effort to understand the Truth within them. What I have tried to do in this newsletter is simply to focus on that which is spoken of within the Scripts...

The Source - The Father - The Son - The Creation
The Order of Man - Our Soul, Our Connection
Darkness & Light - The Sifting & Sorting.

I have tried to express it in words that would make you think about it... because the Truth is not written upon these pages... it is within each one of us, within our own hearts and Souls, for that is where our life truly exists. It is not simply in reading the words, but in going beyond the words to the "Living Truth" which they represent.The "Source", is not just a word or something in some far off place... the "Source" of all life is there, within each of our lives and in all life around us in every single instant. We need only put forth the effort to "awaken" - to "remember" the direct connection, and therein the separation ceases to exist... forever.

The Light so often spoken about is there within each of us, but we must put forth the effort to see it. Yet too often we look "outside" ourselves for something spiritual, for something or someone who will do it for us. But the "living fragment" need not look to others, nor need it look to "things" such as Crystals, Pyramids, vortexes, lay lines, star names, UFO's, or anything else in order to be spiritual. The "Living fragment" need only look to the "Source" of the very life which it IS... for therein is all that we seek, and all that we will ever seek.

Therein is the awakening of our own direct connection... our Spiritual awakening

Excerpts by Sananda

I have given unto thee commandments (within the Scripts) which ye have not lived to the fullest. And ye shall this day begin thy search for the key which lies within these commandments. And ye shall be as one which has betrayed himself when ye pass them by lightly. I say, ye shall turn back each and every page and find them one by one, and practice them until they become thy very nature. I say this is thy key into the secret place of the Most High Living God, for none enter into His place of abode' unprepared. So be it that He has accepted thee, and yet ye shall not enter unprepared.

* * *

Too I say: This is the day of preparation, and I say all within the place wherein I am, have come that ye may be brot in, yet ye and ye alone shall prepare thyself. And when ye are so prepared one shall come unto thee and give unto thee as ye are prepared to receive

* * *

Each one has his own will - it is not lawful that I trespass on that gift so freely given. Now it is come when each and every one shall choose his course. He either chooses the hard and dangerous way of darkness, or the sure and safe way of light in which I abide. Thus I am prepared to bring everyone which gives unto me his hand willingly. I ask of no one anything except obedience unto the Law of the ONE I have spoken of this Law... simple it is, and often overlooked.

* * *

And now it is given unto them which seek Truth to be given these things which shall be unto them their Shield and Buckler within the days ahead. For now I say unto thee, "Unless ye ask, it shall remain hidden" and therein is wisdom. For it is the Law that when ye are ready ye ask, and the Father stands ready to supply thy needs. And it is such that not one shall be forgotten or overlooked, for there are many within thy midst which can pluck thee out at any moment and give thee that which is necessary unto thee.

And so shall ye seek within thine own self for the Light, that ye may be alert unto thy brother's Light. For light is like unto itself, it attracts more light - and for that have I made myself manifest unto them which have sought me. And as they have sought me their light has expanded, and it has been added unto mine that the whole Earth might become a sun. And therein is great revelation unto thee, for as the man of Earth is lifted up so is the Earth that she might fulfill her mission. And be ye fruitful unto The Father, for He has given thee permission to be within the Earth for the fulfilling of this age... and that is a privilege given unto thee of God The Father.

And it is given unto me to speak unto thee as I have not for the past years of the "Silent period". And the silence shall be broken in all the lands of the Earth, and again I shall walk the byways and the hiways and be as ye. And as ye come into the age of comprehension I shall sit and counsel thee, and I shall teach thee the Precepts of The Father which has sent me unto thee that ye might awaken unto thy own "Sonship" and be as the wayfarer of Satan no more.

And it is indeed wise to ask of The Father that ye might receive me, for in no wise shall I intrude upon thy free will. And yet it is the will of The Father that I bring thee out of darkness; and for that do I wait that ye may come as ye are called, and by thy own free will. This is for the ones which have as yet not learned the wisdom of saying - "Father, Thy Will be done in me, thru me, by me, and for me" - for therein is the KEY unto thy legirons which have bound thee. Be ye as one which knows wherein ye are bound, and wherein is thy freedom I shall be unto thee bondsman, and I stand ready to loose thee of thy bondage at thy request.

Ye have but to seek the Light which is of the Father.

* * *

Everlasting Freedom

Sori Sori: Mine beloved, I am come at this hour that all mankind be awakened, for it is now come that the sheep shall be separated from the goats. The ones which are prepared for to come with me shall be as ones lifted up, and these shall no more go in to bondage... freedom shall be their portion forever!

I have said, many are now come unto me as mine flock, for they have listened to mine speaking and direction. These are the ones which are the greater light, which shall go where I go, and we shall rejoice that the day of deliverance is come. By thine own will ye shall be brought out. I am declaring unto mankind, that I am come for the purpose of finding the lost and delivering them into their rightful estate. I have given unto mankind many gifts, that they might see and know that there is a greater "Source" in which they are part or have their existence. This is mine intent... to give unto each and every one which has the will and the mind to accept, mine gift of total Freedom.

While I come as man, man has given unto me many names, and fought for their right to bow down before their images of their gods... yet they have given their "little gods" power to destroy and leave them in desolation. I see and know their plight... I Am the "Living Light" they seek. While they profess to know me, they have looked in the dark shadow world for signs and miracles, which are but the lesser manifestation. It is now come when they shall see, hear, and feel the power of the Greater Light in which they have their being.

It is said many times, that there shall be great and sudden changes, which shall be as the will of the Father. Many shall be as ones come alive and remember mine words... yet there shall (also) be the laggards which have stood steadfast and declared their "god" the only one. These which have denied me as the one sent of the "Source" shall find their Images shall fail to give unto them that which they had imaged or hoped for. They shall find that they have been hoodwinked, misled... that they have been as puppets of the lesser gods to whom they have builded great and impressive Altars and prayed for their enemies destruction!

I Come... yet I come not to bring peace! I am come bringing with me a host of lighted beings, and we carry with us the light of the Living God. We need no metals, no armor other than that of "Light", in which All have their being, their Eternal being, which is indestructible. This is that which I would have all mankind know. For this I come, that mankind, mortal man, see and know himself to be as I... ONE with his Source, even as I. I come not to bring unto thee great and fraudulent speeches to deceive thee, that enhance thy greed, thy gluttony, thy hatred for thine brothers with which ye are bound.

I find that ye are seeking solutions for thine woes and thy failure to accomplish that which they think is the answer to Peace. Peace, my dear ones, rests not on peace-pacts designed by man's mortal mind. These so-called solutions are but appeasements... yet even so, he, man, is better for the effort. Many a one hast been sent from the lighter/higher realm to teach and direct/lead him as a nation/country as a whole, in Unity and Brotherhood... one for All, All for one... in Love and Harmony. This is the basis for Peace... which is not in sight at this late date.

I come crying, Come! Come, I have for thee a great gift, <u>Everlasting Freedom</u>, when ye are prepared to receive it. I give unto thee in the many ways, yet the only sure way for lasting peace is... "<u>Love Ye Thine Brother As I Love Thee</u>". This shall be thine code of Arms. Art thou prepared to walk with me? Or are ye content with thine lot? So be it as ye choose! We shall not impose upon thine sacred gift (of free will) ... Sacred indeed it is!

I Am the Wayshower

* * *

From the Fountainhead

Sori Sori: Mine beloved, I am speaking for the good of all, that each one might be prepared for his part in the great plan which is now in operation. There are ones which have heard the word yet not understood the meaning thereof. They have given themself credit for understanding, while they do not see that which is going on about them. They see not the way of the traitors, the bigots, the hypocrites... neither do they see the ones sent of the Source which shall overcome the darkness.

When I say, "There is a time for all things, the sowing and the reaping"... now is the day of reaping, the gathering in. It is not done in one of man's days or even years, yet the ones which have eyes to see shall surely learn that there are changes which are afoot. Be alert and watch with an open eye and an understanding mind, and ye shall be the one to overcome the darkness of unknowing. To learn of the light of the "Source" is to see the Light, to understand the word which I the Lord God give unto mortal man for his well being. He hast but to listen and follow mine way without any preconditioned opinions. Empty out thine cup and ask for pure water from the fountain head, the Source, and it shall be filled... yea, to overflowing...

* * *

The following is an anonymous writing:

The Lamp

"The time alas is come... Let all who know the light go forth, and let the light be seen. For the Lamp is lighted, the time is now, and the working order is: Light Ye Other Lamps...

Go ye forth my carriers. Go ye forth among the multitudes, and let not thy flame be hidden. And those who have spent their time wisely, and who have laid up their lamps with oil, who say unto you: "*Give unto us the Light, that through myself I might cast out the darkness, and be as a beacon unto others*". And Lo, the light shall be given them, and they shall become. But unto those who have foolishly wasted their time, in deeds to satisfy themselves at the sake of all others, who shall say: "*Give unto us the light also, that we too might see the Lord*". Ye shall pass them by as the wheatmen pass the thistles. And when they cry out after you saying: "*Lo, why hast the lord forsaken us, that we are his children*", ye shall turn and say unto them: "*Nay, Nay, the Lord has not* left, but hast been driven out, for it is YE that hast forsaken HE. For even the bud of the Rose, though it captures the whole of the mind's eye, knows that it cannot stand apart from the bush upon which it grows - for were it to sever itself from its source, it would surely bring the wrath of death upon itself, and lay the blame thusly"..

Concerning Sister Thedra

Since the last newsletter, many of you have written asking if we had heard anything from Sister Thedra. We can only tell you that the woman who brought through those first messages is going through personal difficulties in her life at this time, and so far has not been able to commit her time fully to this assignment. We must all remember, that the higher ones never impose themselves upon us, nor do they try to coerce us. They guide us, but they allow us our own choices and await our decision. If all is not in alignment they simply pull back and allow us the time necessary to go forward at our own pace.

In her very first communique Sister Thedra said to me: *Please remember, that the promise my covenant with the Holy Father embraced while there, still encompasses my devotion to truth and light. A suitable channel for the combined effort of bringing the heavenly perspective and my earth perspective as Sister Thedra together, has not satisfactorily manifested. Several false starts have been in progress, but please do not fret over this. All is in divine order, and the end times will proceed as planned by the Most High Father of all.*

- - -

... "In the beginning, "Source" breathed forth a thought of pure Light, (as a Being), which we the awakened ones know as "Father". First the thought, second the stirring within the Father/Mother womb or Matrix. These did not have bodies of dense matter, they were pure Light, yet with all of the attributes of the ALL, the "Source". They had the mind of their Source, and also the endowment of the Source, such as the power to create by Thought"...

THE STAR MAKER

A Glimpse into Eternity

I AM, and because I AM you ARE. I have ALWAYS BEEN and I shall ever BE, for I am without beginning, without end. I am Life itself, for I am the very Source of all that IS. I brought forth all life within me, and I sustain all life each and every instant that it exists. Nothing can exist outside of Me, for I am the Source, the FIRST CAUSE behind all that IS. Great Beings who are Creators in their own right, who have their existence in dimensions of life that are presently beyond your ability to conceive, have brought forth worlds, whole universes of matter... they have populated them with young Souls like yourselves which have come forth from the very substance of that which I AM... Yet ALL have their Being within Me, for I AM the one and only First Cause. Nothing can exist outside of Life, therefore nothing can exist outside of Me, for I am the very Source of Life itself.

There exists, within the vast dimension of the cosmos, beings beyond count... from Great Beings of infinite power whose very thoughts sustain whole universes of matter, to young Souls like yourselves who are just now beginning to awaken to their Oneness with life itself... yet ALL have their being within Me.

ALL are of one substance, the very substance of Life itself... you are all Light! You are of Me, and because I AM you ARE. I was never created... I am the FIRST CAUSE. I AM THAT I AM, the Source of all that IS, WAS, and all that shall ever BE.

Your book of Genesis reads:

... In the beginning, God created the Heaven and the Earth.

...And the earth was without form, and void and darkness was upon the face of the deep...

...And God said, Let there be Light, and there was Light."

...And God saw the Light, that it was good... and God divided the Light from the darkness.

That was in the beginning.

God said let there be Light, and there was Living Light... there was "Life"... and it was set apart from the darkness, for it was Light!

That was the beginning... but it was only your beginning, it was not mine... for I have Always Been, and I shall ever BE.

So ask yourself... what WAS before the beginning, when void and darkness were upon the face of the deep? Did life exist?

I existed, for I have Always Been, and shall ever Be. I was never created, for I AM the First Cause.

The beginning, as you think of it, was only the beginning of time as you know it, for I am eternal. You calculate life in years, but life itself is eternal, for I AM beyond time. The vast unfathomable cycles of time are but fleeting seconds to me, for I am the eternal NOW. To perceive Me you must go beyond time and glimpse the Eternal Now.

In your present embodiment you are 20, 40, 60, 80, maybe even 100 years old - your recorded history goes back 4000-5000 years - you are told that early Man appeared 2-3 million years ago - you are told that the Earth is 4 billion years old - you are told that the universe of matter is 16 billion years old... but where did that matter come from? What existed before that? What existed 20 billion years ago? 100 billion years ago? A trillion aeons ago? Did Life exist?

I existed, for I AM, without beginning, without end. I am the Source of all that has EVER existed, and all that will ever BE. Nothing can exist outside of Me, for I am the First Cause, the ONE and only Source of all that is, was, or ever shall be. All life exists within Me, for I am the source of Life itself.

You exist because you are a part of Me... you exist within Me... for there is only ONE Source. There is only ONE. Look to the very center of all that you are and you will find Me there, for I am Life itself, the First Cause of all that IS. Apart from Me there is only darkness and void, for I am the Source of Light which is Life itself. Step outside of time and look into eternity and you will see only Me, for I Am Eternity itself. Even Eternity does not exist outside of Me, for eternity is an expression of all that I AM.

Did I exist a trillion aeons ago... a trillion times a trillion? Yes... yet I only exist NOW. In me there is only NOW. Time as you know it is only an illusion, a concept that only exists in your own thinking. I am not a concept... I am Life itself... I am Living Light. I AM... I have always been and shall ever BE.

If you let go of your attachment to your limited Identity of "Self" and see yourself as part of Me, in each and every moment, you will then come to live in the here and now, which I AM.

Today you say, tomorrow is coming... yesterday you said this would be tomorrow... but each time you said it you were here NOW. You can only exist here and NOW. Life is only experienced here now, for Life is ever in the present. Life does not exist yesterday or tomorrow, for it is ever present, here NOW.

Does the past exist? where is it... show me! Does tomorrow exist? Where is it... does it live? Yesterday and tomorrow hold no life, for they are only memories and concepts in your thinking... for Life is ever present, and ever shall it be. Events may pass or events may be in the future, but events are not life, they are only the circumstances oi life... they are not life. Life is ever present, and ever shall it be - for I am ever present, and ever shall I be.

So if I am ever present and only "time" had a beginning, then when did Life begin? Genesis tells you that in the beginning God created the heavens and the earth, but did he also create Life? Where did Life begin? Did life exist a trillion aeons ago Yes, life existed a trillion aeons ago, yet it was the same life as the present... continuously present.

If you let go of your concepts of time you will see that before the beginning of "time" I existed... other beings existed also, for they too were beyond time, in the eternal present. Yet they existed only because I exist, they existed within Me, for I have always been and shall ever be the First Cause behind existence itself. When you truly perceive Me within Eternity, then you will also perceive me here within all that you ARE, for I am ever present. And when you truly perceive me Her and Now, you will also be looking into Eternity without beginning, without end. Creation changes yet I change not. I am eternally the same, for I AM ever the First Cause of all that IS.

You know life in this instant because you ARE of the substance of that which I AM. You are part of Me, for there is only ONE. You are Light, and have set you apart from the darkness, for you are Light. You do not yet realize it, for you are asleep in flesh, believing you are flesh. But you are no flesh. You are Spirit, you are Living Light, for you are of Me and I am not flesh, yet all flesh exists within Me, just as you exist within Me.

You, as an individual identity, did not exist a trillion aeons ago, yet that which you ARE existed, for you are of Me, and I have always been. A trillion aeons ago is but a moment to Me, for I am eternally here NOW. I am the ETERNAL NOW, for am life, and life is ever present and ever shall it be I created time for you, yet I am beyond time... I am always present.

Man searches for Me in the past, in persons of the past, in beliefs and in writings from his past... yet I do not exist in the past, I am eternally present, even as life. When man lets go of the past and seeks Me as I AM in the present, at the center of all that he IS, he shall find Me ever present.

So what existed before this present cycle of "time" was created? Being flesh, and viewing Life within limited concepts of flesh, it is impossible for you to see that which is the eternal order, the Grand Cycles of life, so I will put it into a concept that might let you glimpse a random possibility.

Stretch your minds a little and ask yourself what was Life before your present cycle... in those vast incomprehensible cycles so long past that whole universes have been created, served their purpose, and have turned to the dust from whence they came?

Well perhaps... and just perhaps... in a cycle that is so far distant, so long past in cosmic time that it is beyond anything that you could possibly comprehend... that a fragment of that which I AM, this very fragment which now speaks to you, was then as you are now... a young Soul just beginning its journey, thinking itself separate from all else, not yet aware of the First Cause, and not yet aware of its own Oneness within ALL THAT IS. Perhaps it too began its journey in a creation somewhere in the vastness of the cosmos.

Perhaps it too may have evolved upward through various forms, though infinitely different from that which you now know. Perhaps it too went through its early experiences of separation, until it came to realize that it was more than form... it realized it was Spirit. Perhaps it went beyond form and became a spirit, and thereafter dwelt within those higher spirit planes as it grew into greater and yet greater realization of the infinite vastness of life itself. Perhaps for countless cycles it existed as a spirit, wherein it grew in awareness, grew to reflect greater and yet greater Light. Then, as the vast cosmic cycles continued on in their endless journey, it grew in spirit into even greater understanding of that which it was... it transcended even the lofty planes of spirit and came to realize that there was more... it came to realize that it was more than a spirit, it was a living Soul... it was pure Light, a living fragment of the very the Source itself... it was Living Light!

Perhaps it finally went beyond the spirit planes, moving into greater and yet greater dimensions of life, where awareness expands to include whole regions of the cosmos, which included not only the myriad of spirit planes associated with each planet, but the higher dimensions of life beyond all planets, beyond all form. Perhaps it dwelt within those greater dimensions beyond all matter, beyond all form, as it perceived yet greater and vaster expressions which lay yet above it, greater dimensions to explore and to experience as Life ever unfolded in its majestic plan. Perhaps through untold cycles it moved ever upward through cycles so vast and ancient as to seem comparable to eternity itself, yet ever upwards in ever greater experiences and expressions of life. Perhaps it finally came to know the very essence and magnitude of creation itself, and therein participated in creation... wherein it came to realize that it could create nothing outside of itself, for there exists only ONE, and it was part of that One.

Perhaps through these eternal cycles it finally transcended all need for individuality. It let go of individuality and allowed all that it was to flow back into the First Cause, the Source of all that it was... that mystery of mysteries, the unknowable, unfathomable First Cause, wherein there is only ONE... which now included the sum total of all that it had ever been and known, on all planes and in all dimensions it had passed through on its return to the God-head. The drop of water had merged back into the Ocean from which it came, yet it added to that Ocean all that it had become in its journey.

Perhaps countless cycles again came and went wherein it was simply ONE with the very Source from which it had come. It was without form or individuality, yet it somehow still was... for it had finally awakened as the First Cause itself. Perhaps it thought that this was the end, the ultimate climax to Life's grand expression.

Ah, but not so! That was but one of the Grand Cycles of Life. A new cycle was to begin, and it was to come to know this as just the beginning. The whole process which it had known was simply one of an endless number of Grand Cycles... the out-breath and the in-breath of the First Cause. Each out-breath is sent forth by 'Thought", which begins and ends all movement... first the Thought then the movement.

The Thought is the pattern as the Breath of life moved out into the Cosmos, out into those regions where only darkness and void were on the face of the deep. Therein, after many cycles, a universe of Star systems, of Suns and Worlds come into being, including the countless planes of spirit... all brought into manifestation by the Thought. When the entire universe of matter has actualized into manifestation according to the Thought sent forth... and as that cycle of the out-breath neared its completion and all was ready, a group of young Souls, which included the very fragment which now speaks to you, went forth into that creation to begin its development. It went outward and after numerous smaller cycles finally took on form, though not flesh as you know it. With each new cycle it developed upward, each time developing a greater and ever greater awareness of itself.

When the Thought had manifested to the very last detail, bringing forth creation as it was to be within that place, including the Souls that were to inhabit it, then the out-breath ceased and the in-breath began... the in-breath, when all Souls within that creation would began their journey back towards their unity with the God-head.

Thus did this fragment which now speaks to you began its journey in ages long past. And within the in-breath of that Grand Cycle it would reach the maturity of that cycle and returned to the God-head from which it went forth.

Know that there are cycles within cycles, countless smaller cycles that exist within greater cycles... and countless greater cycles within each and every Grand Cycle. With the final completion of each Grand Cycle there is a cycle of rest within the cosmos, yet it too ends and a new cycle begins. A new cycle for all those who had completed their return within the previous Grand Cycle.

I, who now speaks to you, was that fragment... and as that fragment I returned to the God-head from which I had come. Yet, I was to go outward into creation once again within the next out-breath... yet this time it would be My Thought which would pattern it. As ONE with the Source, it would be I who would send forth the Thought which would manifest within that out-breath... wherein an entire universe would become my "form", and the billions of new Souls which would inhabit it would express my "individuality".

We would be ONE, just as I am ONE with He who sent me forth. The breath of life would once again go out from the First Cause, sent forth by my Thought, into a region within the eternal expanse of space, wherein "darkness and void were upon the face of the deep". I would say: *"Let there be Light, and there would be Light." And I would see the Light, and see that it was good... and I would divided the Light from the darkness....*

There I would bring forth planets, Galaxies, and Star Systems, and I would be the Father of your creation, just as another had been mine... yet in truth there exists only ONE, the one and only First Cause wherein we all have our being. I would create a cycle of time and a plan for the unfoldment for all young Souls conceived therein. The Angelic Orders, who are of Light Substance, with no will of their own but to serve the Source of all Light, would guide and assist in the great over-all plan. I would be the Father behind the out-breath, the Thought behind the creation... yet it would be vastly different from all that had come before, for Life never repeats itself, and never will.

Perhaps... and just perhaps... a trillion aeons ago I sought to know The Starmaker, only to become The Starmaker... wherein I not only created Stars, but a universe full of potential Starmakers. And so it would go... on into Eternity... Worlds without end!

Foolish you say? Surely, as a lowly being seeking for understanding, you will never become a Starmaker!

Look around yourself! Look at Life as it ever moves forward. Life never stagnates or stands still. So where would you have it stop? At what point would you say: *"I am finally there... I have reached the totality of my expression, of all that I can ever be. This is my highest expression, therefore I will remain here forever, without change.* Wherein do you see Life without change?

Too, look around yourself. Does the First Cause produce each and every new generation? Does not the present generation of trees produce the seeds for the next, and does not each new generation produce more beautiful blossoms, with sweeter fruit which contains the seed for the next generation? Are you not greater than the trees?

Did not the past generation of humans bring forth this generation of children, and will not the present generation of children grow to maturity and bring forth the next generation? As above so below. Children are brought forth by parents... parents by grandparents... grandparents by great grandparents... As Above So Below!

So too did the past Starmakers create the present Starmakers. So too do the present Star- makers now create future Starmakers... and so it would go... Worlds Without End.

With each new out-breath, Souls would go outward into manifestation, to experience ever greater aspects of creation... and with each new in-breath that which went out would return to its Source, yet vastly greater than when they went forth, in an endless expression of Life, ever upward. With each new Out-breath would come forth new expressions, yet each one as individually unique as the individual fragment which sent it forth in the beginning. Each vast and incomprehensible cycle creating billions of potential Starmakers, wherein Life would express itself in an endless array... Worlds Without End!

For you on your world this is the great change spoken about. Within your lifetime you will experience the cessation of the out-breath and the beginning of the in-breath, beginning your journey back towards the God-head. The magnitude of this change is presently beyond your comprehension, but soon you will know. Those of you who so choose will step forth from the darkness which now clouds your vision, into a Light so glorious that it is beyond your ability to comprehend presently. That Light will dispel all darkness, and you will KNOW that your journey homeward has begun.

Realize, that it is a very long journey, this return journey... so long in fact that whole Star Systems shall return to the dust from which they came. Yet when that Light breaks through the darkness of your present lives, the Light which is now beyond all comprehension will fill your every breath with joy. It will accompany you forever afterward, and you will soon find that the greatest joy will be in the very journey itself.

Be glad... for as sure as the sun will rise on the morrow, this great change is coming.

If you have now begun to see that which I have said, you might ask: "But a trillion aeons hence, what of the next out-breath? When My Sons and Daughters are as I am now... what will I be? What will that next cycle hold as My expression?

I cannot say, for I am here now, just as I AM. But Eternity! Oh, wonder of wonders! Life IS Eternal! It has ALWAYS BEEN and will EVER BE... for there exists that mystery of mysteries, the First Cause behind all that IS.

As for those eternal cycles beyond creation... they are known only to those who have gone through them in eternity past. They are presently incomprehensible to Me, even as the First Cause is ever beyond all comprehension, even to them... for it simply IS the unfathomable Cause behind all that IS... without beginning... without end.

Oh Wonder of Wonders... Oh Glory of Glories... Mystery of mysteries! Life is Eternal. Life just IS... and EVER SHALL IT BE SO!

* * *

The following words of the Christ Spirit are from *The Golden Scripts*:

> *Abide ye in me and fear not that I shall fail you I say unto each of you...there is too much business of a vast importance for harm of a petty nature to inflict its spiteful mischief on you. We are brethren for a purpose. There are worlds in the making... I say lives untold shall exist and perish on them. We go upward through the cycles... we do mount world upon world... and behold the day cometh when we reach the Father's mansion. We are brethren I say, for the Program Eternal.*

- end excerpt -

In the last Newsletter we looked at the pathway of creation, from the Source, outward into creation, to our own lives here upon the earth.

THE SOURCE - THE FATHER - THE SON
THE CREATION - THE ORDER OF MAN
- OUR SOUL, OUR CONNECTION -
- THE DARKNESS & THE LIGHT -
- THE SIFTING & THE SORTING -

Now, if we were to stop right there, and we were to awaken the "living reality" of that foundation within ourselves, individually and as a whole, it would probably be all that we would need to transcend the bondage of flesh. Many of you have written to say you truly profited from Newsletter 70, and have asked when 71 was going to be sent out. Since the 16 pages in the last newsletter simply would not allow space to go into finer points, this newsletter will go into some of those points.

***

Cycles

We often hear the word "Cycle" in many of the communiques from those beyond our time-frame. They have said that they do not calculate life by years as we do, but rather by events and by cycles. We must realize that these cycles are beyond all time... they are not founded on a given number of years, but rather on a given series of events that will unfold within the progression of that cycle. The cycle is complete only when a given series of events have come to their fullness.

We might plant a garden and tend it as it grows, but who can say on what day the first tomato will ripen, or on what day the roses will first bloom? We know that the rose must go through a certain cycle before it blooms... yet the duration of the cycle depends on many variables such as the soil, rain, sunlight, temperature, etc... which are unknown in advance.

So too with cycles of life... yet there are many lessor cycles and also greater cycles within the Grand Cycles of Creation... and each cycle produces given events which mark the progression of that cycle.

We, as man, have been through many cycles up to this point in our existence, wherein we are now capable of understanding our unity with the rest of creation. The higher ones seek ever to guide us upward, yet Man has free will, therefore none can truly predict exactly what he will do. Ever greater spiritual teachings are given to him within each cycle... when he accepts them, his cycle of development goes forwards... when he rejects or ignores them the cycle proceeds more slowly, until finally he awakens and takes that next step. If no one man is completely predictable, then how predictable are 4 billion men, fragmented by different natures, beliefs, and opinions?

The Father

The message within 'The Starmaker" reflects the Source, the "First Cause" behind each and every being in existence. There is nothing more that I could add concerning that aspect of creation... therefore lets look at the Being who most closely reflects the Source. Consider the following excerpt from "The Golden Scripts", given by the Christ Spirit:

20 When I speak then of the Father, I speak verily of one who ruleth the Host of all Thought Streams... a Spirit so aged that no man knoweth its antiquity.

21 This Spirit in power is beyond even my conceiving, even as I was temporarily beyond your conceiving whilst in mortal flesh.

22 This Spirit existeth and endureth... older I say than any known to the host of those of whom I have knowledge. He is not God as men conceive God (the Source itself), nevertheless He is so wise in His conceiving that His power transcendeth that of any spirit projected onto any plane of which we have wisdom.

23 When I say that I am Son of God and refer to the Father, invariably I refer to this Spirit, because with Him I am in touch and know no greater beyond Him.

24 I tell you beloved, I believe others to be beyond Him, but of them I have no knowledge and probably never will have knowledge, for they ever receding (in stature) as we approach them.

37 What I would tell you this hour is this: There is one God in respect that there is a Ruler of the planetary systems. This ruler, I say, is an old, old Spirit, older than any of us have a knowledge.

39 Behold I do go unto Him for instruction at intervals... a Living Entity who hath so great a power that for Him to speak is for creation to consummate.

49 ... for verily ye do have two rulers; He who was Jesus of Nazareth ruling you immediately, and He who ruleth over the Order of which Jesus of Nazareth is a member and in whose household He standeth well."...

- end excerpt -

There is another excerpt from the Golden Scripts which reads:

10. Whence cometh the Father, you ask? I tell you that no man knoweth, except those Beings older than He in point of understanding.

11. So goeth it... we are creatures of graduations in eternal time. And now we come to the heart of our discourse...

12. It is essential to your missions that ye tell men this: Man hath a responsibility unto the Father, the true God of his species by point of seniority. The Father Himself would have it discharged.

13. Even as an earthly father desires that his sons be like unto himself in attainments, so doth he make them attentive to him that he may increase them in stature by his wisdom.

- end excerpt -

This is the Father of creation as we know it, the creator of all that we are. He is ever prompting all within his creation to become even as He, for within the smallest of seeds is always the pattern and the potential of the tree from which it came.

Too often we struggle with our own growth as though we were the only ones to have ever gone through this process, yet consider the following excerpt from Newsletters 56 & 61, concerning the First Born Sons of the Father:

From this Thought (The Father) was made or created a being (The Son) of the same Power and Substance as the Thought set into motion. From this motion another Thought created a likeness of the first being (now two Sons). These two Beings were also set into motion, which in endless ages took form, yet not dense bodies of flesh and bone. Another period of creation came about by this breathing In\Out, in which these two took upon themself another change, wherein they became aware of themself as ONE, of One Source. This Source gave unto them free will, and as they became creatures of the will, they desired to create as the Source, in Light and Power.

... These are now known unto thee, mine beloved, as Sanat Kumara and Sananda. These are known as the "First Born" of the Father, yet there are none in mortal form which can tell this unspeakable story of The Beginning. Even the greatest of parables are not sufficient, therefore by one feeble step at a time ye awaken from thine deep sleep...

- end excerpt -

Note: Realize that "form" does not always mean bodies of flesh. Those on the high planes of Spirit manifest in etheric "forms", yet still it is form. When Sananda appeared to Sister Thedra, he appeared in visibly tangible form, yet it was not flesh and bone.

So these First Born Sons did not just come forth as creators... they too went through vast cycles of development before taking on form.

After which, they went forward through another cycle of the Inbreath and the Out-Breath, wherein they came to be given free will, wherein they finally came to understand their Oneness with their Source. It was only at the completion of that cycle that they became creators in their own right.

Yet, they did not just go forth and create as they wished. Having become ONE with the Father, they sought to be a part of His creation, to do His will, to bring into manifestation the Original Thought as sent forth by Him in the beginning. They became his hands and his feet that his will might be brought into manifestation through them. This is the essence of asking: *Father, Thy will be done, in me, through me, and by me.*

So at this point in creation, the Son began to manifest the Will of the Father, to bring forth creation as the Father had intended it to be. The Out-Breath was sent forth into creation again... yet this time the Thought was sent forth by the Son... this time the Thought was sent forth from within creation itself, therefore it projected yet further out into the creation... beyond the dimensions of Spirit, beyond etheric form, into denser forms of matter... of Stars systems, worlds, and eventually into flesh itself.

It was at this point that the Order of Man was brought forth, as described in the following excerpt:

The Son - Creation - Man

..."*Now in this period these first two entities which emerged within the ALL, became two sperate entities. One was given the mind to create planets, systems of star patterns, and fashion the heavens about, which is called the firmament. The other was given the privilege gift of overseer, the "Guardian Spirit"...*

Now, within him (The Son) the desire to create like unto the Source became manifest as a conscious entity which was called Man. This Man became, after aeons of countless changes, a creature prepared to take physical form, a dense body (of flesh). This became an age in which man was given free will, and a plan on or in which to work as he progressed...

- end excerpt –

Therein we see the pattern of creation repeating. The pattern of development which the Son followed, we too now follow. Yet as creators they projected the will of the Father into new fields of creation, into Star systems and Worlds of dense matter. Into this universe of matter went Living fragments of the Source itself, as Man... who, after his development would become the hands and the feet of the Father within this universe of matter. When man finally completed his development and awakened to that which he truly was, the First Cause itself would awaken for the first time, as Man, within a universe of matter.

Since Man, first began to take embodiment within forms of flesh, we have progressed upward towards that far-off divine event. Perhaps that is why Sananda has said; "*You are privileged to be upon the earth at this time... and it is a privilege given unto thee by the God the Father*".

The following excerpt is from the book entitled "The Third Millennium", by Ken Carey:

... The coming turn of the millennium will begin the final decade of My awakening into the field of collective human consciousness. It will be the last decade of a process that has taken many centuries. It will be a time of great change, during which a large percentage of humankind will choose to enter this stream of consciousness, leaving forever the realms of history...

... This level of awakening is already complete for some of you. It will be complete for the species as a whole shortly after the turn of the millennium...

- - -

Too often we feel that our entanglements within flesh make us unworthy or incapable of greater understanding. But consider the following excerpt from "The Golden Scripts":

2. Lo, there are millions unto trillions of essences in existence who have passed beyond all sense planes as ye do understand them, but who have not attained as yet to incarnation in universes (of matter).

4. They are not as ye. Great are they verily in concept of knowledge and application of wisdom gained through experiencing, but this thing happeneth:

5. They have failed to perform that which would entitle them to create for themselves that which they would inhabit.

- end excerpt -

The Order of Man

So here we all are as Man, rubbing our sleepy eyes and as we begin to awaken from our dreams in flesh. We are Man - but what exactly is the Order of Man? There is a quote in the Golden Scripts, from the Christ Spirit, which reads: ... Receive ye my presence, all ye who are Worldly! Rise up and rejoice with me... for behold I say unto you... I Am Man as he shall be.

Sananda has often said, "I am your Elder Brother... yet there are also beings within the Order of Man who are referred to as our Elder Brothers... so who are they, and why do they know a far greater expression of life than we upon the earth plane?

Shortly before Sister Thedra's passing she began receiving information for a book concerning the origin and development of "Man". Not just mankind here upon the earth, but what is called the "Order of Man", which had its beginning in the long distant past. Within the Order of Man, she was given symbols which represent specific "Orders" within the Order of Man. These symbols signify the progression of the various Souls within these Orders, and taken as a whole they paint a far greater picture of "Man" than we ever imagined.

The first part of this manuscript was printed in Newsletters #66, 67, & 68. At first it might not be clear just how these Orders fit into our present understanding, but let's take a closer look.

The Symbols

ℯℯℯ The first and highest of these Orders are referred to as our "Elder Brothers, for although they are part of the "Order of Man" just as we of the earth are, these beings underwent their spiritual evolution and grew to maturity within much earlier cycles than ours, long before the earth existed. Having gone through their development and having come to understand their Oneness with the Source, they are not bound within flesh, but have their existence within higher dimensions of life, in a universes too vast for us to presently comprehend. As our Elder Brothers they have watched-over and guided the progress of we younger brothers throughout this cycle here upon the earth, and they now seek to assist us in our ascent, from the bondage of flesh into greater freedom of spirit, which is our inheritance as sons of God.

ℱℱℱ This Order had its origin here upon the earth, and is the next highest Order to the above Order. Although the ones of this Order were originally of the lessor Order described below, this higher Order consists of those who went forward into greater development and understanding, thus they were set apart from the slower ones. This Order is often referred to as the "shepherds", as they have helped and guided those who were slower to develop.

ℐℐℐ This is the third Order, sometimes referred to as the "Sleepers" and laggards. This Order was the first Order upon the earth, and was the first to begin to manifest within primitive forms of flesh. And while it has progressed much during its long sojourn here in flesh, this Order still consists of those who progressed slowly in their development. Despite the unceasing efforts of the above two Orders to awaken them, these have resisted any change through the centuries.

The following excerpts from Newsletter #67, will help us to better understand these orders.

The "Orders" of Man

Be ye not confused unto these Orders of mankind, for they are but the symbols by which ye shall recognize them. We of the 𝒞𝒞𝒞 are the progenitors of the 𝄞𝄞𝄞. We are the parent of the 𝄞𝄞𝄞 which have been the first to walk upright and find that they could use the mind to bring forth like kind of their specie. From these came the next in order, the 𝓅𝓅𝓅... these are now the higher intelligence and of greater understanding of themself. They have now learned to love their progeny and train them. These made greater progression in a shorter cycle of time.

This next cycle begins a new phase of each of these Orders. While they exist as one whole, side by side, each in line teaches the other that they might be the stronger and wiser, prepared to move on unto greater knowledge, greater heights. And for this is the 𝒞𝒞𝒞, the over-all Council, making itself known unto the first of these Orders of Man that they be given their inheritance. They are now being brought into greater awareness of their potential as "Man". They/it (speaking as a whole) shall, within this new period of time, come into the realization that they are of the same Source in the beginning, from the same Spark of Life, the ONE.

However it was given unto the 𝒞𝒞𝒞 to be the progenitors of the 𝄞𝄞𝄞 . This Order 𝄞𝄞𝄞 was the first to walk upright and find itself capable of sound, and pointed the way for the next cycle of time, when they become endowed with greater mental power, as their 𝓅𝓅𝓅 inheritance.

Now it is come when the 𝒞𝒞𝒞 hast made itself known unto the Order of the 𝓅𝓅𝓅 which hast become conscious of their progress here in this cycle in which man hast become both 𝄞𝄞𝄞 - 𝓅𝓅𝓅 walking side by side, with the identical Spark of Life which enables them to progress as living beings, which empowers them to come into the fullness of their specie. From cycle unto cycle the higher Order watches over the lesser as brothers.

Now as I, of the ҽҽҽ, speak for the lesser Order, I say unto thee which have reached this age of accountability and reason, that there are the co-mixture of these Orders within thy present day now. Yet, there are few which now know that they have an inherent ability to grow *within* the Source of all light/life, unto the greater light of all-knowing and freedom from bondage....

end excerpt

In order to understand the whole picture, let us put this into perspective with that which we are familiar with.

Since we are told in Newsletters 66, 67 & 68 that the ҽҽҽ watched and guided the ᎠᎠᎠ-ΓΓΓ here upon the earth as they progressed in their ability to walk upright and to use the mind, and with each new cycle they gave them greater abilities such as speech, reason, mathematics, etc., we might assume that the creation of these Orders coincide with our own findings of early man.

Scientists for decades have studied "Early Man" such as Neanderthal, Homo sapiens, and Cro-Magnon, yet they have been unable to find what they call the "Missing Link" which would show the evolution from one species to the other. In fact science has been perplexed to explain why fossilized findings show Neanderthal as very early man, followed by Homo sapiens, followed later by Cro-Magnon, yet are baffled to explain how this could be, since Homo sapiens were the most evolved, most intelligent of the three.

It is quite probable, from what we have been told, that the "missing link" is not a physical evolution, but rather the genetic creation of a whole new form, with greater inherent abilities and greater capabilities... created by the ҽҽҽ as more progressive forms for early man. This would explain how the ҽҽҽ could be the progenitors of the various species or Orders (we are speaking about physical forms here, not the creation of Souls) meaning they genetically created new forms with greater intelligence and abilities, in-which Souls of expanding abilities might continue to progress. If we, in our limited understanding at present, can genetically alter both plants and animals to produce a product more suitable to our needs, it is not that great a stretch to imaging that ones of far greater understanding might easily create forms more suitable for evolving Man? The following excerpt seems to imply the same:

...It was at this point of their progress that we, their guardians and progenitors came unto the ♂♂♂ to bring out from this Order the most intelligent of the specie. We gave unto these of our energy, insight and desire, and that which would enable them, as individuals, to progress into a higher mental and physical Order (♀♀♀)

"Now, know ye that these were primitive beings, as ye hast learned through thy record left to witness of these beings. This shall be as strange and unacceptable unto many.

- end excerpt -

Lets assume for a moment that Neanderthal was in fact Early Man as ♂♂♂. Then at the end of that cycle, those who showed remarkable progress, the best and the brightest of the first Order, were selected to become the seed, for a whole new Order ♀♀♀, which would be given a new form (Homo sapiens) to accommodate their more developed abilities. After another cycle the ♂♂♂ who were the slower to develop, would finally have progressed, as a whole, to where they too were ready to move forward. But since they were still far behind the ♀♀♀ who had continued to progress, the ♂♂♂ would be given a form suitable to their slower evolvement... that of Cro-Magnon Man. This would explain why scientists are baffled at their findings that the more intelligent of the three came in the middle.

Thus would Man have begun his experiences in flesh in the primitive forms of Early Man... and as Man progressed, so too would the forms ever evolve upward, even unto to the present.

The following excerpt is from Newsletter 67:

The Parable the Sifting and Sorting

... "When a man goes into his garden to plant, he carries a bag of seeds. He knows the seed he carries, and also the soil he hast prepared to receive the seed. He watches with care the growth and development. When the harvest is come, the best of the seed is saved for the future sowing. Nothing is wasted, for he knows the sown to be good, fertile.

Now, within the harvest he finds some (seed) hast brought great promise for yet more abundant yield, a more pleasing product... therefore, he sets aside the most likely seed to be his choice for the next sowing - as this is his intention, to bring forth a more perfect harvest. Therefore, he chooses the most favorable of each harvest until he is satisfied that he hast found a stable and suitable product that he could rely upon.

His experiment has been favorable for the present season, yet, as the seasons (cycles) come and pass, the once perfect seed begins to become contaminated, and again he seeks out the best of his harvest, and there is once again, a sifting and sorting. As the seasons pass and again the best of the sowing, the greatest of the harvest is plucked out... and once again he finds new soil and moves his experimental garden into fresh new soil. Therein again he oversees the results of his labors.

He now stands as one to give himself credit for the wisdom and for the assistance, from the condition of the soil, the rain, and his labor. He is not as yet finished, for there is another garden prepared in which he, in proper timing, sows his new garden according unto the signs of the heavens, and the blessing of Solen Aum Solen...

- end excerpt -

It should humble us all a bit to think that long ago we all may have been thumping along as Neanderthals... but if we are "Man"... and they were "Early Man"... then we are they.

The Fall of Man

So here is Man beginning to incarnate into these primitive forms of flesh. But lets stop and back up here for a moment. We need to realize that this was NOT the original plan brought forth by the Father. Man was never intended to incarnate into these primitive ape forms, nor was he intended to possess the destructive and selfish nature which has caused the downfall of countless civilizations throughout his long dark history here on earth. This was the result of the "Fall of Man" from his once high estate, as spoken of in the following excerpt from "Star Guests":

... Man as Man, however, had deteriorated so far (from his former state) that only through untold millennia and much instruction could he win back his former standard of intelligence. He began reincarnating in the form which the Host itself had employed (created)... a sort of sublimated Ape, or physical man as you know him today... slowly working his way up through the aeons...

- end excerpt -

So this was not the original plan for Man. He was never intended to inhabit the ape-forms of early man. This is why the pattern changed for Man of earth... because he had "deteriorated" from his intended state. So how is it that Man fell from a higher estate? What was the reason for this fall?

Now we have all read about Adam and Eve, but this is not about gender or eating an apple... it is about the knowledge of good and evil.

If we look back at all that has been said, we see in fact that there were more than just two "First Born Sons" of the Father. It appears that the First Born Sons are an "Order" of beings, made up of many other beings who came forth in later cycles, after the first two Sons brought forth creation as we know it. These would also be of the First Born of the Father, meaning they came forth from the Father Himself... and one of these was a Son called Lucifer, as described in the following excerpt from Script 10:

..."For he had the power invested within him of God the Father to create worlds, yea, to create and to populate them"...

... "He was of the Father born, and he had received his inheritance in full, yet he had the audacity to call himself "Father of all that is and was. He used the Law for his own end, and gave no heed unto the warnings of the Father....

- end excerpt -

So Lucifer was also among the First Born Sons, and within the cycles that followed the creation of matter, he too became a creator in his own right.

There is a quote from Star Guests which reads:

..."*And at the apex of them all stands a coterie of beings whom we might best describe as Super Angels, of such extraordinary capacity spiritually that they can manifest in any form desired for the accomplishment of their purpose. Lucifer was one of these, and well known is the story of how he used his transcendent powers wrongly.*

- end excerpt -

It is also quite possible that those who we have called "Archangels", such as Michael, Gabriel, Uriel, etc., are in fact First Born Sons of the Father, the Order of the First Born, and not of the purely "Angelic" Order... for the Angelic Order are described as: "*having no will of their own, only to serve the Source of all light and energy*".

In the past we have called all beings of the higher dimensions "Angels"... When in fact there is a specific Order which have been designated as the "Angelic Order", who do not have free will or the Power of creation, but rather are beings of pure light who serve only the Source of all light.

- - -

So at some point within the unfoldment of this creation, one of the First Born Sons decided that he had a better way. One of those First Born, who was called Lucifer, became "puffed-up" with himself. Having received the Power of creation, he came to believed himself to be the Father's equal, and saw no reason why he should continue to do the Father's will. Since the First Cause ever remains unknowable and unfathomable, he concluded that there was no over-all plan, and felt that the plan which creation was following was weak.

He saw no reason why a "creator" should be a servant unto the creation, or why those of greater attainment should spend their time nurturing and guiding those of lesser development. He felt that the "creator" should not serve the creation, but that the "creation" should serve the creator. He turned from the Father and sought to experiment with creation, to bring forth his own plan for creation... wherein the creation would serve its creator, wherein the weak would serve the strong. He sought to use creation to his own end. He rebelled against the Father and rejected the Plan of the Father, and therein created the first "separation" of the creation from the Source of that creation.

Yet having been given free will, not even the Father would revoke that privilege. Instead it was decided that all would be allowed their free will choice. Those who chose to turn from the Father and side with Lucifer would be allowed their free will choice... and we are told that one third of the angels of heaven chose to follow him.

Yet they would not be allowed to destroy or retard the rest of creation... instead, they would be confined to a region wherein they might come to know the fruit of that tree (the knowledge of good and evil). Such rebellion would be allowed to run its course, that all might come to see the futility of separation. It would not be conquered by force, but rather, they would either be brought home again through unconditional Love... or they would be allowed to experience the fruit of their own actions, to bring about their own destruction if they so choose. Evil would simply be allowed to destroy itself.

The following excerpts is from Script 10:

... And when he, which is called Lucifer, was given the ultimatum, he called together his followers and said unto them: "Ye have seen my work... have I not created these things, have I not given unto these things life, and have I not been with you these days? If ye follow me I shall make of thee great a wondrous beings"... And when they gazed upon his handiwork they fell down and did worship him. I say great was and is their sorrow, for unto this day do they pay the price"...

- end excerpt -

So who were these "fallen angels" who followed Lucifer? Who were "A third of the angels of heaven", who chose to follow him? Some were of the First Born Order who were beguiled by his words... but for the most part they seem to have been part of the Order of Man, those who had already attained their divine inheritance as Sons of God within previous cycles. Remember, that Lucifer was then a high Son of God who was called "The Bright and Morning Star"... Man would have seen Lucifer as a great being of Light, a creator in his own right who promised them a great and glorious existence if they would but follow him.

But the previous excerpt also goes on to say:

..."Now when the war in heaven was but begun, Prince Michael was the one which came forth as the defender of Truth and Justice. It was he which gave unto Lucifer the ultimatum which banished him into the world of darkness... for even then, when the earth was in a different part of the firmament and before her axis was changed, she was a dark planet, for little light went out from her. Now when this was accomplished, that Lucifer was cast out of heaven to the dark planet earth, he set about to all manner of experiments".

- end excerpt -

Now it is more than likely that the earth was not just picked at random... but rather that Lucifer was already experimenting with creation here, and that he had already interfered with and altered the natural order here, thus he and his followers were "confined" to the earth.

Too, it was not just the fallen ones who were affected by this event, but also the young spirits upon the earth who were in their early infancy of development here, as Man. Their development was forever altered, and they too became caught up in the fall. This is referred to in a quote from "Star Guests":

..."It has been many ages since the spirits that have since become known as men, arrived upon this earth-plane, and engaged in creative mischief with the spirit particles developing here, and imbedded qualities into their composition that were never intended to disclose here.

- end excerpt –

Thus, these younger spirits were also turned from their Oneness with the Father and with the rest of creation. The following excerpt from Sananda was given to Sister Thedra in 1954:

"... They were as the time of the experimentalists with the UN (the greater mind) in the sense that they were of the mind to improve upon the work of the creator. The ones who were the scibes (the experimenters), the ones who accepted in the name of the false god scibe (Lucifer) were as ones who were cast down by their own hand, with Lucifer, to their laboratory earth"...

"Unto this day their treal has been to return to the Father's house. To many who call themselves "Adamics", it is told that they are the first of these to reach the earth. To this it was cast that they find their way as a carter, or one who carts himself. There is no savior to cart him, he must be his own. To this we of the Host are coming to the earth, as ones who have been watching for those who are ready of their own treal (will), to take the sice (form) as the sice and the King as the King. To you I have revealed the past.

- end excerpt –

This apparently was the event upon which the story of Adam and Eve was based... and as such Sananda refers to these "fallen ones" as "Adamics".

Yet remember, that Lucifer's original intent was not to destroy creation... it was to rule over creation, to experiment with creation by bringing forth new forms.

There is a quote in "Star Guests" which reads:

...They were not exactly vicious in what they conceived to be the occupancy of forms for their own purpose. Those changes came gradually in their thought concepts. They saw what could be created by the Power of Thought and experimented to see how far their own experiences in manifesting organisms could carry them. But soon they were plunging into sensuous enjoyments and naught else.

Sensuous enjoyments occupied all their "thought time", to the exclusion of spiritual educating. They "forgot themselves", we might put it. They forgot who they were (Sons of God) and for what creative and constructive purposes they had first sought the earth. And it still goes on today, in those extremely self-centered people who care nothing for the rights of others, but concentrate solely on having a good time, no matter what the cost to others. Thinking about others appears foolish or infantile....

- end excerpt –

So now we have two different casts of beings inter-mixed upon the earth... those young spirits who were indigenous to the planet, and those who the Bible refers to as: The Sons of God who *"Looked upon the daughters of men and found them fair, and chose of them wives"*. These were the Fallen Sons of God who began to take on biological forms. Yet they did not just take on the existing biological forms, but sought to experiment with the creation of new forms that were more pleasurable to them. The following is also an excerpt from Star Guests:

... Long ago it was decreed that man should meet with mishap. That is to say, the forces of ignorance and mischief, too often called "evil", had gained such ascendancy over the race that Man was losing his identity. Bestialities and abominations, the crossing of animalistic forms were producing a race of hybrids so terrible that something had to be done about it. The work of cleansing mankind was well-nigh imponderable of execution...

- end excerpt –

In "Star Guests" we are told further, that the biological forms became so intermixed that there came to exist "Angelic looking animals, as well as beastly looking human forms inhabited by these once divine spirits. Yet in occupying these various form for their own gratification, they becoming more and more engrossed within matter. These once high spirits eventually "forgot themselves"... they lost their memory of the high planes they once occupied, their once glorious existence as Sons of God.

But there was yet a third group to enter into the process. These were the Sons of Light... a group of 144,000 beings who had not separated themselves from the Father. The above excerpt from Star Guests goes on to say:

... Into this turmoil of insufferable satanites were called Radiant Beings from another system of creation. This creation had gone through the same - or similar - experiences in evolution in another world order, trillions of years before...

... These beings came to earth from other planets within other world systems... 144,000 of them, under a leader whom men have called Christ. He was their leader because he was furthest advanced in wisdom, compassion, understanding, and general character-nobility...

- end excerpt -

These were the 144,000 spoken of in the Bible. They volunteered to come to the earth, to anchor the Light upon the earth throughout the cycles that would follow. They would hold the Light for Man, until such time as he would raise himself up again. They would live as man and be as man... yet since they had not separated themselves from the father their hearts would remain open to the voice of the Father. This group would hold what little Light was present upon the earth, and with each new generation they would add to it... until with the closing of this present cycle the way would be open to all who would choose to return to the upward course, back to their true Oneness with the Father and with the rest of creation.

Thus a new plan for the earth was brought forth... one which would allow the regeneration of these fallen spirits, as well as the young spirits who were evolving here. But before this new cycle could go forward the earth needed to be cleansed of the abominations which had been brought forth through experimentation.

It was at this point that the Great Flood spoken about in the Bible came about. The reason for the flood was to destroy the "Bestialities and abominations, the crossing of animalistic forms, which had produced a race of hybrids so terrible that some thing had to be done about it".

The Following excerpt is from "Star Guests":

... When the catastrophe (flood) was over, he (man) began reincarnating according to the direction of the 144,000, in the form which the Host itself had employed (created)... a sort of sublimated Ape, or physical man as you know him today... slowly working his way up through the aeons...

- end excerpt -

This was the new plan for the redemption of the earth, wherein all would begin at the beginning, without memory or former knowledge. This too, was the beginning of our history as we know it... the origin of "Early Man", the primitive forms spoken of earlier. This was the creation of the first Order ᛥᛥᛥ into which Man would began to incarnate in his long ascent back to his former glories. This is spoken of in the following excerpt from Star Guests:

... the essential part of the plan was this: Man has inherent in his spiritual nature, much of his lost heritage, but is forbidden by Thought Forces superior to him to use it until he has reached that time when he is so spiritually balanced that he will never again employ his knowledge selfishly or malevolently. That time is far closer at hand than men suppose.

- end excerpt -

The Great Flood was the first step in cleansing the earth from the abominations of the previous cycle. It was the event upon which the story of "Noah's Ark" was founded... wherein the original genetically "pure" species were to be preserved, while the abominable creations were destroyed by the flood. Yet, from what we now know of the Elder Brothers and their technological abilities, their Crafts and Saucers, etc., we might assume that it was not accomplished in a wooden boat or an Ark by just one man, for that would have been well-nigh impossible considering the tens of thousands of species.

Thus was the plan for cleansing the earth and redeeming the fallen begun. Yet they, beginning as primitive man, would go through many long cycles of development before they were once again capable of real intelligence, and even greater cycles still before he was finally ready to know the truth of his existence.

The Cycle of Darkness

We must remember that the Father's plan for the earth had its origin in Light, as did his plan for the Order of Man. Man, in his original state, was never intended to inhabit dense bodies of flesh. Such forms of flesh and bone were intended to be animal forms. Man was to inhabit forms of finer matter, such as those used within the spirit planes of earth. He was to become the Father's hands within the universe of matter, to enjoy and to oversee the biological expression of life here.

The darkness and suffering which we have experienced over thousands of years here upon the earth was not the original plan of the Father, nor was it the will of the Father... it was and is a direct result the Lucifer rebellion.

This present cycle was initiated so that what had been made crooked might once again be made straight... that man might return to his high estate if he so chose. Throughout his many cycles within these ape-forms of flesh, man would be guided ever upward, ever working out his nature, gradually losing his beastly nature in embodiment after embodiment... until such time that there were sufficient numbers who were prepared to once again begin hearing the truth.

That time arrived 2000 years ago, when the Christ Spirit took on physical embodiment as Jesus of Nazareth, and for the first time in mans long dark history since the fall he was given the Truth. Christ knew that all would not change overnight, yet the Truth was once again anchored upon the earth, and man would be given yet another cycle in which to slowly understand and assimilate it, to incorporate it into their hearts and lives, and finally turn his eyes upward once again.

Now, although Lucifer and his followers had long since lost their power, many of them had not lost their original intent... that the creation should serve them. Although they were confined to the earth, they did not want to destroy the earth or mankind... they sought to make man their servants. They became the wealthy and the powerful of the earth, the tyrants who kept the masses in servitude and ignorance.

Through lies and distortions they created within the masses a misplaced allegiance to "King and Country", instead of to the Father. Age after age they have used the masses as pawns, sending them forth to conquer, destroy, and enslave whole races of men, hell-bent in their endless desire for ever greater wealth and power. They did upon the earth that which they had intended to do throughout all of creation... to make creation serve them, above all else... that they might rule creation as "Great and wondrous beings".

Consider the following excerpt from "Star Guests":

... The "beasts" still incarnate and perpetuate their beastliness, hating the Avatar and his people. The "beasts" want to be let alone to dominate the planet and to do as they please. They lose no opportunity to disparage, smear, imprison, or kill anyone whose endeavors mark them as one of the Christus assistants. Even when they have their own way at times, it brings them no lasting satisfaction - for domination is one of their major obsessions.

- end excerpt –

The Truth and Light which Jesus taught was a direct affront to all that they desired, for he stirred the masses from their lethargy in servitude and ignorance, to turn from the superstition and lies... and to look once again to the One True Father of all creation. Lucifer and his followers had no power over such Truth and Light... they could only hope to conceal it by keeping the masses fragmented and ignorant, in a muddle of falsehoods and lies.

From their high places they sought to ridicule and discredit that which Jesus was and what he taught... and although they succeeded in destroying the body of Jesus, it was truly the event which sounded their death-knell... for even the lies and distortions could not keep the Light which he represented from spreading within the hearts of man. And even though men did not understand the depth of what he said, they saw it as Light within the darkness, and they sought that Light.

Realizing that an enlightened mankind would mean the end of their reign, these fallen ones have tried to strike at the very heart of the Truth, seeking to use it to their own ends. They sought the places of power and lost no opportunity to control the masses through blind obedience, turning man against man. Nowhere in our long dark history has there been more cruelty, bloodshed, oppression, and wanton destruction than that perpetuated in the name of God and Christ. The inquisition... the holy wars... the wanton destruction and enslavement of whole races portrayed as "heathens & savages"... all instigated by arrogant men with no love in their hearts but for power, and absolutely no respect for that which God or Christ truly represented. They openly manifested darkness... and they called it Light!

But the heart of Man is founded in Light, and the majority of man responded to what little light was available, century after century. Lifetime after lifetime the 144,000 Sons of Light took on embodiment as visionaries, as new-thinkers and teachers, as great artists and composers, as inventors, and as the founders of freedoms and liberties... and with each successive generation mankind lost more and more of his beastly and rebellious nature.

He began to resist the yokes of oppression and ignorance, he overthrew the thrones of the tyrants and demanded an accounting. Man was gaining knowledge of himself, and set out to establish greater principals based on the rights and freedom of ALL men. And although the fallen ones had so corrupted some of mankind that they were now dark spirits in and of themselves... the majority of men had allowed truth, light, and honesty to flourish within their hearts, and were once again becoming spirits of Light. And this brings us to the closing of this cycle...

The following excerpt is from "The Third Millennium":

... This world is like a seasoned garden on the eve of the harvest. The weeds are thick among the melons and the corn. Potato vines, withered and brown, are almost lost among the amaranth, datura, and morning glory. The garden has produced well, the harvest will be good... but the gardeners of this world sense the fullness that could be... a potential greater still if they wait just a short time longer. The weeds can do little harm now. But a brief wait could add substantially to the quality and quantity of the yield... By the year 2011, humankind will have reached its due date for the cohesion of its collective consciousness...

- - -

The Sifting & Sorting

We have often been told that the great change which is just ahead is beyond our present understand to fully comprehend. If this newsletter holds any reflection of it, then it is truly the turning point for all of mankind.

Yet before this great change transpires, there must first be a sifting & sorting process. Each one must be allowed to choose the way which he she would go. Ignorant men will ever argue that their ignorance is the height and epitome of all knowledge... yet each must now choose: either to cling to the darkness, refusing to acknowledge anything above and beyond their own ignorance... or to return to their Oneness with the rest of creation. Sananda has referred to this in the following excerpt:

Each one has his own will... it is not lawful that I trespass on that gift so freely given. Now it is come when each and every one shall choose his course. He either chooses the hard and dangerous way of darkness, or the sure and safe way of light in which I abide. Thus I am prepared to bring everyone which gives unto me his hand willingly. I ask of no one anything except obedience unto the Law of the ONE.

- end excerpt –

We might assume that the 144,000 Sons of Light who volunteered to come here in selfless service, to suffer the darkness for the sake of others, would not be bound to any karmic debt incurred here. They would finally be released from their self-imposed bondage, wherein their memory would again be restored in full that they might once again return to their lofty home. Yet all others must now choose. The following excerpt is from The Third Millennium:

...Those few who may choose to remain behind will not be un-cared for. They will experience an age of further history, (within another place) much like the history that humans have experienced in the past. There will be good time as well as times of hell, as they gradually wind their way through the same learning process that now find the majority of you ready to migrate beyond the shadows of illusion to the conscious shores...

- - -

With the closing of this cycle the Light and Truth is now coming forth in its fullness, sent forth by our Elder Brothers and all those within the higher dimensions of Light. It is becoming evident to all who choose to look. The dark ones have power ONLY over those who choose, of their own free will, to reject this Light and remain in ignorance.

But remember too, there are also the many spirit planes associated with the earth, and those spirits are Man also. Although many of these are high planes of spirit inhabited by bright spirits, these are not the "higher dimensions". They are spirit planes associated strictly with earth life, wherein disincarnate entities reside while not in embodiment. These "astral" planes, as they are sometimes called, are of many varied "vibrations", both high and low, Light and dark, which coincide with the spirits which reside in each of these planes. And while many within these high planes of spirit assist us in Light and guidance... so too do those within the darker astral regions, the "trouble makers" as Sananda has called them, bring through false and distorted teachings, which only adds to mankind's confusion.

Realize, that as this cycle now draws to a close, each and every being, not only upon the earth but also those within these many astral spheres which surround the earth, will be part of the sifting and sorting process, for the earth will be cleansed of these dark astral spirits also.

I would like to end this newsletter with the following excerpt from "Star Guests":

...By acknowledging and being interested in these matters, you are identifying yourselves as spirits who are either winning out in the fight over your one-time beastly ingredient... or you are spirits (the 144,000) who came to this earth planet originally to aid in the task of cosmic regeneration of your fellows. But try to keep this in mind... which-ever you are, you are a focal point for the spreading of Light and knowledge for which the world suffers most in its present extremity. Coming into earth life again and again, we tell you, for the Sons of God, is never any hardship... it is more to be regarded as a privilege.

* * *

The Following excerpts are from the book

"The Third Millennium"

... I assure you who may feel trapped in historical situations, that there is no human force, no agency, no influence what-so-ever, that can keep you from discovering the current of My consciousness within you, once you are aware of its existence and choose to look for it. My thoughts flow into your consciousness in each and every moment, within each breath. On the current of your awareness they enter. Lift your eyes from the conditioned interpretations... look up... and see clearly again.

- - -

... You are already living in the dawning hours of the Age of Planetary Awakening... it is here now for those sensitive to its fragrance, texture, majesty, and vision...

... Though there will be much awakening of individuals prior to the final unified movement of the awakening planetary organism... this (final) movement, like a first breath, will occur in but a single moment. It is then that the Starmaker will consciously awaken within all the systems of (individual) human bio-circuitry capable of sustaining universal awareness.

... The consciousness that will ultimately emerge will be the consciousness of the Eternal One, the Creator, the Being who IS Life, awake and aware for the first time inside a material universe...

... As this reality comes fully into human consciousness, all illusion of a destructive nature will be dissolved. Though there have been many centuries leading up to this movement, when that movement comes it will be decisive. There will be a great shift... a single moment of quantum awakening...

... This is the event that is central to all of human history...

- - -

... There are externals yet to come... signs, signals from the nations... But the essence of the prophecies is within you now. Do not look for validation outside yourself... experience it within you, as your Soul remembers, as your spirit settles fully into your awareness and opens its eyes, your eyes, to see.

- - -

... Do not think you are unworthy or unprepared for so great a step. In some ways you have always been prepared... in other ways there is not, nor could there be, any preparation.

... Long have I observed you from within, from be- hind your thoughts and feelings. I know the moment when the odds are in your favor, when the likelihood of your making the choice of eternal life is greatest.

... Now is such a time. You are ready to make the vital decision. You now have all that you need to release the conditioning of history and to ride the ascending wave of consciousness beyond the spell of matter, into an awakened life...

- end excerpts -

* * *

This last excerpt from Sananda says it all:

Mans Total Freedom

When it is given unto man to be prepared he shall be as ONE with the whole of the lighted Order. He shall have the privilege of going and coming between worlds, and as one of these he shall be without limitation of any sort. He shall have knowledge of all creation, just as we of the &&&. He shall be as the Father created him for to be... this is his inheritance.

Let thine time be spent profitably, for the Call hast gone forth, "*Come! Come! Come ye out*". What think ye is meant by this call? It means, now is the day of awareness. Time is short... give heed unto the call and hasten to prepare for thine departure from the Mother Earth, for she no longer shall carry thee upon her back. She is now prepared for her new berth within the firmaments. Her time is come that she bring forth a son which shall foster another generation (*see: Mine Intercom Messages from the Realms of Light*), while she, the Mother Earth, shall be free of the spores and whores which have tormented her. She shall be free, even as man which is so prepared to arise into the light as spirit, free from pain and sorrow. So shall it be as the Father wills. No longer shall the sons of man linger in darkness and unknowing, in ignorance of his inheritance, his origin.

Behold ye, Oh man, the signs of the time. The day is come when ye shall move. Ye shall be as one come alive and come out from under the 'black hood' which hast blinded thine sight. Ye have been <u>hoodwinked</u>! Ye have followed the dark one down the primrose path! Ye have been tantalized by his bewitching speeches, his fetching ways, his glamor and all his false promises.

I say unto thee that hast followed him to the brink of destruction: It is now time that ye heed the instruction which is coming forth from the "Source" of thine existence. Be ye not concerned through which, or by what means, we of the lighted messengers choose to give thee instructions or protection. We use any means available unto us. Know ye that we have all power and intention to use it for the good of ALL! Yea, this 'ALL' indicates other realms of light also, for earth is not alone in the family of the many planets and Stars of the universe... Yea, universes. All are as One, one power, one whole, composed of many Orders of creation/life. Life is continuous throughout all space.

Man, as he is at this time of his earthly existence, is but the shadow, the shell shall I call it, of himself, which is his eternal being, like unto the "Source" of his being. At present, the age in which he finds himself as flesh made manifest is but the age of awakening from his long sleep wherein he forgot his "Source". Long his weary wanderings... Sad his plight!

Now we of the Cosmos have come nigh unto the earth in concert... as light we come that man be made aware that he is not alone.

* * *

Abide in me and fear not that I shall fail you. I say unto each of you, there is too much business of a vast importance for harm of a petty nature to inflict its spiteful mischief on you. We are brethren for a purpose. There are Worlds in the making... I say lives untold shall exist and perish on them. We go upward through the cycles... we do mount world upon world... and behold the day cometh when we reach the Father's mansion. We are brethren I say, for the program eternal...

* * *

All of you have read the messages given by Sananda through Sister Thedra. Some of you may have read only parts of it, while some of you may have had a sincere enough desire for understanding that you have read through all of them, perhaps even more than once.

Have you ever wondered how this will profit you once your earthly time is finished and you finally pass on into those planes of spirit so often spoken about? It would be of great benefit if only we might speak with someone who had previously studied these Scripts in earnest, and who had then passed on to those planes of spirit. We might wish to know just how it all relates, both during and after the transition. Wouldn't it be wonderful to hear from such a one? The following is an account which I think will answer some of those questions.

The Story of Judy

Judy lived and worked at the "Gatehouse" at Mt Shasta, CA in 1973-75, and was an integral part of the work there. She was 39 years old, and had come to the Gatehouse to study and to help out with the work of A.S.S.K. She was vibrant, she was always overflowing with smiles and abundant energy, she was devoted to her study of the work there, and she was greatly loved by all.

Towards the end of 1974, she herself began receiving messages from Sananda during her meditation, telling her that she had completed her work there, and he now had greater work for her to do within another place. She assumed that this meant that she would be leaving the Gatehouse, and thus she began to prepare herself for a change.

On Good-Friday, 1975, she and her son went up onto the snowy slopes of Mount Shasta to go sledding for the day, on what seemed to be just another day. In what appeared to be an accident, she and her sled went off a high embankment, crashing down onto the roadway below. She suffered severe head injuries and was rushed to the hospital.

Sister Thedra immediately went to the hospital, and upon seeing Judy in what was obviously her final moments of life, Sister placed her hand on Judy's brow to comfort her. As if from Judy's own lips Sister Thedra's inner hearing heard the words: "*Don't worry Sister, I set it all up myself*". Judy left her body completely a short time later.

Sister Thedra returned to the Gatehouse and told us that Judy was gone. She explained to each of us that the next three days would be a crucial time for Judy, and that although grief was an inherent part of such a process, we were not to focus on anything which might hold her back. Instead, we were to send her thoughts of encouragement, thoughts that all was in completion with each of us, and that she could let go of any attachments and focus her attention fully on going forward. For the next three days we all sent her loving thoughts of strength and encouragement.

One day six months after her passing, Margot, who was also studying the work at the Gatehouse, began receiving messages from Judy during her morning meditation. Being apprehensive that it might just be her own imagination, she sought Sister Thedra's counsel... Sister encouraged her to trust in herself and to see where it would lead.

Judy then began sharing her experiences, both during and after her transition. She explained how she had been called by Sananda to greater service within the spirit planes above the earth plane. She explained how, at the time of her "supposed accident", that she was lifted out of her body as if by the downy softness of unseen hands... and how, without any attachment, she had watched as her body continued down the snowy slopes and over the cliff.

She also explained that (in spirit) she had previously been given the choice... of being removed from her body by the powers that be, or she could choose the time and place herself. She had chosen to leave her body on Good-Friday, high up on the sunny snow-covered slopes of Mount Shasta.

After reassuring us all that her passing had truly been an uplifting and joyful transition, she began to relate a few glimpses into the spirit planes and the lessons she was now learning. She also shared some of her experiences within her new place of abode. She explained that although she was now involved in her schooling for her new work, she was being allowed to be a liaison between the realms, that the work of the Gatehouse be even more anchored within those higher planes of spirit. The selected messages which follow are some of those communiques...

FROM JUDY IN SPIRIT

Recorded by Margot
Begin communiques, Sept 6, 1975

Sananda speaking: Your sister of light, Judy wishes to speak with you at this time.

Judy: Beloved Sister

Tis I, your friend Judy, wishing to break through the heavy veil to be in touch with my dear family (at the Gatehouse). Be not afraid that it is a mistake, for I am real and do wish to be in touch now.

You have all helped me more than you can know, through your love and unity with one another. The freedom that comes to one while making the transition from the earth plane to another plane is truly greatly enhanced by your (ones brothers and sisters of earth) attitude and loving service to the light.

All that we studied together has helped me greatly... most especially the Scripts, which I carried with me in my heart and which sustained me, especially during my transition.

Joyful I am that you have taken up the pen to serve as a liaison between the realm. Do share this with my beloved Sister Thedra, to whom I shall always be devoted. Do not be afraid (of errors), for it is not that important a happening. I have been in communication with others too, in other ways (silently) and will continue.

Bless you, one and all, this glorious fall day.

Your sister in the light... Judith

- - -

Sept 7, 1975

Sananda speaking: Hear now my child, as once again thy sister comes to thee.

Judy: Dear Sister Margot

Greetings from the outer realms. How joyous am I this day... praise be to our Father, and blessings to you all. Holy, holy is his name.

Be at peace and poise, for there is much to be accomplished through our contact.

Set it up I did, just as Sister Thedra knew, for much work awaited me here. Although it seemed that I was needed there, the need here was more pressing, and I was assured that all would be taken care of, as it has been.

How I love you all and appreciate the part you are playing. If you could only see it from here... boy oh boy! I know this is new to you, but don't forget, it is new to me too. Together we can work as fledglings... won't it be fun?

If you (at the Gatehouse) could only see your little campfire shining so brightly in the midst of all that darkness, a candle in the dark night. Yes there are other campfires... but yours - ours - is the prettiest. Work we shall, but the lightness and the joy need not be kept out, for it is a vital ingredient in the Father's recipe for divinity.

Your studies, books, and lessons are all right-on, and know that it is all true. Tell Joseph not to forget to water the plants, and give him a hug for me too. Love to dear Sister Thedra. Bless you all.

Your blessed sister... Judith

- - -

Added Note: *All the messages which follow begin with Sananda opening the door for each communication, similar to the above messages. Because of limited space, I will not include the openings with the remainder of the communiques.*

- - -

Sept 8, 1975

My dear sister of the Light.

Be at peace this day and let the light shine upon thee. I come as a liaison between the realms bringing you information and energy from my new place of abode.

How can I relate the vastness and the glories that surround me? It is a freedom that is difficult to relate. We here are all pulling for the little green emerald (earth), which is so dear to our hearts. Be not afraid that you will interpret my messages or words incorrectly, for we all rest in the Father's hands, and in this way we cannot fail.

- - -

Sept 9, 1975

My dear Sister

My joy is ever increasing, as is my love and gratitude to He who makes all things possible... our beloved Father, Solen Aum Solen. I now wish to share with you all the experiences of my passing.

Somewhere deep within, I knew of the events which were to transpire, and I felt the intensity within as my instructions came through (from Sananda) with more force, and my preparation did indeed seem more urgent. My spirit knew of course, but protected us all from the knowledge of what was to take place. How merciful is our heavenly Father, and how gently He leads His children.

(*Judy's son's name omitted*) ... was chosen to be with me for a special reason which I cannot reveal at this time. Great has been his sorrow and suffering, but I can now accept it as necessary. Love him and be of good cheer, for he has an inner strength that even he does not realize, which will see him through.

The day was, of course, carefully chosen (by me) as the anniversary of the crucifixion of our beloved Lord and master Sananda. What a privilege to leave on such a day. I had no fear, and thank God for my wonderful preparation. As you read in my messages, I was told over and over to be at peace and poise.

You were right... the episode preceding my leaving was a test to see if I was ready, and as I shared with you on Sunday morning, I did pass the test with flying colors. God bless Joseph, my beloved husband, for his quick action and his help made me KNOW that I would always be protected, and that there was no need to fear... ANYTHING.

I will continue at our next meeting. Bless you dear sister. God be with you... each and every one.

Your sister in the light... Judith

- - -

Sept 10, 1975

Greetings from the other side. Sharing is what it is all about... be discriminating of course, but share without hesitancy with those who are trustworthy.

And so my tale continues: At no time did I doubt, for long ago I gave myself to God and I knew that he would lead me aright. Such a simple thing to do, and the rewards are so immediate... that inner feeling of fulfillment and overflowing. To leave while "at play" seemed to be my own unique choice... to be lifted up was His.

The pore or body continued on down the hill, but Judith was literally lifted right off that sled, with the softness and gentleness that I had never known before, nor can I describe it. Like the down of a new born baby's head - like a kittens paw - soft and with loving care was I lifted. The fact that the body or pore continued down the hill concerned me not... although I did observe it from my new vantage point. Fortunately I was not to have need of the experience of the so-called "sting of death", for there is no death. I am living proof of that! No pain... no fear... no suffering.

I was permitted to view the events of that day and my concern for Sister Thedra was great. Yes, she DID hear me as she viewed that battered old body in the hospital, and I so much wanted to comfort her. Thank God for your sensitive inner ear, Sister Thedra. The vigilance, the love and closeness I felt from all of you, the unity of brotherhood, made me know that it was just as it should be, each and every step of the way.

To feel the support at that time is so vitally important, for it reinforces the decision that has already been made by the one leaving, and frees his mind to concentrate on other matters. Believe me, it is a very busy time. I was helped in accepting (son's name omitted) part... it took a while, and I was given great comfort as I viewed his suffering. Your silence and your peaceful attitude helped me with this too... isn't that something?

The way was well prepared for my transition. I but needed faith to let it happen in its natural way, for only I could create a blockage in my path to my new home. How many times have we heard the words "Prepare - Prepare"... how important they are!

This part needs to come in small doses. Let us continue at our next meeting. I love you all. God bless you, and let us rest in the Father's hand, together.

Your loving sister in the light...

Judith

- - -

Sept 14, 1975

Greetings to you this day. Hosanna in the highest. Sing praises in His holy name, for He lives... He is all Life.

And so the story continues. The three days of transition are important to regard well for many reasons. During this time, because of free will, the one passing is calling many of his own plays, even though he has help ever at hand.

The decision is his to make at this time, as always, which path he will follow. Any disturbance on the earth plane amongst his loved ones, or to his body at this time, can influence that important decision. He is especially vulnerable and easily distracted at this time, as is anyone at a time of transition within their life.

To have friends and family remaining at peace and poise, holding especially loving thoughts of the one making the transition, is the nicest gift they can give. To cremate the body is also very helpful, for the consummation by fire is so cleansing. It is a clear symbol that that phase has ended, and it helps remind the passing one not to turn back. So I had the best possible send-off.

Held so gently in loving arms, I was permitted to observe the Sunday morning breakfast service at the Gatehouse, and I shared the love and devotion so gratefully received. You all helped me so much, and strengthened yourselves in the doing.

We shall speak again...

Your sister in the light...

Judith

- - -

Sept 17, 1975

Here in this holy place do I now reside. My vision is much greater... my memory has been restored. My cup is continually empty, and continually it is refilled with the water of life and light. My praise and devotion is a constant action, pouring forth from within. With ever increasing intensity do we here endeavor to serve our almighty Father/Mother God. There is no separation here, for we live within Him, and know this to be so.

Holy, holy is His name, Solen Aum Solen. Sacred is all that He has created, for His perfection is ever present. All who seek the Light with a sincere heart will find it, for such is His mercy. Service to Him, to serve with one's total being, is to become one with Him.

This day be of humble nature and give thanks for your being, and for His ever flowing mercy, Let thy light so shine that it may light the darkest night, and the dawn will surely follow. Be at peace, for you are not alone...

Your sister... Judith

- - -

Sept 20, 1975

I am blessed indeed, for my heart fills with love of our heavenly Father... Praise His Holy Name.

Through your hand I present myself to prove that life is eternal. There is no death... only in the minds of men who refuse to accept such living proof such as I. There is nothing to fear, except being afraid. Life pours forth in its various creations, beauteous beyond belief. From the fount of His eternal fountain does it flow, ever expanding, ever growing, ever changing. All that we can do is worship Him through prayer, praise, and devotion.

The work at the Gatehouse is ever more important than you can imagine. To spread the living word of God throughout a darkened sleeping planet at a critical time in its development is the highest of endeavors.

Were it not for your work and others of a similar nature, the burden on those of this realm would be very heavy to bear. You are all receiving constant help and protection from here in the higher realms. Sananda's plan will not be foiled nor will it fail, for it is the Father's will that it be executed. You (at the Gatehouse) are a vital link in that plan... go forth as ones knowing that it is so, and carry on the work without ceasing, for you go with the love and support of the heavenly host.

My new abode abounds with flowers of every conceivable color and fragrance. Would that I could share it all with you... especially the white roses. The colors are not flat, but each have depth and seem to vibrate and dance with light. Each flower is loved and cared for with great tenderness, for it is recognized to be His creation, and they seem to reflect that recognition.

Be ye blessed this day... each one of you.

Your beloved sister... Judith

- - -

Added Note: *I, like everyone else at the Gatehouse, felt a great sense of loss at Judy's passing, yet because of Sister Thedra's guidance I was able to put it all aside and send her positive thoughts of completion and of encouragement.*

In the three days following her transition I felt as though I was able to experience first-hand some of the process which she was going through. I mentioned this to Sister Thedra several times, and she encouraged me to experience it instead of talking about it.

- - -

Sept 21, 1975

My dear sister

Today let us rejoice, for this is the time of abundance and of thanksgiving, a time for renewal of faith in our merciful Father, who is ever giving of himself that we may BE. There is no separation from one realm to another... nothing dividing us except our own diverse thoughts and the clouds which we create around ourselves.

At the time of my transition, those who were not wrapped in their own self-created clouds of grief, pity, fear, and pre-conceived ideas, were able to feel my experience, at least in part, and were uplifted by it.

Those whose clouds enveloped them were unable to feel me, for there was a definite separation caused by their own motivation. To see these self-created clouds is to know how impenetrable they are. Only from the inside-out can they be removed, and only by the one which is creating them.

Bathed I was in fresh clear effervescent water, which doesn't feel like water on earth, for their is no weight to it. It feels soft and wet, yet it is weightless. Until then I had not even thought about my new body, only that I had slipped out of the old one.

(Added Note: This is also described by William Dudley Pelley in the book "Seven Minutes in Eternity") Now I became aware for the first time since leaving, that I felt strangely different. I was totally cleansed and I felt lighter than a feather... no weight, no heaviness. Inside I felt the same, but the outside!... still me, but so much more than before.

How can I explain the freedom and the exhilaration that comes with the "light body". It's as if it were there all the time, but the outside layer of grossness and heaviness being shed allowed it to step forth into its full expression. I guess Sister Thedra knows full well the feeling, from hearing her tell us all of her episodes at night and of reentering the gross body in the morning.

Its all true, what we read and studied, but to experience it first hand is something else again. Now I understand the difficulty of the Sibors in trying to communicate about these experiences in words. I will try my best because I want so much to share it all with you.

Movement is effortless. I seem to glide around rather than the old heavy walking. Yet it is not exactly floating, for each intended motion is specific, but with such total ease. Everything is more vivid and exacting here than it is on earth, including my new "light body". It does take some adjusting, but what a delightful time it is. As you can imagine, I spent a lot of time giggling and laughing during this adjustment period. I don't have wings... but who needs um?

The garment too, that I was adorned with, was of the same light luminescent quality, and feels as though it's not even there, yet it is. When we learned about the more refined energy and the higher vibration, I guess this is it!

God bless you, each and every one. I am so happy to be in touch with you all again.

Your sister in the light... Judith

- - -

Sept 24, 1975

Dear sister in the light

Be at peace and poise, for your suffering is not in vain. Every battle fought is worth a thousand fold on another plane. To clear yourself now is wise, believe me.

My love encompasses you all. The work you would undertake at the Gatehouse is of the greatest of value upon the earth plane. To be about the Father's business, putting it above all else, is to rise above the bondage of materialism. The yoke you have worn for so long seems to be a part of you, and you have no idea the weight you are dragging around.

We all live in the Father's mansion... in it are many rooms (planes), each suited to the inhabitants therein. Observe well the room in which you reside, but don't forget that there are many other rooms as well.

Praise be our Father/Mother God. By His divine grace do we live. I am your sister in the light... Judith

- - -

Sept 24, 1975

Blessed be this day and all that it contains. To give thanks seems too small an offering.

Yes, laugh we do, and often... for the Father loves joy and laughter, and encourages it among us. But there is sadness and tears too, primarily for the ones that are lost and the laggards, yet also for the trials and tribulations of those we love so dearly... for it is our sole desire that all God's children be gathered in... soon!

Remember our conversation (prior to passing) concerning a feeling on both our parts, of wanting to remain free and unattached from any permanent responsibilities that would prevent us from being able to drop everything in a flash if necessary? We felt that we were "on call" but knew not for what. Now we are performing our new parts, and know this to be the part, at least partially, that we were waiting for.

There seems to be a question concerning my pore (body) still being alive after I claim to have been lifted up. Both are true, and I will explain how. The body is animated by the spirit dwelling within... that is so, but the spirit is not bound by the flesh... it is free to come and go in and out of the body as it chooses. This happens at night during sleep... the spirit is off on adventures of many sundry types. Schooling and counseling are given during this time.

There are many facets to each spirit... the earthly incarnation being one facet only, as one facet of a beautifully carved diamond. When the attention is withdrawn from that particular facet, the experience misnamed death occurs. Now the moment when so-called death is pronounced is the moment when the attention has been totally withdrawn. In my case, although Judith did not experience the "death experience", the spirit, of which Judith is but one facet, continued to animate the flesh in a very minimal way until the body was finally pronounced "dead".

Our Father/Mother God is the real divine animator. Without Him all life would cease to be. To Him do we give our thanks for endowing us with life. Were it not for Him we would cease to be. How then can we turn from Him, and even forgotten entirely that He is our Source of being? Our separation was our downfall.

Now is the time of awakening, the time for remembering who we are and from where we came. It is truly a glad day when the memory has been restored. Rejoice and praise His holy name... Solen Aum Solen, our Source of being.

I am thy sister in light... Judith

- - -

The Planes of Thought
October 1, 1975

Holy, holy is the name of Solen Aum Solen... speak it with reverence and devotion.

I am come this day to share with you some thoughts concerning my new abode. Each dwells here in a structure (a dwelling) of his own choice, one in which he is most comfortable... often fashioned after a favorite design on earth. By "Thought" is it fashioned. By such endeavors does each begin to understand the power of thought, and watches as he actually manifests it (a dwelling) through this method.

Here it is not necessary to toil and sweat with hands and feet to manipulate materials into an order to assemble a structure. We use Thought in like manner, exacting and in orderly sequence, as we build stone by stone (if such be the design of our choosing) with attention to each and every detail. In this way do we learn to use our faculty of thinking directly to serve our purpose.

On earth thought is used in an indirect manner... to acquire the money to purchase the materials, to gather the tools, to put the body into action. Do you begin to see the difference?

Yet, once a design is chosen and the structure is 'Thought" into manifestation, it does not remain as such, as on earth. It is constantly changing, in size, in shape, in color, and even in basic design, as he who dwells within it changes.

I shall continue at another time.

I am your sister, Judith

- - -

Added note: *How many times has Sananda said, go into your closet (within) and clean out all that you have buried therein. If you have wronged someone, set it right... if you buried resentment or anger within your heart, then go within and find it, set it right and let it go. Our heart is a storehouse for that which we will take with us when we leave the earth plane... all which remains therein will remain a part of us and will be glaringly evident when we enter the planes of spirit. While in flesh we might hide our motives or resentments behind a smiling facade, but in spirit there is nowhere to hide that which is within our hearts, and all becomes glaringly evident. In fact, IT will define the brightness of the spirit plane which we are drawn to, for your "vibration" seeks its own kind. Therefore, part of our preparation is bringing out those things which we have buried within our "closet", and letting them go while here on earth Consider this while reading the following message:*

October 2, 1975

I am thy sister Judith, bathed in a new light... radiant is my essence and divine its nature. It is with sublimity and with submission that I now go about my endeavors. No less is my intensity, yet many of the rough edges and awkwardness have been smoothed or eliminated. I am the self-same Judith you knew and loved, yet expanded, broadened, and sharpened as an instrument.

I did sit in judgment upon myself, and watched the "movie" of my life unfold before my eyes, scene by scene, act by act, as I relived each moment. Glad am I that I atoned for my misused energy while still in the body of flesh. Sad indeed are those who let their lives slip by, putting off those things which make them uncomfortable, which are the very things which they come to earth to work on. I tell you, that it is sad to see them here, for their "movie" is long and arduous, and needs to be taken very slowly and painstakingly. Valuable it is to view the composite of your life.

My message I give to you with great compassion is: Prepare now for watching that "movie". Clean your house of all debris... leave no old injuries, hatred, jealousy, or other litter lying about... for here, if not there, you will need to face each and every one and atone for it in your own way. You now have the materials at hand, and help surrounds you on every side. I urge you to take action in this matter, for none other is responsible for your misused energy. Each must account for his own life's drama and how he has played it out. If you "clean house" from day to day, and don't let the dirt accumulate, you will be ever prepared for each new step on your path.

To see ones life in retrospect, if you are so prepared, can be a fulfilling experience, one of richness and reward. Such was my experience on the whole. Grateful I am for the guidance and help I received while in the pore (body) to do the self-same thing I am now urging you to do. The task of watching the "movie" was a brief one for me, though some spend long, long, arduous times here at the place of accounting. Forgive those whom you feel have wronged you... then begin to ask forgiveness for yourself. It is a worthwhile task... believe me.

All who pass from the flesh are presented with this procedure, for it is of great value to evaluate and understand one's own past experiences before proceeding on to new experiences.

Prepare yourself now... "Prepare, Prepare, Prepare! For as you are prepared, so will you receive." Words of great wisdom indeed!

God bless you, each and every one. Give thanks for the life that He has given you.

I am Judith, your sister in light.

- - -

October 3, 1975

Sananda speaking: I present thy sister Judith at this time,

Judy: My dear sister

You are wondering why I always come to you through the introduction of Sananda. In the folds of his garment I have been protected, nurtured, and held, since my transition. I have been greatly blessed by his hand. To follow him while on earth, with total devotion, is to earn thy heavenly passport into his realm of abode. His servants are dear to him, each and every one, and he forgets them not.

To a special work I was called from my earthly pore... and glad I am for the lessons learned of obedience, for I answered the call without question or hesitation, and for this have I been truly blessed. All that is requires is obedience unto the Law.

Many things did I feel I lacked, and I felt inadequate to serve so high a purpose... however, this is not of such importance... in fact of none. For as long as the cup be kept empty it will be constantly filled to over-flowing with knowledge and wisdom... always new and fresh, ever growing in depth.

The treasures contained within the sacred Scripts recorded by Sister Thedra are of greater value than I had imagined. Each portion is filled with keys, with simple truths and instructions that will lead you straight to the High Holy Mount, if you but practice them and make them an integral part of your everyday experiences. The truth WILL set you free.

How fortuned are those of earth to have received these sacred writings at this time. You have been truly blessed that one was sent (Sister Thedra), one from the realms of light, to deliver them in their perfect form, for not a word has been changed. How few there are who are truly attuned to their (The Scripts) value, yet the time will soon come, yea it is now at hand, when man shall begin to awaken and desire to be fed the bread of life, and they shall be fed and nourished thereby.

There is so much I would say as a tribute to the one sent to light the dark night, for it is she (Sister Thedra) who was chosen for the work which no other man could do. It was she who volunteered, for the good of all mankind, to descend into matter and to tread alone with her faith never wavering, her purpose single. Truly has mankind been blessed by her presence. Privileged was I to serve for a short while... and for this joyful service I have been greatly rewarded. She is greatly loved and is highly esteemed in these realms... to serve her is to serve the Father, Solen Aum Solen.

I am thy sister in the light... Judith

- - -

October 5, 1975

My dear sister

Think not that we are never sad within this realm or that we no longer suffer. Our feelings are more acute and now more deeply felt than when in the dense body of flesh. Our sorrow is for man and his ignorance and stupidity.

To see him groveling in his own filth when the light draws nigh and surrounds him on every side is sad indeed. To see them turn from their only hope for freedom, their beloved Master Sananda, is hard to bear, when all they need do is look up and receive. To see the masses in their contented emptiness, drinking their old stale wine (of beliefs), and ignoring the offer of sparkling fresh water (of truth) makes one sober indeed.

Light thy lamp and shine it ever brighter. It may make them uncomfortable, for their eyes are not accustomed to the light, but their discomfort will serve to awaken them, and it is good.

If only they knew what poverty they have allowed themselves to become accustomed to... to what depth they have sunk. But they have forgotten, and they think themselves among the fortunate. Yet their hearts be empty and their lives filled with trivia and frivolity. We do weep for them... and we rejoice when one begins to rouse himself and rubs his sleepy eyes from having slept too long. Be up and about the Father's business now, for you are much needed in the work at hand. Blessed are the torch bearers... blessed are they who seek the light.

I am thy sister in light... Judith

- - -

The Spoken Word
October 8, 1975

He anointed my head with oil... my cup runeth over. To Him am I eternally grateful, for He has given me life in great abundance. Praise His holy name, and speak it with reverence and awe.

He has blessed mankind at this time in this simple act... the gift of His name has He revealed to man. Sorely needed is that vibration on earth at this time. By the spoken word, His Name (Solen Aum Solen), will the speaker be blessed, as well as all within the realm of the vibration of the sound.

The power of sound is little understood to man. It has been a great and wondrous revelation to me. Each sound uttered carries a vibration, which has the power to arrange and re-arrange atoms and molecules into new and different patterns. Each sound has its own vibration and touches upon the ethers in its own unique pattern.

The spoken word was a divine gift from the Father, to be used to glorify him, but how it has been mis-used and abused. Its purpose has been forgotten long ago. Man goes about blathering words upon words, knowing not what he is doing yet in truth he is responsible for each sound that is omitted from his lips. He is the creator of whatever he speaks, be it for good or evil purposes, or a mixture of both.

You can see what a perfect and effective instrument you can be for the good of all if you do nothing else but select your words carefully, making sure that each is purposeful in its creation for glorifying the Father. You may even feel that you need to stop talking for a while in order to sort things out... not a bad idea!

Praise His name, Solen Aum Solen. In this you cannot go wrong!

I am thy sister... Judith

- - -

October 10, 1975

My dear sister

Lost... lost in the world of their own trappings. They long for light, yet they do not accept it when it is offered. My heart aches for those who hold out one hand asking for the bread of life, while keeping their eyes tightly covered with the other hand.

Do not waste your time and precious energy on those who remain divided within themselves, for they straddle the fence and are lost in the confusion which they have created for themselves. Your words will be listened to momentarily, yet will be forgotten with the next breath they breathe. The fence straddler must choose on which side he wishes to be... until then, he will remain immobilized by his own indecisiveness. He must desire the truth and freedom with his whole being, and be ready to surrender his will to that of the Father. He must take the first step by his own effort, by firmly placing himself on the side of the fence of his own choosing.

There are ones who nibble at every fence post along the way, asking of man his opinions concerning eternal truth, not willing to work for it himself nor to listen to the Source from whence it emits... that still small voice within. It feels "safe" to draw it in from the "outside" where it can be spit out before it reaches home. Sad is their lot, for hungry they remain.

Be no part of their silly game, for you have work of greater importance to perform. Be discriminating in thy sharing of the knowledge which you find to be true... share it only with those who come seeking in full sincerity. You are bringing forth light... but of what use is a television set that has been left on while the viewer, although watching it, is not focusing their full attention on it? It is your choice of how you administer your knowledge, but to be effective you must be discriminating.

Never forget from where you receive your understanding, the truth which you are learning. From the Source does it flow, from the creator of all things, the All in All... thy Father/Mother God, Solen Aum Solen. "For He so loved the world that He sent His only begotten Son, that who-so-ever believeth in him would have life everlasting". He is a merciful Father. Praise Him... Glorify Him... Love Him, and give unceasing thanks unto Him.

I am thy sister in light... Judith

- - -

October 11, 1975

Dear sister

All weakness must be cleansed... be thankful for the opportunity to do this on each and every point of truth you are learning. In no other place is the opportunity so great for trying, testing, strengthening yourself, than on earth. A school for gods it truly is.

Hold high the banner of truth for all to see. Be not discouraged in thy daily tasks, for although they may seem to be interfering with the work to be done, it is a vital part of the preparation for the days ahead. Be at peace and poise. Look to the example set by our Lord Sananda when he walked the earth as Jesus.

Listen well to his words of wisdom which he imparts to you, and study well his teachings within the sacred Scripts recorded by Sister Thedra, for therein lies the questions and the answers to what you would wish to know. He is the wayshower, and in him you will find the comfort and the solace which you seek.

In him and through him flows all truth, which will help you through all problems. Through him do all blessings flow. Turn to him... depend upon him... ask him to be your guide and your sibor. Place your trust in him who is trustworthy beyond question. Give thanks to the Father who has sent him to show you the way. To him go all praise, honor, and glory. Love him with all thy being, then love him more.

I am thy devoted sister in light... Judith

- - -

October 12, 1975

Dear sister

To you I address myself, yet to the many do I speak. Hear my voice dear ones, and listen well. I come as a reference... I come to refer you to the teachings which will be food for your hungry soul. So long have you hungered that you no longer heed the pain, thinking it to be a natural part of your being.

It is NOT natural to be in pain, to be lonely, to go about hungry (for understanding) without ceasing. Through your own separation from your Source you have created this condition yourself. Now you are being offered teachings which will set you aright and show you the way. Sananda, our blessed Lord, has given of himself at this time to be that wayshower.

He holds out his hand to each of you, offering you assistance. What a blessing is being offered to you... would you be so foolish as to refuse his help? Would you scoff at his teachings, his words, calling them rubbish? If so, then you cut off your own life-line. There is no other way... this is it!

He has lent himself to releasing his words of wisdom for the new age, the new dispensation, which are given to man at this time for his own salvation... yet he (man) treats it as just one more radical and strange cult. He has not the discrimination nor the trust in himself to know the truth when he sees it. He listens not to his hungering spirit crying out to be fed the bread of life.

I come as a reference, to refer you to the direct path home... the path on which travels Lord Sananda, Son of God, for he is come to show you the way. Heed his call... do not wait nor seek thy brother's opinion. Have courage and faith in your self, that the still small voice within you is the best guide... it is your spirit speaking to you, directing you to the food for which it hungers.

Do not place your faith in me, for I follow him. It is he you must follow and trust. I am but one of his faithful servants.

My love encompasses you. I am Judith, your sister in light.

- - -

October 13, 1975

Be ye blessed of the Father, Solen Aum Solen, in whom you live and have your being.

I come to do a special work. Much preparation have I been receiving for that which lies ahead. Much help is needed in every realm at this time, but only those who are adequately prepared can be of use... those who have been taught to go about their business with singleness of purpose and unflinching in their demeanor. Those who become rattled and thrown off center by the unexpected abrupt changes in circumstance must better prepare themself before they can be effective as a servant of the Father. How can you wonder concerning the preparation when it has been spelled out in detail for all mankind in the Scripts? Only those who read them without concentrating can feign ignorance concerning their preparation.

Receive with gladness each new experience placed before you... for your own expression, your own uniqueness, is becoming more clarified with each event, as you interrelate with each of life's circumstances. Never will the same event be repeated in the same way. Your expectations in this regard (trying to repeat an experience) will only place obstacles before you, making the new experience unclear because of the preconceived ideas you have regarding it. Predictions of future events then, will create obstacles in the path... for the formulation of pictures and thoughts concerning those future events begin to shape the mind, causing problems when the actual event occurs.

Welcome the unexpected! Be open to the newness and freshness that life offers. This is one of the beauties of the eternal plan if you could but realize it. There is nothing to fear or dread once you realize, once you KNOW once and for all, that ALL is of the Father sent... that there is nothing new under the sun, and that the Father is kind and merciful above all.

So much to learn... for you... for me... SO MUCH! Yes, the learning never seems to cease, but the purpose becomes ever more clear, and the Love of the Father ever more wondrous and expansive.

I am thy sister, Judith.

- - -

October 16, 1975

Beloved sister

My divine nature is of a feminine quality, for although we are each components of both male and femaleness, my female nature has predominated and continues to do so. To be a receptacle for his work, to be "worked through" so to speak, is my greatest joy. To provide comfort and love as a mother hen enfolding her chicks within her soft protecting wings... to provide love and comfort to all who are troubled, all who are suffering, all who seek solace, fulfills me and nourishes me.

May all who seek the Light of the Father allow these female qualities to shine forth, while at the same time tuning into the maleness of creativity and discrimination, of standing forth strongly for that which you know to be true and just. To create a balance in this regard is a never ending process... one which was achieved by one who came to earth so long ago in a body of flesh, as a living example of his God-given perfection. Look to him as your teacher of all you strive to become. Allow him to show you the way, for through him did the Father manifest as a perfect example set before mankind.

He is now returned, as you have been told often... yet you do not quite believe it to be reality. It is true! He walks among you and you know it not! Your preconceived ideas and expectations of him (from the past) limit you... it stops you from acknowledging his presence of today. He comes in love, the Father's love. If you could but know how blessed you are in this.

My love surrounds you.

I am your sister, Judith.

- - -

October 20, 1975

Dear ones

To see one so great, so perfect, so filled with the divine essence of the Father Mother God... and to see him (Sananda) unrecognized and ignored, pushed away and spit upon as he enters the world of men, is a heavy number... for he is loved and greatly respected by all who are privileged to know him in these realms. He is served with untold joy, and it is the cause of much sorrow here to see this taking place on earth).

Prepare the way my brothers and sisters, that he, Sananda, our Lord and director, will be recognized as the one who has come to show them the way home. In this way would you be serving him and your Father, Solen Aum Solen, of whom he is sent. Prepare the way by helping to eliminate the preconceived ideas and opinions concerning him, which blind them to that which he truly is. Prepare the way by being a living example of one who knows, and one who knows that they know.

Each in his own way will go about his special preparedness. Each will be a shining orb, joining with others and still others. Your part will help greatly in the plan which has been so carefully prepared and held in readiness. Be of good cheer, for it will not go astray. Praise be our Source and creator, the ALL in ALL in whom all rests and has its being.

I am thy sister, Judith

- - -

October 21, 1975

Dear ones

My mission is presently as a liaison between the realms. I come to show you that there is no barrier, no walls or barricades. These exist only in the mind of men... and as you release them within yourself the path becomes a clear and unobstructed roadway for you to travel.

The reality of the material world, which presents daily obstructions and holds your attention so solidly, is only an illusion... it will pass and be no more. Daily it shifts and changes into new and varying objects, each demanding your attention, each screaming that it is of real substance, but it will only trip you up. The only thing that does not change, the ONLY thing on which you can depend, is the spiritual nature of all. It is the cause behind the material world, and it comes of God the Father, in whom we all have our being.

Put your energies then, into that which is lasting... do not waste yourself on that which is only transitory. Deal with it you must, and responsibility concerning your material surroundings is necessary... but assess your values correctly and act accordingly.

Always look to the spiritual CAUSE behind the material illusion, for in this there is much knowledge to be gained. Just as this printed page contains only the symbols (letters) for the real spiritual communication between us, so too is the material world symbolic of the real spiritual meaning behind it. Never forget to take it one step further, to the Source and Creator of all spirit... our Father, Solen Aum Solen, and allow the awe and wonder to fill you to overflowing.

I am your loving sister, Judith.

- - -

October 22, 1975

Beloved ones

Many is the time I would cry out to you, for much do I see that I would make right and help you with. Yet, it is only through your own "doing" (or un-doing) that you learn. Each must tread his own path... that which he molds for himself. Guidance is ever at hand, but only through asking, of your own free will, will that guidance be received... for your free will is not to be touched or tampered with, even if it leads you to your own destruction.

Turn towards the light, and seek the knowledge spilling forth all around you. The truth surrounds you if you but acknowledge it. Work you must, for there is no easy way to enlightenment... but every small gesture you make towards that goal will return to you many times over.

I know, for I see it happening. No longer do I believe this on faith alone as I did when in my flesh body, but I can now observe it taking place from my new improved vantage point. The plan, so perfect in design, is simple, yet imaginatively conceived to be self-operating, self-destructing, self-repairing.

Seek the guidance you need... NOT from your fellow man, for he too is as limited as you are. Go directly to He who has devoted himself to showing you the way. He holds the keys to the gate you are seeking, he is our blessed Lord and director, Sananda. He asks nothing from you, only your obedience to the Law. Give him your hand and he will lead you ever so gently.

I am your sister in light, Judith.

- - -

October 24, 1975

Greetings from my home to yours

I am still but a fledgling in these realms, and I am diligently striving to learn through study and observation of so much that is necessary to my preparation. Think not that preparation is complete when one leaves his earthly body and makes the transition to another realm, for your environment here is dependent upon your preparation while on earth. Each gravitates towards his chosen environment which has been self-determined by his own efforts, or lack of such.

Many there are here who do not yet understand the necessity of preparation. Their false notions and distorted views of "heaven" have contributed towards this warped and unrealistic attitude. Just to rid themselves of their preconceived ideas and expectations in this regard, takes much work and effort. Many continue to cling to their false beliefs for the longest time, wasting their energy in the duration.

The civilized world thinks itself to be so wise, so right in its theories, attitudes, and beliefs... yet if they only knew of their overwhelming ignorance and the undoing that lies ahead of them. Would that they begin now to awaken to the true nature of things as they ARE, rather than how they view them. So much can be accomplished on the earth plane... so much!

To have faith in the creator of all things, of all life, and to believe in the divine nature of His works, gives me hope. I rest in His hands... my will is His will.

I am thy sister, Judith.

- - -

October 25, 1975

Beloved ones: The universe is constructed on the principle of perfect order, each particle accurately timed and placed for the best use and its best growth. As the parts grow and change, so too does the whole develop accordingly.

When each particle realizes its place within the great and glorious whole, it then radiates forth its perfection from within. It becomes all that it is and so much more, for it knows itself to be part OF the whole as well as WITHIN it. Its purpose then becomes expanded, beyond its imaginings, and nothing can prevent it from attaining its glory. When it goes from a selfish (self-centered) to a selfless (without thought of self) purpose, it takes a giant step for the whole, which includes each part.

Sananda, when in the body of Jesus of Nazareth, never deviated from his inner motive of serving the whole. He recognized himself without question, without any deviation, as being one part of the perfect totality of ALL THAT IS. In this way did he demonstrate to all mankind that by serving the ALL, the Source, the whole, you ultimately serve each and every part therein.

Through man's habitual "thinking" himself to be separate, he has created for himself a world of matter so dense that he now reinforces that thinking within his surroundings... each taking the appearance of being separated and divided, one from the other. Only by great effort on his part to expand his vision once again, to lift himself to a higher vantage point, can he see reality as it truly exists.

Strive then to regain your previous vantage point dear brothers and sisters, and let nothing deter you from this goal, for it is well worth the effort. It will allow you to see the truths you are learning daily as a living reality, as actual reality, more vivid and well-defined than you can imagine. To lift your head above the fog-mist while your feet are still treading the sod of mother earth, is truly an accomplishment.

I am your loving sister, Judith.

- - -

October 25, 1975

My dear ones: Many is the time I am with you, and if you wish to feel my presence you have only to desire communication and contact. I am not afar off, and I respond to any call for light where I can be of assistance, for in this way do I serve my Father/Mother God.

It is only you - through your own fear of the unknown, through your own doubt in the eternal nature of life, through your preconceived ideas of those who have passed on - who create the barriers which prevent the contact which you desire. Learn to trust in the Father, to trust Life itself, and trust in yourself that you are an integral part of it all.

As each one prepares himself, so shall he receive. As he strives to remove the barriers which he has constructed, so shall he be rewarded in the doing by experiencing a freedom and a peace he has not known before. Nothing can take this peace from him, for he will have earned it and it is rightfully his.

As we of the Host draw closer to the earth, each is prepared to be of service in the places where he can be most effective. Each will minister unto his own, where he can do the most good. By letting your light shine forth you roll out a welcome mat to we your brothers, who have come to work with you, hand in hand, for the good of all. In the dark night, one small candle is easily seen... let you light so shine as to light the dark night.

I am your sister in light, Judith.

- - -

October 29, 1975

Grateful am I that we are able to commune together, closing the gap between the realms, a separation which is existent only in the mortal mind of man. I tread lightly and with surety of foot that knows its way. Much do I have to learn... so much... yet the self-created pressure of earthly existence no longer is a factor, and I am able to absorb knowledge with much greater ease and enjoyment. My mind is clear, my memory more keen, both of which are important factors in the process of learning.

Through experience do we learn here, as do you also... but here the lessons are offered direct and first hand, rather than through the second hand methods of earth, such as books and the opinions of men. Learning is a great joy here, presenting ever new challenges and fresh material. Seek to learn directly, my dear ones, from the Source of thy being. These obvious lessons surrounding man of earth are too often ignored or neglected, and precedence is given to the more arduous, roundabout methods of learning the same thing.

Ask that you may receive of His knowledge directly... then be open to receive that which will be forthcoming. At first it may come so rapidly, so immediately, that you are not prepared for it... but with continued practice you will be able to receive in this way. Never was it intended that learning should be a struggle, a difficult task. With joy and delight should the discovery of new ideas, new concepts and lessons, be received and absorbed.

I am thy loving sister, Judith.

- - -

Added Note: Both darkness and Light carry their own distinct "vibration", whether it be in a person or the written word. We can be misled by words, but the "vibration" behind the words always represents the motive, and is discernable once you feel it. Words speak only to our minds, but the vibration speaks within our hearts... and to discern that "vibration" is to come to know the true from the false.

The Written Word
October 30, 1975

Dear ones

How can I express to you that which I wish to share, that which is in my heart and longs to reach you? Although Truth becomes ever more clear, words are ever less adequate as a means of conveyance of the Truth. It has become clear to me now that it is not the words that are of importance, but rather the 'vibration" which they carry from one person to another. The words are only the conveyance for the deeper message. They are only one means, but at the present time on earth it is the accepted method of the "transportation" of thought.

So much emphasis has been placed on the written word at this time in the history of man that it in and of itself, is thought to be the authority. The false worship of the intellect (instead of the spirit) has led men to this misconception, and consequently the written word has been used as a tool by the forces of darkness to sustain and to spread ignorance and confusion throughout the world.

Be aware of the vibration carried by the written word, and let this be your guideline, your means of learning. Be discriminating in what you read. Through your intuition will you know immediately the nature of the vibration conveyed within the material.

Turn aside from that which you know to be false and designed to lead you astray... give it no energy. Use your time and energy to enhance your growth, to increase your knowledge, to cut through the forest of ignorance, by reading only the words that touch you as a soothing balm, as nourishment for your spirit.

I am thy sister in light, Judith.

- - -

October 31, 1975

My dear ones

Be blessed of the Father, for He is all merciful, all kind, all loving. Through Him do all blessings flow without pause, without ceasing. He blesses constantly all life within Him... you have only to receive that blessing.

Those who choose to turn their backs and to keep their vessel tightly closed have the free will to do so. Then they wonder why they hunger and are never satisfied... why they thirst and remain parched and dry... poor hungering souls! Turn towards the light and open your empty vessel... only in this way can you receive that which will nourish you and bring you peace.

Can you not see that there is only one way home to your Father Mother God from whom you went out so long ago? The blueprints for the journey home are being offered to you in their original form, unadulterated, unchanged in any way. Painstakingly have they been received for your benefit by she (Sister Thedra) who has served with utter devotion and obedience. The sacred Scripts which she recorded are yours for the asking... and in them is contained all that you have need of knowing at this present time, to guide you safely home. Few there are who have chosen to benefit themselves in this way... fewer still are they who receive these Scripts and take them seriously, making them a part of themselves.

I have not come to preach to you... yet I see a need so great, with the fulfillment of that need within reach... and I see it being rejected. I cannot help but to cry out to you for your own sake: "Give yourselves a break!" Relieve yourselves of all that pressure you have created for yourselves... for your load is heavy and your backs grow tired under the strain. You have been endowed with free will, and nothing can take it away from you. The choice is yours to make... I pray that you choose wisely.

I stand as one who has submitted my will long ago to God the Father. Since then I have been led through chaos and confusion, turbulence and strife, with a calmness and knowingness I had never before experienced. Trust in the Lord, for on him can you depend. He will not let you down.

I am your devoted sister, Judith.

- - -

November 1, 1975

My dear sister

Concentration is a lesson so important that it is well worth some consideration. It is a gift with which man is endowed. Watch a baby in his efforts to manipulate his new and awkward covering (body) he finds himself encased in... his concentration is intense, his effort single of purpose. How else could he learn to walk, to talk?

But through the process of growing up he allows himself to become distracted and his energy to become dispersed by the opinions of others and by the world of mortality. He loses his beautiful ability of perfect concentration.

Some, feeling their purpose more strongly than others, remain heartstrong and buck the obstacles, thus keeping a hold on their gift of concentration. These are the men of accomplishment... observe them in the world around you. Others, having lost the gift, must work to regain it... for it is not truly lost, only obliterated by the distractions that the "Self" has allowed in its way. Now, through effort, the path must once again be cleared of debris that this quality be permitted to come forth. To be able to concentrate yourself totally on the matter at hand is essential if you wish to be of use to the Father at this time.

The distractions on the earth plane are countless and demanding of your attention. To learn the skill of concentration while still in the physical body is of no small accomplishment, and will hold you in good stead for any future endeavor. Consider it an important part of your preparation, and the effort it may take is worthwhile... believe me.

I am thy sister in light, Judith.

- - -

November 2, 1975

Beloved ones

We of the higher realms send our blessings and our love to you in a constant flow, as a fresh stream of water containing all the vibrant colors and the harmonizing sounds so much needed on the earth plane. In unison do we work for the good of all mankind, and for our beloved friend, earth.

It is beautiful to watch as it penetrates the thick layers of dark thoughts which are like an ooze, dark and heavy, encasing the earth, encrusting her very soul. The light does dispel the darkness... as a two edged sword it cuts through with an ease hard to imagine.

That which appears impenetrable is only a show, an act, put on by those misguided souls lost in the web of their own illusion. Be not fooled by the appearance of hopeless situations, for the negativity is often but a display of deep and hidden fears, confusion, and a lack of direction.

Do you not see that even one thought of a strong purposeful nature, one of clarity and purity, will cut through and dispel the gloom? Such is the power of light... of such is His glorious universe constructed. Is it surprising then, that it has continued to exist and to run smoothly throughout eternity?

Do not be fooled then, by appearances. The gloom may be just a cover-up for those who have lost sight of the light and of their own inner knowingness. They may even have forgotten how to look... but with a thought, a prayer, a gentle word spoken, their hope may be restored, their vision cleared, their hardened hearts softened. Do not underestimate the power of the light. It is within each one of us for the use in serving and glorifying our beloved Father, Solen Aum Solen.

I am Judith, thy sister in the light.

- - -

Added note: At the Gatehouse in Mt Shasta, all during the 1970's, we used to have a meditation service at sunrise each morning. Any who wished be un-synchronized with the whole for long, for its imbalance is felt clear to the outer realms, as ripples created by a single drop of water falling in a still pond.

The forces of all creation, continuing on in their progress, will overcome that one which is out-of-sync, and it will once again be set on its true course. All must progress according to divine Law in its unfoldment and development. All must finally, at some time, acknowledge its own divinity and its need to operate according to the Law of Love.

The world at present is in a state of disharmony, it is out of sync with the rest of the universe. Watch the necessary changes occur as the balance is re-established, and God's perfect order once again prevails upon the planet.

By holding peace within your own heart, by knowing that all is working for the greater good, you will help the earth in her present dilemma to resume her rightful place within the universe. Were it not for the divine mercy of our Father who loves each fallen sparrow with infinite tenderness, the earth would have perished long ago.

Give thanks to him for his mercy and his love. Acknowledge those serving Him, those who devote themselves to the task of aiding the earth and her people, especially their leader Sananda. Grateful am I to be part of his divine plan.

I am thy sister, Judith.

- - -

November 10, 1975

My dear sister

Little is known of the work that goes on here, for although many attempts have been made throughout the ages to enlighten man concerning this matter, he still has only a limited ability to receive and understand the fullness of the activity here. He had been given many smatterings, but the whole picture he has not been able to grasp.

Do not let this discourage you in your endeavor to receive and to understand... let it be a constant inspiration to you, leading you ever forward and onward. Communication is essential between the realms. In order to work closely together for the good of all, it is necessary to have full knowledge of the existence of these realms.

Has Sister Thedra not shared with you many times her experiences of being called to help in other realms with which she is unfamiliar? She does not stop to ask questions, nor to increase her knowledge while there, for she is aware of the purpose for which she was sent, and she goes about her service with her eye single upon that purpose.

Her limited knowledge of life within these realms (during her embodiment on earth) does not interfere nor have a bearing on the good she accomplishes while there. By being an obedient servant, by being dependable and trustworthy, she accomplishes that service for which she was sent. Through her total faith she is able to submit herself totally to the matter at hand.

Be not saddened by her present condition of health (frail of body, and in constant pain) for she understands the deep underlying cause and accepts it totally. Let her life be as a shining example to all those fortunate enough to have been touched by her loving vibration. She has chosen her path well, and it is not an easy one. She will reap her reward in all its fullness.

God be with you, each and every one. I am Judith.

- - -

November 15, 1975

How merciful is our Father to provide us with this guidance and direction as to the way home. But man is ungrateful, and gives no credit to Him... in fact, man discredits Him and thinks himself to reign supreme. Yet help is never withheld from those who are ready to receive it, no matter how wayward they have been. Is this not mercy beyond anything the earth has known?

Few there are who ask. Fewer still are those who listen... and although those who listen may hear, many do not obey... and those who obey are fewer still. Give unto them your love and compassion, for they are your brothers and sisters. In unity there is strength, therefore, be not divided one against the other. Work out the small interferences that come between you, and remain strong in your brotherhood with each other.

I am thy sister in the light, Judith.

- - -

November 16, 1975

Don't be contented for one second with your small distorted views of life, for you are indeed looking through mists and veils created over aeons of time by men's muddled thoughts. Strive always for a clearer sharper view of the greater reality. Have no opinions of how that view will or should look, only hold yourself open to its vastness and its ever surprising newness. Those who hold tightly to certain views of what they will find, confine themselves to seeing that view and that one only... like the ostrich with its head in the sand, declaring that there is only darkness in the world.

You have yet to begin your trek through unknown territory. Seek it out... nobody will bring it to you. You must make the effort to break out of your confining shell and walk into the sunlight. There is nothing to fear, for the light will protect you so long as you ask for protection.

I tell you, you cannot hope to lead others through this unknown territory until you have gone through it yourself. Until you have become familiar with the newness and the brilliant clarity, you will be as blind, offering your hand to your blind brothers. Better not to offer it at all than to lead him astray when he puts his trust in you. Let us all put our trust in the one who has come for the purpose of showing us the way, of guiding and directing us... for he, our Lord Sananda, knows the way well, every leaf and pebble on the path. He has been sent by God the Father expressly for this purpose. I am thy sister, Judith.

- - -

November 17, 1975

Blessed am I to have been given the opportunity to serve in my present capacity. It fills me with joy to be able to serve more fully than when in earthly garb. My vision is much greater and more clear, my mobility is virtually unlimited, my responsibilities much greater.

It has become ever clearer to me that one's motivation to serve, one's inner most intent, is that which determines his path to greater service. If his motive is pure, then he is given - or rather, he attracts to himself - that which he desires to do while serving in his limited capacity with joy and devotion, his desire to serve in a still greater manner is attracting to him ever greater responsibilities, with which he is presented when he has completed the former and proven himself to be trustworthy.

And so it goes, on and on, with the capacity to love and to serve ever increasing, ever expanding according to the will of the server. As he continues on his path his knowledge increases, his joy is boundless, his foot is continually seeking the next higher step. The plan is orderly and exacting, yet at the same time the opportunity for greater freedom is endless. With a humble heart and total submission to our Father Mother God, I give thanks that it is so. I give thanks for being a part of Him, the ever merciful one.

I am thy sister in light, Judith.

- - -

November 19, 1975

Dear ones

Blessed is he who takes no credit for his accomplishments, remembering always that it is the Father working through him.

This is a pitfall on the path which ensnares many. They give themselves in loving service to their creator, then as the work begins to manifest through them they forget their original vow, and begin to take credit for that which the Father has performed. This stops the flow, for it creates a blockage within the servant. The once sparkling flow becomes stagnant, and there is no room for the fresh new water of life. Sad indeed is he who betrays himself or his trust.

Be as the silent one, doing good works with no thought of reward. Remember always that it is a privilege to serve the Father in the way that He sees fit. Be ready to recognize and accept Truth when it presents itself to you. It may come in the most unexpected way at the most unexpected time. Nothing will surprise you if you are ever alert and watchful, expecting only the unexpected.

We may visit you in a way you have not anticipated, at a time when you least expect it. We come only to those who seek assistance, and whom we can help. Privileged are we to serve the Father in this manner.

I am thy sister, Judith.

- - -

Added note: Always remember, that "beliefs" and "opinions" are formulated within the mind... while TRUTH speaks directly to your heart, not needing words. We form beliefs based on opinions", because we do not know the Truth.

Think about three men not long ago, discussing their "beliefs" about the world. One "believed" the earth to be flat, that if you sailed far enough you would fall off the edge. He was sure of this, for if the earth were round then those on the bottom would fall off. He had done much "thinking" about this and fully "believed" it to be true.

The second also believed that the earth was flat, yet believing the earth was obviously the center of all of God's creation, he "believed" it was without end and went on forever. He too had reasoned it out for himself, and was sure he was right.

The third, having observed that the sun and the moon were round, 'believed" therefore that the earth too must be round. He didn't understand why people did not fall off of the bottom, but none the less he argued his "beliefs".

None Knew the truth, yet each argued his opinion. All three had their own opinions, and all would argue to their death to uphold them. Such too is the plight of mankind, that we are full of opinions, while remaining ignorant of the truth.

Today we would say to them: "Your opinions have no bearing on anything... let go of your opinions and I will tell you the truth. The earth is round... I am telling you what IS."

The higher ones KNOW the Truth and they have come to tell us what truly IS. But mankind is already full of "opinions" as to what they believe concerning things spiritual, and most people will reject the truth because it contradicts their opinions. I can't tell you how many times I have heard someone claim to believe in Sananda, yet in the same breath they reject something he has said, because it does not fit into their opinions. Do they think Sananda speaks falsehoods? Do we think that he is just spouting off opinions like we do?

If we really desire to know what is true, then we must first be willing to empty out our cups, so long willed with misconceptions and distortions. We must first empty out the old muddy water... and then ask that our cups be filled again with the clear sparkling waters of life, the sparkling clarity of TRUTH, uncontaminated by the distortions of man's "thinking". Consider then the following:

November 20, 1975

Beloved ones

Blessed are you this day... this day which is bursting and overflowing with the wine of new life. It is being distributed to one and all alike. Just as the sun shines on everyone, so too does the eternal love flow forth. As you are prepared for it, so will you receive it.

Those who choose to hide in dark corners they have created for themselves through their own thinking, will reject it because of their own opinions. Yet for those who willingly open themselves to receive of it, they will be filled to overflowing. Keep your cup ever empty of the old, cleanse it daily, yes even moment by moment, that you be ever ready to receive your new portion.

Let the sacred Scripts be your guideline for living at the present time. They will answer your every question if you truly seek the answers within them, turning from the opinions of men and giving these words of truth your attention. They are the word of God, spoken through his Son, Sananda. What better Source could you consult?

Let peace reside in your hearts. I am you sister, Judith.

- - -

November 22, 1975

Dear ones

Let your hearts sing a glad song, for he lives... our Lord God Sananda lives in the hearts of all men. He lives and performs a mighty work by day and by night, and blessed is the earth and all mankind for his presence and his caring.

Long ago did he take upon his shoulders the yoke of this planet and her people. He is true to his trust and he will complete his task just as he promised. Mankind has no comprehension of what this means... that the Son of God has seen fit to concern himself with this world, so small in the heavenly spheres, so darkened and disgraced by its own wayward children. It is a blessing you cannot begin to realize.

This is the time of action... the more complete the preparation on earth for this action, the greater will be the acceptance and the transformation. Do not concern yourself with tomorrow, for as long as your preparation has been sufficient for this day, tomorrow will take care of itself.

In your hearts find and abide in peace, and live totally within this peace in each moment. Let nothing or no-one change this in any way. Remain strong within it, with a knowingness that only a child of God can feel.

Give thanks that the Father has seen fit to send forth his Son to an earth in distress. Give thanks... and then give more thanks.

I am thy sister in light, Judith.

- - -

Added note: Although the above messages are only a few of the communiques received from Judy, it is enough for us to see just how important Sananda's words have been to her, even after her transition from the earth plane. If you are one of the ones who read only a few of the Scripts and found them too tedious or boring to continue... let these communiques be a word of encouragement from one who KNOWS their true value.

The Freedom of Spirit

I will add these last communique just to give you some idea of the true unlimited nature of our spirit. It is one of the many communiques received by Margot from Sister Thedra during that time. Even though Sister Thedra was still in flesh, and even though her physical embodiment was not fully aware of this communication, her spirit, operating independent of the limitations of her body, often spoke to Margot during her meditation and offered her words of guidance and encouragement. This not only happened with Margot, but also with another woman in Florida who was also in training at the time.

- - -

January 28, 1975

Thedra speaking

Sori Sori: Unto you I come this day, bringing my offering of love and service to all mankind. The more that is given of yourself to serve the whole, the more you will receive... such is the Law.

I am able to share less and less of my spiritual experiences as time passes by, as they are "wordless", to the point that attempting to talk about them seems pointless, an insult to the experience itself, so to speak. Yet, I will speak to you this day of that which can clearly be put into words and clearly understood, that there be no mistaking what is said.

Be ye concentrated in and on the Light. Keep your attention focused upon God the Father, whether it be admiring a flower, feeling love for the suffering, or contemplating His divine plan. If you would grow towards Him you must give Him your attention... seeing His handiwork in ALL things, great and small. It is only when we withdraw our attention from Him, even momentarily, that we falter along the path and become blinded by our own forgetfulness. Always turn to Him for counsel and guidance, for help and sustenance, continually thanking Him for His many blessings. It is said over and over again... yet how many actually live IN him, remembering at all times wherein they are staid?

I have come to remind man wherein he is staid, not to offer him a bed of roses. I have chosen a rugged earthly path, full of thorns and pitfalls for a purpose. The fulfillment of that purpose you will come to know in time. I choose it not for masochistic reasons, nor to be a martyr, but rather that I might glorify God the Father to the fullest of my capacity in the shortest time possible.

Be not turned off by that which is seen to manifest on the physical plane, but search for the unseen deeper meaning behind the physical, and pray for greater capacity for understanding of that which you see.

Praise His holy name (Solen Aum Solen) given to us as a gift for the upliftment of all mankind.

I am Sister Thedra

- - -

Added Note: The earth and the myriad of spirit planes associated with the earth are made up of ones of two different natures... those who are yet asleep, with their attention absorbed in "Self"... and those who have awakened to their Oneness with the Father, and who work without ceasing to awaken those who still sleep. The only difference is that one is awake to their Oneness with the Father, and one is still asleep within "self", dreaming their dreams of separateness. The only thing necessary to awaken, is the effort required to ask, and then taking the time to listen within your own heart... to look to the Father each and every day for guidance and understanding. Is this too much to ask for the gift of eternal life?

- - -

February 5, 1976

Thedra Speaking: As it was in the beginning, so it is now... worlds without end. The presence of God the Almighty Father remains constant in all things... manifesting and not manifesting, yet ever present. His divine hand has been ever present in the creation of all things, from the very minute, to the gigantic beyond the scope of man's mind. His perfect plan has proceeded from the beginning, unfolding bit by bit through the aeons of time. His infinite mind has conceived it all, worlds without end, in its multiplicity of forms and formlessness.

In awe do I stand before His plan. In awe and wonderment do I stand as a child, privileged to behold even a minute fraction of it. I only wish to be granted the privilege of serving Him more fully. To be accepted as a servant to Him is the greatest of honors. To become that for which I was originally created is my goal. I give thanks for the opportunity to be a part of His great divine plan.

I am Sister Thedra, of The Order of The Emerald Cross.

- - -

February 12, 1976

Beloved ones

Why tarry? Why hesitate? What is it that holds you back from totally submitting yourself to the divine will of the Father? Do you feel too unworthy to consider yourself one of His own?

I say unto you this day: Judge not thyself or any other man. Only the Father knows... only He can judge. In humble submission present yourself to Him, asking that His Will be done... then let it be. Just <u>allow</u> it to happen.

Yet, of what use is the submission, the asking, if one does not allow the space for the answer, for the receiving, for the guidance? In the silence of your heart wait with calmness and surity, listening well with thine inner ear, with thy whole being... alert, awake, and prepared. Yet, to you I also say: Be not passive in thy submission... be awake, be attentive and poised. To submit does not mean to be spaced-out. It is an activity which needs much work, much patience and discipline. Listening has nearly become a lost art in these noisy hectic times.

Be ye as ones blessed. Be ye prepared for more purposeful activity requiring greater responsibility, greater strength than you have experienced.

I am Sister Thedra, of The Order of The Emerald Cross.

- - -

February 17, 1976

Thedra Speaking: In the days ahead there will be great changes. Thy present problems will be as naught... only how you have prepared yourself will be important. You have chosen your own path for yourself... others have chosen their particular path. Do not have concern for your brother's path... concentrate your attention upon your own and this will be enough.

Look not backward, for the answers are not hidden up in past experiences. The answer to every one of life's problems are available in the NOW. All wisdom necessary is contained within you, and can be retrieved by willing it so. Ask for the wisdom you desire... then <u>listen</u> for the answer. Listen well and you will hear that still small voice within speaking clearly yet ever so gently, with truth and wisdom. Your inner knowing will confirm that it is Truth, and you will have no reason to doubt.

I come in love and truth as one who has walked the self-same road. Thy problems are not unique, and the solutions are within thy immediate grasp if you but listen. Be ever alert to the still small voice... for only when you ask, and then have faith in its wisdom and ability to guide you through troubled waters, will you be privileged to receive. Prepare yourself for to receive... for in the same measure that you are prepared will you receive.

Bless you this day as you go forth in full confidence that all knowledge is within you. Place thy hand in the hand of the Lord thy God, and trust in his divine guidance.

I am thy sister, Thedra.

* * *

THE PLANES OF SPIRIT

In the last newsletter we read a series of communications from Judy, who had diligently studied the Scripts of Sananda while here on earth, and who had then made her transition into the higher planes of spirit. She described her new place of abode in glowing terms of the light and freedom which she now knew, and also shared some of her experiences within her new place of abode. Her joy and new found freedom were more than she could convey in words, yet her ongoing desire was to continue to serve the great plan of the Father, in helping those still struggling within the limitations of earthly existence. Since her account was received 20 years ago, she has no doubt completed her time within that plane and moved on into yet higher planes of learning, yet such accounts inspire us to want to know more... to know the pure joy of life in ever greater light.

Many accounts have been recorded over the years concerning life upon the spirit planes. These accounts often vary in their portrayals, for there are many spirit planes, and also many regions within each plane. Most accounts reflect only the perspective of the spirit giving the account and that which he has personal knowledge of, which usually includes only the region or plane which he is now on and those planes below him. Very few accounts actually come from the highest and brightest spirit planes, for it is easier for us to comprehend and to accept the communications from those within the intermediate planes, which are a closer reflection of our own lives upon the earth.

With so many varying accounts it is often confusing, so for those of you who have not read these numerous accounts, I will try to present an over-all perspective. Realize that this is only a very brief sketch, for the vastness and diversity within all of the spirit planes is far more than can be conveyed in a single newsletter.

Spirit planes - Thought planes

Realize, that the spirit planes which surround the earth are all simply reflections of differing levels of light within the human spirit.

Each spirit plane simply reflects the light (or lack thereof) of those who dwell therein, each within their own environment, with others of like nature.

In the last newsletter Judy told us how these were "Thought Planes", where ones thoughts created and reflected within that which existed around them. Unlike the earth where the laws of nature govern the expression of dense matter, the spirit planes are comprised of much finer matter, called ethers. Etheric matter, unlike dense matter, is not defined by the laws of nature, it simply responds to thought, creating an expression of the thoughts of those who dwell therein. While those within the lower planes may no longer be bound by flesh, they continue to be bound by their own thinking, for they do not yet understand the power of their own thoughts.

If we are to understand the higher spirit planes, it is important that we first understand the range of spirit planes. Just as all spirits while on earth do not express light, so too, all spirit planes are not of light and joy, yet it is important to understand that these too are an integral part of man's development.

The Darker Planes of Spirit

... To those who have (light), more shall be added... to those who have not (light), what little they have shall be taken from them...

We can all bear witness of the many violent or criminally minded spirits expressing themselves upon the earth, both the obvious ones and also those who hide their motives behind a outer facade of respectability. We have also witnessed ones who invoke the name of God to carry out acts of terrorism and violence... ones who speak of God, yet whose hearts remain filled with the blackness of hatred and revenge. While Judy spoke of how the love and joy within her own heart was reflected in the environment around her, so too do those whose hearts hold thoughts of hatred, revenge, malice, cruelty, arrogance, greed, etc... create their own environment. These are the darker planes, the "compounds" spoken of by Sananda, inhabited by spirits whose thoughts and motives have become obsessed with their own destructive natures.

To give you some idea of the environment of these dark planes I would like to print an excerpt from a book which is now out of print, entitled "A Wanderer In The Spirit Planes". It is a factual account from one who wandered these dark regions helping those who were beginning to ask for light. He relates the following:

... As we emerged we found ourselves in a land of night. It might have seemed like a bottomless pit of desolation had we not stood on solid enough ground, while above us was a dark sky, like blackened smoke. How far this country extended it was impossible to know, since the heavy atmosphere like a black fog shut out our vision on every side. I was told that it extended throughout the whole of this vast and dreadful sphere.

- end excerpt -

Consider too, the following excerpt from the book entitled "Excursions To The Spirit World" concerning the lower regions:

... On one occasion I was taken into one of the spirit planes where the vibrations were low and miserable. Suddenly I was struck by a whole host of vicious and vengeful thoughts, and saw a group standing about twenty yards away within a lurid and dirty orange glow. Some had sneering grins on their faces, others absolute down-right hatred. I sensed that they knew where they were and had been there for ages, and would probably continue until the futility of such a state dawned on them...

- end excerpt -

We need to realize that these darker regions were NOT created by God as punishment, but are created and sustained by the thoughts of those who dwell within them, and each willfully chooses to remain bound therein by the very things which he continues to hold within his heart. While such spirits are not bound by the limitations of flesh, they continue to be bound by their own thinking, for they have not yet learned that life and light are synonymous.

Such glimpses are not very inspiring, yet I would like to print one last excerpt from "Excursions to The Spirit Planes:"

... One of my more distasteful visits was to a town inhabited by those unfortunate spirits with quarrelsome habits. I was put down on a street, and as I looked around I saw people violently quarreling. As my awareness became more acute, my spirit received their thoughts, which were vicious and pitiless. It was a hopeless place to be in, as each individuals nature was worsened by the collective thoughts of all the others within that dreadful place.

- end excerpt -

The Lower Planes - The Dull Planes

Above the darker planes described above, begin what are called the normal planes of spirit development. It is often said that there are twelve of these spirit planes surrounding the earth, each progressively brighter, each a reflection of the thoughts of those who dwell within them. The lower planes are often called the "dull states", or the "planes of illusion", for although ones here may not be dark in the sense of being hateful, cruel, or vicious... yet they have incorporated very little light or love into their spirit throughout their long sojourn upon the earth. Throughout their many embodiments they have never cared to look beyond their own lives for any greater light or understanding. Here within the spirit planes they are no different, for in their lethargy they still do not seek light. These are the ones Sananda has referred to as "dullards" or "laggards".

In the book "Excursions To The Spirit World", the author begins by saying:

... Many seem to think that every trip to the spirit world must be full of excitement, with many new wonders and strange things to see, but this is not al. ways so. In my early projections I was taken to the low,

unprogressed states many times, and as these are just like earth and the inhabitants do not know of anything better, their activities were often banal and boring.

... Although life within the spirit planes is based upon projections of thought, I have several times been to a lower region within these planes, where not enough thought was used in any one direction. It was inhabited by those who, during earth life, did not trouble themselves to extend their minds beyond their own dull lives, nor were they interested in anything in particular. On entry into the spirit planes they gravitated to this lower region, where there were street after street of uninteresting houses... creating a condition which caused me to feel extreme boredom.

... Once I found myself outside of a small house, and asked my guide what place this was. He said: It is the Land of Low Thoughts. He began to show me around, and I saw what appeared to be a dreary endless landscape. Here and there were sad looking people, some walking slowly, some standing still. The vibrations of this place were wretched. I was not kept there long, and as usual, I was taken to a brighter plane before returning to the physical body.

- end excerpt -

Sister Thedra often went into these lower planes at night on what she called "mercy missions", to try and help those who might be willing to learn. One morning she asked me if I knew such and such a man in Mt Shasta, who was quite old and who lived somewhere in town... which I did not. The following is her account in her own words, as I remember them. She told me:

.... I was returning from my work behind sleep last night, when I was drawn downward into the lower spirit planes by a vibration that was familiar to me. I soon found myself within a small hovel of a shack with only an old dilapidated table and chair inside. There on this wooden chair sat (this man), looking very confused and disoriented. I felt that he had probable passed from the earth that night, but he did not yet know that he was "dead". He knew that everything was somehow

different, but it was all still confusing to him and he did not know why. I approached him and spoke his name, wherein he looked up at me bewildered. I asked him: "Is there anything I can do for you? Would you like me to fix you a fruit salad" (symbolic for life-giving food... light). To which he replied: "No'oooo, I think I would just like a cup of coffee" (a continuation of his old lethargic habits).

- end excerpt -

Even in spirit, such ones continue to be bound by their lack of motivation, remaining oblivious to the light and love which continues to lie dormant within their own Soul. The book "Excursions To The Spirit World" goes on to say:

... In these lower spheres are spirits of varying degrees of ignorance, and some have not the slightest idea that they have left the earth. Others have the impression that they are living a different life, but it is dream-like and not very positive. These people carry the same mind-set which they had on earth, and "spirit" is just as vague to them here as it was on earth. Many remain contented in their ignorance, therefore their minds do not seek for, or know of, anything better. These cannot be "pushed" forward, for in spirit the Law is, that the urge to seek must come from within themselves.

- end excerpt -

Realize that these spirit planes are vast spheres, each containing many regions, which are as diverse as the earth itself. They surround the entire earth, and within the lower planes each culture and country defines a region, each according to their own beliefs and thinking. Within the planes which are further removed from the earthly pattern, spirits become more unified in their thinking, and all spirits begin to awaken to a more unified expression of life's greater purpose.

Too often we think that all who leave the body immediately see the light, but this is only true for those who have awakened that light within their own spirit. Those who "Do not want to hear it" upon the earth, still "Do not want to hear it" in spirit, for they are still the same spirit. They do not seek for greater light, for their own un-willingness to learn has kept them from progressing beyond these lower planes throughout this long cycle. The absence of light within these lower planes is a reflection of their own lethargy, and since all within these lower planes are of the same nature, the overwhelming apathy there provides little in spiration. It is only in embodiment on earth that they are exposed to the diversity of spirits from all of the spirit planes, which allows them to see and feel the light and love in others which they themselves continue to lack. And it is only through repeated embodiments that they might finally begin to seek within themselves for that same light and love which they see in others.

While most within these lower regions remain bound by their own un-willingness to seek for greater light, when one does put forth the effort to change, he is helped to move forward by those from the brighter planes above, as described in the following excerpt:

... In these dull astral towns I often saw ones neatly dressed in ordinary cloths, but their features and eyes had a brightness that made them outstanding in such a locality. I sensed that they were advanced helpers on their various missions into these dull planes.

- end excerpt -

So it is with each and every plane, as ones reach back to those below them, and give a helping hand to those who have learned to ask for help.

The "Summerlands"

The bright planes which stretch out above these dull planes have often been called the "summerlands", for although they are still a close reflection of life on earth, the gross vibrations of ignorance and lethargy become far less. Those who come here from the dull planes below move first into the lower regions of these summerlands, making their transition more gradual... while those who come here from the earth carry such limitations within their own thinking. The following excerpt from Excursions To The Spirit World, describes the lower regions of these summerlands:

... Spirit life is the great revealer, as the prevalent thoughts of the inner person always come to the forefront. Ones "self-image" or "thought pattern" during earthly life can become 50 ingrained that it can delay their progress in these spheres.

... I was once taken to a lower region of the summerlands, and at first glance it appeared to be a pleasant park, with ornamental gates set in stonework. There was a small pond and wooden benches here and there, yet I noticed there were no plants or shrubs of any kind within the park. There were a few people walking about, while others sat upon wooden benches. They were all smartly dressed, but each assumed an attitude which was supposed to represent the height of dignity and elegance that only an exclusive set might have. Those on the benches were sitting stiffly and formally, with set faces, as if fearful of being caught relaxing. All had a look of frozen nonchalance ingrained in their habits of thought, brought over from the earth.

... I then saw a man enter through the gates, and I could see at once that he was an advanced teacher from the planes above. He began to speak to some of the people, but he had just begun to tell them of other places within this plane which were better than that which they now knew, when two men began to escort him out through the gates. They were gentle with him, but they were saying: "Really old man, park speeches are hardly the thing for our class of people... do be a good fellow and go away."

... I should point out here, that all my experiences in the spirit world concerned the British and European states, as being from Britain I could more easily follow the line of thought and way of living of my own kind.

- end excerpt -

Realize that this is but one small local within this one region of this lower plane, yet it attests to how our own thoughts continue to define our lives, even in spirit. Also, the reference above to the plant life within the spirit planes is very common... for the lower the spirit plane, the more void they are of living plants, while the higher brighter planes become increasingly filled with a vibrant array of plants, trees, and colorful fragrant flowers. This is a direct reflection of the abundance of life and love within the thoughts of those who dwell within the higher planes.

The upper planes of these summerlands become increasingly filled with fragrant flowers and trees, for these upper regions are inhabited by those who have incorporated more Love, Light and Joy into their spirits. While life on these brighter planes is very pleasant, ones here still do not understand the need for effort in awakening to yet greater light. Although they know that they are now in the spirit planes, they do not yet realize that this cycle will come to a close, and most do not yet realize that there are many brighter planes yet above them. They have not yet awakened a desire for greater light, for they do not yet understand that there IS greater light.

Some here choose to reside in small cottages, amid the perpetual summer-like environment, while others gravitate to small towns or villages, with quiet streets lined with quaint little houses and flower gardens. These regions are also called the "family planes", for on arrival into these planes most are greeted by friends or loved ones who now dwell there. Once arriving spirits have adjusted to their new home, they begin to relax and enjoy the peaceful summer-like environment, free from the turmoil of life as it was on earth.

In the book "Excursions To The Spirit World", these intermediate planes are described as follows:

... Apart from the lower dull planes, there are a number of spheres of normal brightness, quite earth-like yet in a better way, where spirits enjoy themselves and become accustomed to the spirit world. It is difficult to describe these easy-going states, as they are neither backward nor advanced. Generally speaking, spirits on these spheres keep to their habits of thought and ways of living, just as during their earth life. The countryman prefers the open spaces, townspeople the

many towns and villages. Relatives and friends who might reside within this state begin to contact each other, and spirits here soon begin to form a circle of acquaintances.

- end excerpt -

Within these spirit planes there is no division of night or day, for the sky overhead continually reflects a brightness (or darkness) consistent with that region or plane... the higher the plane, the brighter the sky, Time within these planes is not consistent with that of earth, for time is seen only as the passing of events. Children who come here from the earth grow to maturity within a short time, while those who are older soon begin to reflect the youthful appearance of their previous embodiment, and soon find that they never grow tired or fatigued. Since these are Thought planes, they sometimes feel mental fatigue, but this is reversed by rest and relaxation. To most who come here this seems like heaven, and many spend years here enjoying such peaceful contentment. Yet eventually they begin to wonder if this really is heaven. They begin to wonder why they still have no greater understanding than they did while on earth, and why they do not see the myriad of angels and the glories of heaven they had so often heard about. Sooner or later most spirits within this plane become restless in what they first thought to be heaven, and begin to bestir themselves to seek for answers. For some this happens quickly, for others it takes a long while. Consider the following excerpt from "Excursions To The Spirit World".

... Life in the "summerland" does not in any way resemble the vague "heaven" pictured by orthodoxy, and though pleasant, it does not have a deep significance for many. Those who on earth would not think of attending a lecture on spiritual truth, do not suddenly become enthusiastic in spirit, because the idea of greater truth is not yet within their thinking.

Judy spoke of those within the lower spirit planes who had still not prepared themselves to receive greater light, thus they were now having to do in spirit, what they failed to do here on earth. Remember her message telling us:

... Think not that your preparation is complete just because one leaves his earthly body and makes the transition to another realm, for your environment here only reflects the degree of your preparation while on earth. Each gravitates towards his chosen environment, which has been self-determined by his own efforts, or lack of such. Many here do not yet understand the necessity of (continuing) preparation, for their false notions and distorted views of "heaven" contribute to an unrealistic attitude. Just to rid themselves of their preconceived ideas and expectations in this regard takes much work and effort, and many continue to cling to their false beliefs for the longest time.

- end excerpt -

Most within these sleepy planes do not understand that these are lower spheres, for they have no greater understanding here than they did while on earth. The desire for greater light is not part of the prevalent "thought" within these planes of idle enjoyment... such higher thoughts" become inherent only within the brighter planes above, and only as ones are prepared can they move forward.'

Many have not yet awakened the desire for greater light, therefore their learning process eventually brings them back to the earth, where the earthly struggles and the limitations of flesh might cause them to seek for greater understanding. Yet once in embodiment, those who sleep on in their contentment, soon find themselves back within these lesser spheres, with no greater understanding, and with no memory of their previous times there. Consider the following excerpt:

... After many experiences in the spirit planes, I could see how very necessary it is to gain knowledge of our own spiritual nature while on earth, for it is "much easier to learn it upon the earth than upon entry into the spirit planes. This may seem strange to you, but if the mind while on earth is blank concerning spiritual things, it is blank still on entering these spirit planes.

- end excerpt -

Realize that each of the spirit planes are inhabited only by those of like nature, therefore the collective thought" in these lower planes makes it difficult for ones to see beyond their own limitations. The earth-plane, on the other hand, is inhabited by spirits from every plane, both light and dark, sending forth their collective thoughts. The friction and unrest caused by this admixture of light and dark causes some to put forth the effort to seek for greater truth and light. For this reason is great light sent to the earth, for it is here upon the earth where most spirits progress.

The Brighter Planes of Spirit

Not all spirits have a need to spend time within these lower planes of rest and idleness, for many have passed through those planes long ago, and have long since raised their light and understanding above such simple contentment. The love and light within the hearts of many spirits allow them to pass beyond these lessor planes, to the higher plane where the greater light is consistent with their own. As Judy told us, those who are drawn to the higher spheres are those who have turned their attention more fully to the greater light and purpose behind all of life. In the book "Excursions To The Spirit World" this account describes life within these brighter planes:

... The simplicity of spiritual truth is never more evident than when one is on the brilliant planes. I say brilliant because the whiteness overhead (the sky is something like that of mid-day in the tropics, but without the heat and discomfort. The effect upon me while in these planes is always the same, for seem to understand more and have greater access to knowledge, for within these higher frequencies the mind is always open to higher guidance.

... Yet it is not just by knowledge that ones come here. A person whose inner nature is friendly, loving and considerate of others during their earthly life, would gravitate to that same vibration in spirit, even if that person was ignorant of spirit. The state they were drawn to would naturally be bright, and the spirit would have access to the knowledge of that state, therefore their on-going progress would be pleasant and

easy. Yet they would not be separated from loved ones who were not so progressed, as those from the higher spheres can always go into the lower spheres.

- end excerpt -

Even within these higher planes of spirit, life continues to reflect many aspects of life on earth. I once found myself (behind sleep) walking with Judy through a city in one of these brighter spirit planes. It resembled a city of the 1950's, yet it was immaculately clean and orderly. There was no sense of rush or scattered thoughts as in cities on earth. The over-all atmosphere was that of greater peace and of greater purpose.

Although these are thought planes, realize that etheric matter is just as solid as anything upon the earth. This is described by William Pelley in the book "Seven Minutes In Eternity":

... And now that I had reawakened without the slightest distress or harm, I was conscious of a beauty and loveliness that surpasses chronicling on paper. A sort of marble portico, lighted by a soft opal luminescence. I can best liken the structure to a roofed-in Roman style portico, with heavy smooth pillars supporting the roof. Across from me the wall was open, with three or four steps leading down into a garden that was indistinct in a sort of nocturnal haze.

... Again I found my voice. Looking around me, my gaze come to the marble bench beneath me. I thumped it with my palm, and my next words were: Great Scott! It's Real! "Of course it's real, my friend said, still smiling,

... I cannot make anyone understand how natural it all seemed to be there. It never occurred to me that I was in Heaven, or if it did it caused me no more astonishment than, at some point in my adolescent life it had "occurred" to me that I was on earth.

- end excerpt -

Within these brighter planes the focus is always on greater learning, and these spirits have awakened to the fact that progression takes effort. In the book 'Life Beyond The Veil", a city within one of these upper regions is described as follows:

... The Temple is of use not only for worship, but for instruction of those prepared to receive it. This is much like a "high school" of this sphere, and only those who have passed through the lower schools may come here for greater learning. At various places of this region are other schools or collages, each for some special instruction.

... This city has three of these schools, where those who have passed through the lower schools come to learn higher aspects of the instructions they have received, to seam to combine them together. In many spheres this pattern is followed, yet each sphere is a continuation and also an advancement of the spheres below it, so that from the lower to the higher spheres there is a gradient system of progress and learning. Each and every step implies not only added understanding, but also in learning the enjoyment of using such understanding.

- end excerpt -

Realize that the scope of each plane is vast in its expression, and is far greater than just what is mentioned above, just as life on earth encompasses more than the description of one collage. Ones within these brighter planes understand more of the greater purpose behind their lives, therefore they continually seek to incorporate greater light within their own spirit. When they do take embodiment in flesh, it is usually to strengthen their character, or to learn greater control over the self-ego-mind... to learn to balance the intellect with the greater light within their heart, allowing the pure light of the Soul to express itself through the spirit. In doing so they help anchor such light, love, and understanding, upon the earth for those yet struggling with the lessons of flesh. Yet as Judy explained, upon returning to the spirit planes these too review their embodiment in flesh, wherein they too come to see their accomplishments as well as their own shortcomings, and therein they continue to learn.

We need to realize that our learning and our preparation, no matter how "enlightened" we may now "think" we are, does not end when we leave the earth. We do not just go to God and live happily ever after. These spirit planes are places of on-going preparation for man of earth, as mankind AS A WHOLE prepares for the closing of this cycle. All of us upon the earth have come here from these many spirit planes, and I dare say that none of us have come here from the highest of these planes. The earth-plane is the proving ground, wherein we prove ourselves... yet too often we think that just because we read a few books and remember a lot of information, that we are now prepared to go into the higher dimensions of life. It is not "information" which awakens us... it is awakening greater light within our minds, and awakening greater Love within our own hearts. These are the things which are inherent within an awakened spirit. These are the things which awaken our living connection with the Father. Remember Sananda's words saying: *There are none so foolish as those who think themself wise".*

The Higher Planes of Light

It is said that there are twelve spirit planes which surround the earth, each progressively brighter, yet even the higher planes are places of continued learning and greater service. This is spoken of in the following excerpt from "Life Beyond The Veil":

.... I noticed near the border of the ninth sphere, a large lake bordered with forest, with buildings spread out among the trees. I asked my guide what colony or settlement it was, and ire told me that a long time ago a difficulty arose in those arriving here in this sphere from other regions. While there are some who progress evenly in all their faculties, others do not develop all of their faculties equally in their progress. These are highly developed spirits whose development brings them here to the tenth sphere, yet before they can proceed they must first develop their negligent aspects in the same proportion as their advanced aspects. This is because of the much more complexity of perfection prevailing here than you understand on earth. These people are still of the ninth sphere in some portion of their character, while perhaps of the tenth sphere in others. They are in some ways too

progressed in power and personality for the ninth, jet unable to proceed to the next sphere where their inferior aspects are not sufficient. Thus they abide here on the borderland, where they work at their own progress, while continuing to help others within the spheres below.

- end except -

Of the highest and brightest of these spirit planes, we know very little for life upon these higher planes is too far removed from our own for us to understand while in flesh. While those within the very highest planes have long since gone beyond the need to take upon themselves the cumbersome expression of flesh, yet they continue to serve the great plan of the Father, by using their greater light and understanding to guide those throughout all the planes below them. Since greater learning always entails greater service, ones within the intermediate planes are often sent into the lower regions to help ones who are asking for light, yet they are always guided and protected by those within the highest spirit planes. The general rule is that ones can see and go into all the planes which exist below them, yet each has only fleeting knowledge of that which lie yet above them, until they begin to experience it directly.

In most cases, those who we might call our "guardian Angels", who appear to us on earth, are ones from these spirit planes who are sent to earth on a specific mission. They are usually ones from the brighter planes who understand how to lower their vibration so that their form might be seen by the human eye. Yet they are not concerned only with the earth, for their efforts are also directed to all of the lessor planes.

Spirit Planes & Higher Dimensions

While the brightest planes are inhabited by spirits of very great light and understanding, it is important to realize that these are NOT the higher dimensions of life as we might want to think of them... these are NOT dimensions having to do with all of creation. These are the spirit planes of the earth, as one planet with its corresponding planes of spirit development. All within these planes are part of this present cycle of the earth, and all continue to be part of the earth until this cycle is completed. Remember that portion of newsletter 71, concerning the fall of man, and the plan brought forth for man to raise himself back to his former knowledge, as described in the following excerpt:

... Man as man, however, had deteriorated so far (from his former state) that only through untold millennia and much instruction could he win back his former standard of intelligence. He began reincarnating in the form which the Host itself had employed (created)... a sort of sublimated Ape, or physical man as you know him today... slowly working his way up through the aeons...

- end excerpt -

These spirit planes are an integral part of this cycle upon the earth, yet throughout this long cycle some have progressed no further than the dull planes... these are the laggards. Some have awakened varying degrees of love and light within their spirit and moved forward into the intermediate planes, yet many became complacent and did not continue to reach for greater light... these are the sleepers. Some have worked to awaken greater light within their own spirits, and these now dwell within the higher planes of spirit, wherein they continue to learn and to "prepare" for the closing of this cycle. A few have given their full attention to their preparation, and these now dwell within the highest of the spirit planes, wherein they continue to help those within all the planes below them, including the earth.

When Sananda speaks about earning our passport into his place of abode, he is speaking of dimensions of life beyond the earth and its associated planes of spirit. He is speaking of the freedom within dimensions of Life which are not limited to any planet or spirit plane... dimensions associated with all of creation, wherein there is NO such limitation.

Remember Sananda words saying:

... When it is given unto man (as a whole) to be prepared, he shall be as ONE with the whole of the lighted Order. He shall have the

privilege of going and coming between worlds, and as one of these he shall be without limitation of any sort. He shall have knowledge of all creation, just as we of the ϾϾϾ. He shall be as the Father created him to be... for this is his inheritance.

- end excerpt -

We upon the earth are all just spirits from these many planes, now embodied in flesh for a short time. Realize too, that when ones leave embodiment, they do not just go into the higher dimensions of life... they return to these spirit planes which surround the earth, wherein each continue their preparation.

When Sananda speaks about the completion of this cycle, he is not only speaking of the earth, but completion for those within all of the spirit planes of earth, for he is speaking of mankind as a whole. When the cycle ends and the doors of heaven are finally opened, man of earth, AS A WHOLE, will move forward, each to their own choosing. Remember too Sananda's words saying: ... *And this is the last time I shall lower my light to accommodate the sleepers and the laggards. It is Finished! It is Done! I shall return unto my Father, and those who so choose to follow me shall return to the Father with me. These shall go where I go... and they shall be as 1, free and without guilt or blemish, for they shall be as ones prepared to enter into the place wherein I AM.*

... And the book (of earth) shall be closed, for I shall be as one finished, as one which hast done mine part and taken mine leave. Then another shall fill mine place, mine "office", and he shall do his part (of guiding the on-going progression of those who refuse to awaken), even as I did mine part.

- end excerpt -

The Order of Man

Remember here the portion of newsletter 71 concerning of the "Order of Man". Realize that man of earth, including all within the spirit planes, is only a small portion of the "Order of Man". We are that portion which was turned from the Father by the Son named Lucifer. The term hu-man refers only to the portion of Man which became bound within the limitations of flesh. The vast majority of the Order of Man did not turn from the Father, but remained of the Lighted Order, which Man was created to be. These are our Elder Brothers who have watched and guided us throughout our long cycle of forgetfulness. They have awaited the fulfilling of this cycle, when they might once again remind us of our true home which we have forgotten. This is "our Memory" which will be restored... this is our "Inheritance" which we forfeited, which we have forgotten... our inheritance willed unto us of the Father, which we have also forgotten. This is our return to the place from which we went out in the beginning... for we are the Prodigal Son returning home.

We are told that when the cycle has ended and Man of earth has moved forward, the earth will move out into a new place within the firmaments, where it will be cleansed of all the dross which was not the will of the Father, which man has created. The earth will be purified, wherein it will finally become the shining planet which it was created to be. Remember Judy's message from the last newsletter saying:

... Long and intense has been the preparation here within these realms for the events which will be taking place on earth, the fulfillment of the plan made so long ago for the progress of the earth and for mankind. Sad it is that this preparation is not also being made on the earth plane with the same enthusiasm. Yet this lack of preparation will not stop or even delay the plan, for all unfolds within its proper season within the Father's kingdom.

- end excerpt -

Long ago man of earth, of his own free will, turned from his Source, he turned from the Father who had brought him forth. The separation which we now know is of our own making, and we have been given this cycle that we might see the results of our self-will.

The First Born Son of the Father, who brought forth the Father's will into this creation, has guided us towards this day, when the door would once again be opened for those who chose to return to their Oneness with the Father. Now that that day is here, he has come to show us the Light in its First Magnitude, even as the Father. While there are many upon the earth who are still not prepared to follow him, so too are many within the lower spirit planes un-prepared. These too are our brothers and sisters who do not yet see the greater light behind their lives. There is much work yet to be done on all planes before this cycle is finished, for many who now sleep may yet choose to awaken from their dreams, and move forward towards an awakened life. Those upon the higher planes are trying to awaken all who will respond... and if we profess to know the Light, then we must be willing to embody that light here upon the earth, for remember Sananda's words saying:

... Hast the Father not sent thee forth that ye might glorify him in the earth, even as he hast glorified thee in the Heavens? I say unto thee, no other hands and feet hast he upon the earth other than his children.

- end excerpt -

You and I ARE the Father's hands and feet upon the earth... We ARE an expression of His light, and it is through each of us that he would work if we would but turn our attention to him and ALLOW it. We speak of light, and we speak about Sananda, but are we putting forth our own efforts to help him anchor and spread that light... or do we continue to expect him to do it?

The Earth Planet

Too often we think of the earth as being totally separate from the brighter planes of spirit, but it is only our thinking which has become separate. The earth IS the Father's creation, it is only in our own thinking that we see ourselves as separate.

Realize that the earth is central to all these spirit planes, for they are only temporary dwelling places for Man of earth. These spirit planes were brought forth only to accommodate man of earth as he slowly progressed upward throughout this present cycle, and when the cycle is completed they will have served their purpose. While that which exists within these "etheric planes" is as solid as the things of earth, they are created by the thoughts of those within each plane... while the earth is created and sustained by the "Thought" of the Father. The earth-planet was the original creation of the Father, and will remain as such until the Father withdraws His Thought.

While the vibration on earth is denser than that of spirit, this was intended for the expression of the biological life which was meant to be expressed here in the beginning. Look around at the diversity of animal life... the myriad of plant life which drapes the planet in such a life-giving expression... the great mountains, valleys and canyons which we find so breath-taking to behold... the majestic expanses of the blue oceans which bring rain and life to the whole of the planet... all these are the creation of the Father.

All were brought forth to express the biological creation, as it was intended in the beginning. Remember the words: *The Kingdom of God is spread out upon the earth, but man has not the eyes to see it.* Realize that man of earth sees these things... but NOT as an expression of the Father, created for the upliftment of life... but as things to be exploited for his own selfish gain. Man in his original creation was meant to be the over-seer of this biological creation, but instead he has become the exploiter of this creation, which is just what Lucifer intended.

Realize that the Father has no part in creating the turmoil and confusion which man calls life upon the earth... such is the creation of man and his own thinking. Man has forgotten that which he was brought forth to be, for he has forgotten the Father who brought him forth. Man of earth defines and expresses life only in accordance with his own selfish desires, therefore he has forgotten his true oneness of all living things.

This is the whole purpose for this cycle upon the earth. Man of earth turned from the Father, therefore he has been left to his own means throughout this cycle of darkness which he himself created. He has been left to learn a great lesson, that he might come to know that he is NOT sufficient unto himself, wherein he might once again seek his true oneness with the Father. Man of earth has been given this cycle in which to learn or to reject that lesson, each according to his own will.

Remember Sananda's words telling us:

... This is the time of sifting and sorting, of classifying each unto their own light and class. When I speak of man, I see a portion which are of the darkest evil... then there are ones which are of little light... then there are the ones which are prepared to go with me into greater light wherein they shall find peace, perfect peace. There is an infallible law: "As ye are prepared so shall ye receive". My words have been shouted from every land of earth, for every generation, that they might be prepared to go all the way with me.

- end excerpt -

The Earth Plane - The Place of Testing

If you have read the many accounts from ones upon the lower and intermediate planes of spirit, you may have noticed that their memory includes only the spirit planes they have recently passed through, and their one previous incarnation on earth. This is because as each spirit goes forth to take on a new embodiment it loses its previous memory, and therein must prove its worth according to its own true nature. In losing its previous memory, each spirit is temporarily freed from the burdens of guilt or sorrow from past actions, free from its attachments to the past, and begins each new embodiment with a clean slate... upon which each might write a whole new chapter to his life, if he so chooses.

Realize too, that our memory is not lost forever. Remember the portion of newsletter 70, concerning the difference between our Soul and our spirit. This is an important distinction, and it is the crux of understanding the meaning of "Our Memory". The following is an excerpt from that newsletter:

... Now through all embodiments the Soul remains ever untainted by either darkness or evil, for the Soul is created of the very Substance of the Life itself... it is pure Light. It is a living fragment of the Source,

wherein there is NO darkness. It is only the "spirit", the soul's developing "identity, which must come to learn the greatest of all lessons... that Life and Light are synonymous.

... The Soul is that which is eternal, it is the one constant throughout all of the experience that you have ever had. The Soul retains the memory of every single experience you have ever had, on all planes and in all embodiments, since your inception into creation as a living soul.

We lose our memory with each embodiment because the Soul does not take embodiment - it is our "spirit", our developing "identity" which struggles with the lessons of flesh. Within each embodiment your own free will choices either add to or retard the development of your "spirit", for the Soul ever seeks to guide it upwards towards greater perfection, towards the day when all vestiges of darkness taken on by that spirit are purged, when the Soul and the spirit may finally merge as ONE, an eternal expression of that which it was created to be in the beginning.

- end excerpt -

Too often we bemoan the fact that we are here struggling in flesh, as though the earth were a place of punishment... but it is not a place of punishment, it is a place of self-examination. Remember Sananda's words: *Be ye fruitful unto the Father, for He has given thee permission to be within the Earth for the fulfilling of this age... and that is a privilege given unto thee of God the Father.*

Sananda has also said: *"The earth is a school for the gods"*, - for the earth is the place wherein all must prove themselves. No matter what plane we might have dwelled within previously, our own actions, thoughts, words, and deeds in each embodiment, either bless us with greater light, or burden us with more darkness, each of our own making. We were all created in light in the beginning... of our own free will we chose to turn from the Source of that light, the Father... now, to that self-same light we ourselves must choose to return.

The Direct Pathway Home

As this cycle draws to a close, much effort is being put forth that we might come to see that the vastness of Life's great plan is far greater than that which we have known upon the earth. Many on the higher planes of life are sending us light and understanding that man might once again claim his inheritance which he forfeited so long ago.

As we search for a greater understanding of how to disentangle ourselves from this darkness, we find ourselves confronted with a mountain of purportedly spiritual information concerning many Ascended Masters, Space brothers, photon belts, Ancient teachings, UFO's, lay lines, vortexes, pyramids, crystals, earth changes, past life readings, starships, earth evacuations, etc... etc... etc... In trying to comprehend all of these things we find ourselves with a lot of information in our heads, but with little or no understanding of life itself, and with an unspeakable longing still filling our hearts. Is the true spiritual awakening process then, about filling our minds with information... or is it more than that?

In the last newsletter we read the communications from Judy, who had made her transition from the earth plane into the planes of spirit with only Sananda's words to guide her. She spoke of the things that were truly of importance in making her transition into those bright planes of spirit. In reading her account we come to realize that none of the things mentioned above were of the least importance to her during her transition, and once there, such things were of no importance at all. So we need to ask ourselves... What is important? What should we be giving out attention to while here upon the earth.

In reading Judy's account we see that the only things that were of true importance, was the love she held with her heart, and her on-going desire to return to her oneness with the Father, She told us how during the three day transition process, the one making the transition is calling most of their own shots, and therefore it is important to have clarity of purpose foremost in one's own thoughts. As Judy made her transition, she was not distracted by useless information, pre-conceived ideas, or expectations... she had long since emptied her cup of all such trivia.

She was guided only by the love she held within her heart for the Father and his great plan, and went forward according to His will and guidance. She went upwards into those planes of light and joy because she had no other desires within her heart. So too, if we seek the true pathway home, we only need to give our attention to the one thing which is central to all true awakening... a sincere desire to return to our oneness with the Father... not through information, but by "awakening" light within our own spirit.

If all of the things mentioned above (lay lines, vortexes, pyramids, photon belts, UFO's etc., etc...) have absolutely no importance at the time of our transition from flesh into spirit, then why do we call them "spiritual"... why do we consider them to be important in our spiritual awakening? You and I are LIVING SPIRIT... We are LIVING LIGHT... and within each of us already exists that which we seek. It is not information which we lack... it is not information concerning things outside ourself which awakens us... It is the light we awaken within our own thoughts... and more important, the Love we allow to awaken within our own hearts for the ONE who gave unto us the very life that we each now know. We need only "awaken" our own spirit to that which we already ARE.

The Pathway of Creation

Newsletters 70 & 71 followed the pathway of Life itself, beginning with the very SOURCE of life itself. It followed the pathway outward from the Source of all life, to the Father, that spirit who brought forth the very foundation of creation as we know it. From the Father it went forth again to the First Born Son of the Father, who after receiving his inheritance in full, sought only to manifest the will of the Father within His (the Father's) creation. The Son, following the will of the Father, brought forth the universe of matter (worlds and star systems) and also the Order of Man who was to over-see this biological creation. Unfortunately, before Man had completed his own development, a portion of the Order of Man was turned from the plan of the Father by another Son named Lucifer. They turned from their Oneness with the Father, and sought to express only for "self". And thus Man of earth, instead of becoming the over-seer of the biological creations upon the earth, became the exploiter of the Father's creation. And because of his self-willed separation from the Source of all light, he found himself bound within a cycle of darkness which he himself had created.

This is as simple as I can express it... yet these are only words describing concepts, and the truth is more than believing in a concept. Remembering information is not to KNOW, it is still only remembering the concept. TO KNOW you must put forth the effort to go beyond the words and concepts, and awaken your own spirit to the Living reality behind the words. You must awaken your living connection to, as well as your own individual expression of, the Source of life itself.

What is it that we seek... more information, or greater life? It is not information that frees us, it is awakening to that which we have always been... that which we were created to be in the beginning. For those of you who have read the Scripts, you will remember Sananda saying:

... "And it is indeed wise to ask of the Father that ye might receive me, for in no wise shall I intrude upon thy free will - and yet it is the will of the Father that I bring thee out of darkness. This is for the ones which have as yet not learned the wisdom of saying "Father, Thy will be done in me, thru me, by me", for therein is the KEY unto thy legirons which have bound thee.

- end excerpt -

Why do we continue to think that this is not sufficient? Why do we allow ourselves to become confused by all the information touted by man, when direct guidance from the Father is ours for the simple effort of asking, and then listening. Why is it that we continue to look away from the Father, in search of "mystical teachings" or "spiritual powers"... is it that we are still trying to bypass the Father and become great and glorious beings in and of ourselves? Why is it that we continue to look for spiritual "things" outside of ourselves, when all that we seek is already within our own hearts and minds, waiting to be awakened? Remember the words of Sister Thedra which were printed in the last newsletter, saying:

... Beloved ones: Why tarry? Why hesitate? What is it that holds you back from totally submitting yourself to the divine will of the Father? Do you feel too unworthy to consider yourself one of His own?

... Be ye concentrated in and on his Light... Keep your attention focused upon Him. If you would grow towards Him you must give Him your attention, seeing His handiwork in ALL things. It is only when we withdraw our attention from Him, even momentarily, that we falter along the path and become blinded by our own forgetfulness. Always turn to Him for counsel and guidance, for help and sustenance, continually thanking Him for His many blessings. It is said over and over again, yet how many actually, live WITHIN him, remembering at all times wherein they are staid?

- end excerpt -

Why do we seek for spiritual sounding names or titles, do these make us any more than we ARE. Why do we seek ancient wisdom from Atlantis or Lemuria, when the Father, whose very light sustains us, speaks to our own hearts here and now. In case you haven't noticed, those two places destroyed themselves... was that wisdom? Why do we continue to look to the past when the Living Presence of the Father lives here and now? Remember Sister Thedra's admonition within the last newsletter, telling us:

... Look not backward, for the answers are not hidden up in past experiences. The answer to every one of life's problems is available here and now. Ask... then LISTEN for the answer. Listen well and you will hear that still small voice within speaking clearly yet ever so gently, with truth and wisdom. Your inner KNOWING will confirm that it is Truth, and you will have no reason to doubt. In humble submission present yourself to the Father, asking that His will be done... then let it be. Just ALLOW it to happen.

... Yet, of what use is the asking if one does not allow the space for the answer, for the receiving, for the guidance? In the silence of your heart wait with calmness and assurety, listening well with thine inner ear... with thy whole being alert, awake, and prepared. Yet, to you I

also say: Be not passive in thy submission... be awake, be attentive and poised - to submit does not mean to be spaced-out. It is an activity which needs much work, much patience and discipline. Listening has nearly become a lost art in these noisy hectic times.

... Bless you this day as you go forth in full confidence that all knowledge is within you. Place thy hand in the hand of the Lord thy God, and trust in his divine guidance.

I am thy sister, Thedra.

To remind us of the One True Light behind all of life, the Father has sent one who IS that Light. He has sent his First Born Son, who IS Light in its First Magnitude, even as the Father, for there is but ONE Source of light. To know the Son is to know the Father... for the Father and the Son are ONE, just as the Father and the Source are ONE. They are the Light of the Source, in its First Magnitude... One Source... One Light... One Life.

We have all come forth from that Light, and within that light we have always existed. To remember our oneness we have only to once again look within, to the ONE true Source of all Life.

The following excerpt is from the Scripts:

He is the First Born

There is but one Lord God, and he is the one sent, overall and above all. He is the one which hast given the Law unto Moses in the beginning - He is the one which spoke unto the Children of Israel - He is the one which hast fashioned the Temple of the Inner Sanctuary - He is the one which heads the "Mighty Council". He is the one which is head of the Order of Melchizedek, for he is the First-Born, and therefore he is First begotten of the Father, and none other hast that station. This makes of him the First in line of his Father's Children, and this makes of him the Son of God, and for that hast he first received his inheritance IN FULL. For this hast he first come forth from out the Father, as the First-Born hast he gone forth.

... Now it cometh the time when there shall go forth again the same Son of God the Father, as a Mighty and powerful force, as a great Light, and it shall cut away the darkness. It shall be unto the forces of darkness their banishment, for the forces of darkness shall no longer bind and torment a people which seek the Light.

... And I say unto thee this day, I see them crying out for the Light, they are weary of their lot, and these shall be unbound. Yet I say unto them: Weary not of thine search, for it shall end and thine reward shall indeed be thine liberation. Thine time shall come, and ye shall be glad for thine search.

.... Yet ye shall weary not, for thine waiting (the closing of the cycle) shall be according unto the Law, and no man shall hasten the day of thine unbinding, neither shall he add unto it. Thine days shall end and the word shall be fulfilled. As I have spoken so shall it be, for I know whereof I speak.

... Let thine waiting end in thine victory - then ye shall hear the glad cry: Hail! Hail unto the Victor, for thine waiting hast ended in victory!

- end excerpt -

Throughout the Scripts we are told much about the Laws of Life, and we are told that we only need apply these Laws within our lives and the darkness will fall away.

Many have asked: *What are these Laws? Why don't you just print up a booklet with all these laws listed?*

For over 40 years, Sister Thedra dedicated her life to recording the instruction given by Sananda, 1800 pages of these are printed into 73 Scripts booklets, which are sent out free of charge. Throughout these Scripts he has spoken of - The First Law of Order - The Law of Free Will - The Law of Giving and Receiving - The Law of Asking and Receiving - The Law of Love - The Law of The Spoken Word - to name just a few. He has given it all to us in printed form for any and all who choose to seek it out, and we have only to put forth the effort.

Remember, that while Sananda always seeks to awaken us, he also sees our pattern of lethargy. Do we free ourselves from our lethargy by asking that it all just be handed to us? Is it not enough that he has placed the food before us... or would we ask him to feed us also? Is it too much to ask that we put forth the effort... or would we ask him to accommodate our lethargy and just hand it to us in ten easy steps? That is the same thinking which has kept so many from lifting themselves above the "dull planes" throughout the whole of this cycle... for they too have waited for God to do it for them. It has all been placed in our hands, and we have only to read it with a sincere desire for greater light and understanding, and to ASK for greater comprehension.

Why are we not willing to put forth such a small effort for the gift of Eternal Life? It would seem like a very small price.

The following excerpt is from the Scripts, which were recorded by Sister Thedra

The Brotherhood of Man

Beloved Children: This day I speak unto thee of things beyond the mortal realms. I speak unto thee of things eternal... of the eternal things would I speak. Thou hast been tormented by the things of mortal man, that which he hast brought about and which he hast been responsible for.

This day I say unto thee: Be ye of a mind to learn of me, and I shall give unto thee food which shall nourish thee, which shall be unto thee great manna which hast no equal in the realm of flesh. While thou hast been asleep I have provided a place for thee... I have gone unto mine Father, and I have been faithful unto mine trust. I have kept mine covenant with thee, I have returned unto thee that ye might be prepared for the greater part which is not of earth.

I say unto thee, this (the earth) is the school of the gods... ye shall remember this. It, the earth, is the school of the gods, wherein ye shall be prepared for the greater part, wherein ye shall be prepared to receive thine inheritance in full, and therein is everlasting freedom.

Now for this have I revealed mineself this day. I have given unto this, mine servant (Thedra), mine new name (Sananda) that it might be made known unto all people which doth choose to follow in mine footsteps. I come this day that ye too might come to know me, that ye too might walk in mine footsteps that ye might go where I go.

Now I see thee as ones bowed down in pain and suffering, in bondage, crying out for surcease from all thine miseries. And too, I know that which bindeth thee. I bid thee arise, shake off thine lethargy and be ye up and about thy Father's business. Let nothing deter thee. Be ye alert and know ye that I am the Lord thy God, sent of mine Father that ye be delivered out.

Yet I say unto thee, ye shall have the will to follow me. Ye shall arise and come forth of thine OWN WILL, for none shall bring thee against thine will, for therein is folly. Ye shall be thine own porter and bring thineself as a living sacrifice. Give thine "self" as the sacrifice, for none other can the Father use. For hast he not sent thee forth that ye might glorify him in the earth, even as he hast glorified thee in the Heavens? I say unto thee, no other hands and feet hast he upon the earth other than his children. I say unto thee, he is the Father, thou art the Sons, for he hast breathed forth his breath which hast brought thee forth. He is the CAUSE of thine being. Ask of him naught but Light, for he knoweth thine every need. I say unto thee, he knoweth that which thou hast need of, even before thou hast asked. Ask of Him light, for comprehension of the greater part.

Be ye as one filled with love, for this is the fulfilling of the law. I say, love ye one another, and be ye as brother one unto the other. Share the love which is bestowed upon thee from the realms of light. I say unto thee, know ye all men by their light, and give unto none the bitter cup. Praise ye the name of the Most High Living God and rejoice forever more. Ask of no man his opinion... ask of the Father for wisdom and for comprehension of the Law, the Law by which thou liveth and have thine being.

Yet I say unto thee, thou shall not ask of the Father mercy and forgiveness so long as thou dost hold within thine heart aught against thine fellow man. Seek not to give unto him that which thou dost not want. I say unto thee, give unto him as thou would have him give unto thee. Bless him as ye would that he bless thee, and be ye selfless in the doing. Boast not of thine good works, rest not on thine laurels, and be ye blest by that which ye do. I say, by thine own actions shall ye bless thine own self.

I speak unto thee of the way of the initiate. I speak unto thee of the Brotherhood of Man, under the Fatherhood of God. Be it so as he hast decreed it.

I am Sananda, Son of God the Father, Solen Aum Solen.

* * *

Before we close this newsletter, I will introduce you to one more person who studied Sananda's words for many years and then made their transition into the planes of spirit. He was called "Brother Ponce", and he came to work with Sister Thedra shortly after she began the work in Mt Shasta in 1964, and devoted the rest of his life to this work.

He helped build the Gatehouse, and put untold hours into landscaping and creating the peaceful surroundings. For over 10 years he typed and printed all the Scripts which were to be sent out, as well as all of the manuscripts which were given through Sister Thedra. He was an integral part of the work of A.S.S.K., and he was very much loved and appreciated by all who knew him.

In 1977 he made his transition at the age of 82, and his passing was a great loss to Sister Thedra. She had said that after his passing she had seen him at various times during her nightly work within the planes of spirit, yet the protocol which governed her nightly work did not allow her to speak with him or be seen by him.

In October of 1991, eight months before she made her own transition, she told me the following account, as I remember it:

... I was returning from my nightly work last night in the spirit planes, when I found myself on the top of a high hill, overlooking a beautiful valley of green rolling meadows intertwined with beautiful trees and forest. On one side of this valley was a group of buildings which my guide told me was a school for new arrivals. He then said to me: "Your dear friend Brother Ponce resides here. He now works with those who come over here with little spiritual understanding, and he tutors them in the ways of spirit". My thoughts and vision saw into one of the buildings, where I saw him busy with his work. I felt that he could not see me, yet I sent him my thoughts of love before finally returning to my sleeping body here upon the earth.

- end excerpt -

Shortly after she had returned to her body, Sananda awakened her and asked her to record his nightly message, just as she had done every night for over 40 years. The following is part of that night's record:

... Sananda speaking: As the time goes, it has been only a few hours since I last spoke unto thee, yet much has been accomplished in so short a while.

There is one of the loyal ones which asks to communicate with you... he has within his mind a vision of days past, which he would like to speak of. It has been permitted that he speak at this time... so be it and selah.

Brother Ponce

My Precious Sister: What a joy that I am privileged to speak unto thee. I have been in the service of our Lord for some time now, which is so very fulfilling, for I know that this is what I was prepared for.

I have been a mentor to groups of new arrivals here, and I am content with this assignment, as it is given unto me by our beloved Sananda. I was aware that you were nearby (earlier), and while you did not come into view, it was good to know that you were nearby.

I wish to say this, for it has been on my mind for a while: I have been privileged to have a quick look-see at that which is being done there at the Gatehouse (A.S.S.K.) It is so gratifying to see, for it is the will of God that the work shall prosper. To see the way it has come about is most pleasing.

I had made a few mistakes in the days of my sojourn upon the earth, yet I am now atoning for them. While on earth I gave little credit for the way in which we were disciplined, yet now I am learning that the Law is strict and precise, with no exceptions.

All must accept discipline for their own sake, and until we are ready to accept the way that is set before us, we stay in the lessor class, with the lessor teaching, such as we can understand. Not until we are "prepared" to accept the greater Truth do we move forward into greater Light. It is a matter of comprehension, a matter of one's willingness to learn new and greater things... for there are ones who care not to go forward into those greater heights.

My love and thanks to you. With Peace and Love from the host... I am Ponce.

- end excerpt -

Since I had known and worked closely with Brother Ponce for several years, his message made me realize, that while the work we do "outside" ourselves may be of great value in bringing greater light to others... it is only the work we do "within" ourselves which opens the doors to our own greater light and understanding.

If we truly desire greater light, then we must put forth the effort to awaken that greater light within our own thoughts... if we desire greater love, we ourselves must put forth the effort to awaken that greater love within our own hearts... and therein is our ongoing preparation.

I will end this newsletter with the following is an excerpt from the Scripts, recorded by Sister Thedra:

Sananda

That which is Spirit sayeth unto thee: Behold that which is Spirit, that which is eternal and which is pure. I say that spirit is life... pure in its purity which is of God the Father. by his virtue and by his nature.

Now ye shall be unto thyself true and declare for thyself thy freedom from bondage, thy freedom from darkness. And ye shall cleanse thyself of all preconceived concepts of the Father-Mother God, thy Source, for I say unto thee man of earth, ye have not conceived the fullness of Him the Father nor his handiwork.

For Man has been as one whose head is bound, and he has enshrouded himself in a great mist. He has been indoctrinated through the ages, from the beginning of his sojourn... he has gone in and out of the flesh as a wanderer in darkness, and he returns again and again to find himself entangled within the same web (of illusion). And each has played his part in the weaving, for not one stands alone in his enmeshed condition. I say it is indeed sad, for as a people dost thou go out, and as a people dost thou weave the "web of illusion."

I say unto thee, only thy OWN effort, thy OWN free will, can free thee, for therein is thy freedom. And let it be for the good of all that ye seek thy own freedom, for therein is wisdom.

I say unto thee, great and powerful are the ones now sent to bring thee Truth, Light and Life. More fully shall ye live, greater shall be thy work, and lighter thy way. I say unto thee, ye shall be as ones free from all thy dogmas and creeds, thy legirons of bondage, and ye shall be as ones free forever. Yet I say unto thee, ye shall will it so, so be it and Selah.

Ye shall be as one prepared to receive the greatest revelation, now, in this day, when ye have cast aside thy preconceived ideas of thy Source, of thy God and his Son, and of thy own being and the universe about thee. I say, ye have been given false doctrines and ye have adulterated even them.

Now I say unto thee, the time draweth nigh when ye shall go into the secret place of the Most High Living God bare, bare as a new-born babe, void of anything save thy eternal soul, and it shall be clean, for none other shall enter therein. Behold thyself this day as a child of the Most High Living God. Come as a little child, void of all thy preconceived ideas, of all thy rituals and all thy creeds... and ask of him, thy Father for thy freedom. When ye have asked as a little child, in humbleness and with a contrite heart, he shall have compassion on thee, and he shall accept thee as His own with love and compassion, and he shall be unto thee the Father of love and mercy. So be it and Selah.

I give of myself that this may be my gift unto thee this day. I am Sananda, the Nazarine. Son of God am I, sent to show thee the way. Follow ye me, for I am the one gone before thee that the place be prepared for thee. It is done and I am come that ye may return with me.

Let it be so... I am Sananda.

* * *

PART I: THE CELESTIAL CITY IN THE SUN

In the sun is a City... which I have seen!

This is not the fantastic tale of a professional story spinner, but a conscientious report of something that actually happened to me... and I was wide awake, clear of brain, and spiritually at peace.

I am not a dreamer, but a doer. I have no fantastic visions, no strange predictions. My name is as well known in Africa and Australia as it is in America, as a writer and lecturer. When I returned from a four year tour around the world, my many friends were deeply interested to hear about the countries I had visited and the people I had met. Now, I am wondering if they will be as eager to hear about this stupendous journey of my Soul, through a country no mortal eyes may see, to a CITY OF GOLDEN LIGHT in the very heart of the SUN!

Jesus of Nazareth said: "In my Father's house are many mansions; if it were not so I would have told you."

I have seen these Mansions. Wide awake, so completely awake that not the slightest detail escaped me, I was taken in spirit to the very heart of the glorious Sun, where lies a magnificent City, I was transported in a flash of consciousness, leaving my body of flesh apparently asleep in bed. By my side appeared a radiant personage, who said: "Be not afraid! I am your ministering Angel. You have been in my care for many incarnations, and now it is given to me to reveal to you the beauty and glory of the Eternal City of God."

Side by side, we floated or flew through the ether. About us at front and back and on either side, were hosts of angels. Their faces were so lovely that I tried to miss none of the beauty, and so turned my eyes from face to face continually. Finally, there was a great change in the atmosphere. I had imagined the sun to be as a ball of fire, but deep within its heart the temperature was like a balmy summer day. The air was fragrant, as if from the breath of millions of flowers, and I drank in the sweetness thirstily. I could not imagine my spirit imprisoned again in that far away body of flesh and blood. The remembrance of its clumsiness appalled me, and I knew that it would be easy to sever the slender elastic cord that bound me to that inert body so far away. The Angel sensed this thought, and answered: "Your work on earth is not yet complete. You are given this vision for the one purpose of returning to the earth and relating to humanity all that you shall have seen and heard, all of the wisdom imparted to you".

At last, from a great height, I looked down upon the Heavenly City, whose iridescent loveliness lay below me in a panorama of beauty and splendor too great for words to picture or for all the artists of the world to paint. Farther than eye could see, in the crystal light of heaven I saw terrace on terrace, with magnificent mansions and shining rivers and blooming trees for countless miles on every side. It seemed impossible to reach the limits of that Glorious City.

This, then, was that Heavenly City "not made with hands. Paul was snatched up to it, the seventh or perfect heaven. John visited it in his wonderful apocalyptic journey, and describes it perfectly. I had heard his description many times in the past, but the living reality of it had escaped me until then. Today I read his words with an inward illumination, for I have seen the selfsame City that John saw. I, who am still in the physical body, living on the earth, have walked its shining streets, have entered its mansions, and strolled through its gardens; and its inhabitants have walked and talked with me.

Always by my side floated the beautiful form of my angelic guide, explaining the conditions and the scenes as they changed before me, giving reasons for everything, and answering my question even before they could be voiced by me. For example, I began to wonder how I could possibly remember everything when I returned to earth and sought to redeem my promise to recount everything for the benefit of the world. The Angel sensed my feeling of bewilderment and hasten to reassure me, saying:

"Pay close attention to all that you hear and see; then, as the need shall arise, memory will recall words and scenes, and you will be able to write or speak with authority. Great truths are to be revealed to you. Treasure them as jewels beyond price. Live them with every conscious breath, Teach them to all who will heed your voice. It is your sacred mission to go forth to all parts of the earth, feeding those who hunger and thirst for the living waters of Truth.

"There are many who are not yet ready for your message, who will turn deaf ears and blind eyes. Be patient with such as these. They are the little ones of Spirit. Give to them your love, and reprove them not. Behold in them child-souls to be led gently into adult soul life. Even as the flower bud must unfold slowly and naturally, so must the young soul be given tenderness and care in order to develop into perfection. Give your message and go your way in happiness and peace. Those who are ready will drink of your living water and they will pass the draught to others, in love and faith."

As the Angel talked, we were speeding over the vast, shining terraces of the City. I could feel on my face and hands the gentle caress of breezes that seemed laden with the blended fragrance of many flowers. Moving in rhythm with the Angel, I rose or lowered myself as he changed his course, remaining ever by his side. Actual words were unnecessary between us, for we were speaking in the universal language of thought. Now, as I write, the unspoken words of the Angel return to me as if written on my heart.

"Salvation," he said, "will never be complete until each created being shall live within the Father. So you must return to earth, beloved one, for you are needed there. You must summon aspiring souls to climb the mount of spiritual vision and tear away the veil of ignorance that hides from mankind the face of the Living God. You must lift high the glorious banner of Love and Truth that will have nothing for one that is not for all; for the entire human family is in the image and likeness of God. You must teach that God is always near, to everyone, to all created things. Wherever space is, there too is God, but only through the powers of spiritual discernment can He be seen and known.

When you return to earth, you must teach that all the qualities of God are portrayed there; and it is there that all these qualities of the

Spirit must be understood and developed by mankind. As one lives with God consciously, so does one grow like unto God. The only perfect fullness of joy for man is for him to sense this divine companionship through living the life of a sun of God, returning at last to his Father's house, to live there forever."

Thus spoke the Angel, and his words were as music, and his face glowed as from a light within. As we floated through the air we were at ease, as though firm substance were beneath our feet. We now drew close to the great terraces. Without actually having seen them, it would be impossible for one to imagine the beauty and splendor of these foundations of the City's wall. Each was at least twelve hundred feet high, and the twelve of them extended entirely around the city; and I was told that they were one hundred miles apart.

The mountain on which the City was built gave an appearance of squareness at the base, sloping gradually upward to the summit. The atmosphere of the City was balmy in temperature, and all the inhabitants were joyous, busy and abundantly alive. Every face was alight with purest happiness. I gazed upon the gleaming terraces and glorious faces until a picture of them was photographed on my consciousness. In the distance could be seen a glow as from mounds of opals, and the Angel told me I was beholding the heavenly "gates of pearl." Later, we passed many times through those glorious gates whose soft lustre was like transparent satin through which rainbows shone At last we came to rest on the very summit of this vast mountain, with the beautiful terraced City spreading below... rivers and valleys and trees and flowers in a pattern of living beauty as far as we could see.

Looking into the Angel's face, I saw unutterable sadness depicted there. He began to speak in a very low tone, more as if he were communing with himself than conversing with another. "All of this glory must remain hidden," he said, "from those who do not first fulfill their responsibility to live according to the laws of God. In the dim light of their undeveloped spiritual understanding, they wander farther and farther from happiness and peace, ever stumbling and hurting themselves, and thus retarding their progress for age upon age, until at last these weary souls allow the tinsel trap pings of their worldliness to fall away. And then they come into the light, finding in the shining pathway before them the perfect fruition of their dreams."

For a long time I was silent, thinking upon what he had said. Then I asked the Angel to tell me where Jesus went when he ascended. Smiling almost as a tender mother would smile at a questioning child, he answered: "Jesus came directly to the Sun, His spiritual home, where he sits at the right hand of God, His Father, whom He loved and served and prayed to constantly while on earth. He gave to the world the pure spiritual teachings that came straight from God. There is but one way that leads to perfection, the way of Christ, who is the Ruler and Redeemer of the universe. His abode is here in the Sun, but the Power of His Spirit overshadows the entire universe. As humanity progresses, the teachings of Jesus will become clearer and clearer, and it will become easier to follow Him in daily life. Then, at last, will the living earth bring forth the divine blossoming of love and hope and happiness."

Every breeze gave forth the rhythm of music. The sweetness of lilies and roses came to us. The Presence of our dear Lord seemed enveloping us, until his Glory shone in everything. I knew that I must remember everything revealed to me, so that I might return to earth with a message of hope for all mankind, so I prayed: "Oh God, let me speak with the tongue of a prophet - let me herald Truth to all the world. Let the awakened Christ within me help to heal the nations of their sickness. Guide me always, that I may lead others aright." When I opened my eyes, I saw that the Angel was smiling upon me, and I returned his smile as naturally as I have always smiled upon those I love on earth. The great City of God shimmered below us. Its loveliness seemed a part of me, as if living Divine Beauty were spread over all creation.

- - -

.... We were speeding through the air as easily as the birds were flying, and the panorama of beauty that unfolded before me was more real than the mountains and valleys of the earth had ever been, The Angel said: "See how easily you are receiving into your own consciousness all that I am transferring to you without the utterance of words. In the same manner, many on earth will commune with you in silence. But to the world as a whole you must clothe your divine message in the garment of familiar language. Always speak plainly so that there may be no misunderstanding. Be utterly fearless at all times, for Truth will be your unfailing staff, and your Spirit will be refreshed and inspired as the need shall arise."

"Look upon these great terraces," said the Angel. "Their magnificence cannot be painted in words so that the human mind may vision them as they are. Their iridescent glory is beyond expression. All of the languages of earth, even with the greatest poets of the world garnering from them the richest word and phrase, never gave to humanity even a glimpse of this glorious scene before you now: tier upon tier of beauty and glory, straight from the hand of God.

"But come! Let us descend. Note how light is the feeling of your spiritual body, as if it were one with the elements. Also take note of the fact that you feel no hunger or weariness. In this heavenly region there is no hunger or thirst, and fatigue is unknown. There is neither heat nor cold, but al. ways a gentle warmth."

"To visit any part of the City, we have only to feel the desire in order to be transported there with the speed of thought. The spiritual body knows no limitations of time or space. On the earth plane this limitation is a great barrier. And to further hamper the Spirit, human beings fill their daily lives with countless unimportant duties and senseless pleasures, failing to take advantage of their opportunity for spiritual development. Being clumsy because of constant confinement in physical prisons, they blunder along slowly and painfully, timing themselves by the clock and making no allowance for the Spirit's needs."

"When you return, you will become impatient because of the necessity of adapting yourself to the confines of the flesh again. But be not discouraged. Your physical body will become more and more pliable to your will, as it is used by the Spirit."

As the Angel talked, we were speeding through space so lightly and easily that it seemed as if we barely moved. At last we came to rest on a great terrace, with gardens of flowers and shrubs and trees, and in the distance I could see shining rivers and lakes. There was a smile on the Angel's face. He said: "I have a surprise for you. Behold!"

Even now I catch my breath at the very thought of what I saw before me. A giant fountain sparkled and sang as it sent its rainbow-colored spray thousands of feet into the air! It seemed to be a living thing. It was like a play of fireworks, and the water shone like crystal. And music flowed from the spray! As the waters rose into the air, it sounded as if dozens of pipe organs were playing all at once, and as they came dancing down, there was a sound like the music of a harp of a thousand strings. As the Angel talked to me and I answered him, our voices seemed to be part of the water's song. I stood entranced. The fountain seemed to fill all space. Its spray floated in rainbows over the spreading terraces, sparkled on the lifted faces of the flowers, lay like jewels on the leaves of the shrubs, vines and trees. I felt it like a caress on my face, it shimmered in my cupped hands, but I felt no moisture, only the very spirit of freshness, coolness and fragrance.

Silently, I watched the sparkling waters as they gathered at the base of the fountain and then moved from terrace to terrace in waterfalls of glory. Through the great parks, over the broad boulevards, into the gardens of the shining mansions, raced the beauty of living water, I found myself crying: "Oh, God! Give me words! Give me words!" I knelt and caressed the grasses at my feet, I touched my cheek to a rose.

And all the time my heart was singing praise, and the fountains caught it up and echoed it through the air. Fragrance and beauty and glory were wrapped about me like a robe. Breathless with wonder and delight, I floated above and around the fountain. Its spray kissed my lips and tangled itself in my hair. I could not get enough of it. It was as if I had been thirsty forever and my soul could not drink its fill.

My heart kept singing to itself, over and over again: "Oh, my dear Father-Mother God! Oh, my dear Lord! This then is the glorious home prepared for children of the earth. This is where the hurt ones will know healing for their wounds. This is where the sorrowful will grieve no more, but will know such happiness that will dry all tears forever. This is where the soul may see its holiest dreams come true."

* * *

All about me were angelic beings, taking pleasure in my happiness. Their white robes floated about their bodies in graceful folds, and on their beautiful foreheads shone their sacred names. Their eyes were tender and their lips smiled. Many of them touched me and spoke to me, some kissed me and called me by name. I returned their caresses and talked to them freely. I had lost all count of time. Yesterday was a dim memory; tomorrow was far away.

The Angel came close and took my hand in his. I think he was sorry that I must return to the earth and live there for many years when such glory was unrolled before me. At last, he said: "We must go."

Our direction changed, and soon we were far away from the fountain itself, but its spray was about us still. Finally we stopped flying and found ourselves standing in a spacious garden, with lovely, shining walks that were bordered with such flowers as I most loved. There were roses of many colors, some of them very large.

And there were dainty wild roses of pink and white. Everywhere blossoms seemed to be waiting to greet me. The very leaves of the trees in this particular garden seemed to whisper loving things to me. *(Note: She was later to realize that this was, in fact, her own home within this glorious city, to which she would return when her time in flesh was finished).*

We walked slowly along the broad driveway leading to an imposing dwelling that could be seen through a bower of trees. There were many arbors and pergolas on either side, covered with flowering vines, and having comfortable seats and tables.

At last we stopped in front of the glorious mansion, made of purest alabaster, and shining in the light like a great jewel. The building was square in shape, with great white columns on all four sides of each of the three tiers that seemed to divide it into different parts. The lowest tier was the most massive, and its carvings were large and deep. The middle tier was not so large as the bottom one, and its carvings were more delicate. The top tier was still smaller, and its sculptured tracery of flower and vine and symbolism was limned upon the softly gleaming alabaster so exquisitely that it would be necessary for one to look closely in order to decipher the pattern.

I stood immovable, and gloried in the vision of perfect loveliness before me. At last the Angel led me away, and we entered the mansion through the great front door that swung so lightly on its golden hinges that it seemed to open of its own accord. There was a tremendous hall, with rugs and pictures and furniture; and then we entered a beautiful, spacious room, with carved doorways leading into many other rooms. At these doorways there were lovely draperies of shining brocade. Growing flowers smiled at me from their places near the great windows, through which streamed a flood of light straight from the glowing heart of the Sun.

We passed through a great conservatory where orchids of every color were growing; through a music room where rare instruments waited for the touch of loving hands. As we passed from room to room I felt that I must stop every once in a while to impress certain things on my mind, and the Angel let me have my way.

Finally, we passed into a very large room where there were many carved shelves on the walls. And there were low tables and easy chairs. There was no need for me to be told that it was a library. At once, I visioned quantities of familiar books on those bare shelves; and lo, they appeared in actuality almost as quickly as I had thought of them. But the Angel said:

"It is not from such as these that wisdom's knowledge will come to you, but from the Book of Life, which can only be read with the clear eyes of intuition."

My soul knew this to be true, and with the conviction came that desire to read only that one Great Book, whose divine pages unfold themselves to the seeking eyes of the Spirit, revealing Truth given by God Himself.

Through the great windows we could see the shining City, and since the mansion was situated in the very midst of a forest garden, we could see flowers and trees that were so close we could touch them from the windows. I noticed that many of the trees bore leaves that were heart shaped, and they were green on the outside and silver underneath. There were a great many fruit trees, all of them bearing. The fruits were unusual in size and beauty, the grapes being as large as apples and deep purple or pure golden in color. The bananas were yellow, but the fruit was perfectly ripe. Every leaf and twig was filled with life.

At last I knew that I must resume my journey. The Angel took my hand in his, and with one last lingering look, I followed him.

* * *

PART II: THE PHILOSOPHY OF HEAVEN

Soon, we were flying again, over the shining terraces, over the broad, shimmering rivers and silvery lakes, over the quiet serenity of flower-starred valleys and hills. At last, we came to rest in a great park, where thousands of radiant angels were gathered in groups. Flowers were so abundant that it was necessary for us to be careful lest we crush them as we walked.

The Angel said: "You will notice that the flowers here are much brighter and far more varied in color than the flowers of earth. All plants are marvelously alive in appearance and in reality. Their texture is super-fine, and they are much more fragrant. You will remember that you always talked to your flowers when you planted and cared for them (on earth). Your love entered their flower-consciousness and they responded to you as they could not have done had you felt and acted otherwise toward them. And now in your heavenly home the flowers growing there for you were created by your own love of them and your desire for their beauty.

Had you not loved flowers on earth, they could not have manifested such loveliness for you here. When you return to the world, teach that what is done on earth will be duplicated elsewhere. The law of reaping as one sows is an immutable law of Almighty God. Those on earth can create heaven or hell for themselves, to come into manifestation when they shall have left that planet forever. It is in the school of earthly experience that the soul must learn its lessons of the lower grades of consciousness; and the sooner these lessons are learned, the more quickly will promotion to higher grades be earned by the soul. These lessons must be learned! Unfoldment of spiritual consciousness is inevitable for all. He who plays truant and refuses to learn can only delay his destiny.

As you traveled from continent to continent on earth, your work of hastening soul development was recorded; and when you finally reach the haven of the City of God, to depart no more, those whom you have led upward in Spirit will surely find their way to you here. Those same brave souls and many others who are now awaiting your teachings on earth, will be your companions and students in the higher spheres, and will eventually reach this Holy City and find their way to you through gratitude and love. Such ties that are made on earth are eternal ties. They break not, through the centuries of centuries, and they tarnish not. In the shelter of your arms, sorrowing ones on earth have found peace. Your love has reached them in the depths of sin and pain, creating for them a holy radiance in which they felt the divine urge to rise to the heights, with you. And so you are blended with them eternally through the spiritual alchemy of love, and they became your little ones of the heavenly fold, ever seeking greater and greater unfoldment, because of the divine spark alight within them, which must finally burst forth in glory here in the garden of God."

As the Angel talked, I noticed that the scattered groups began to come together. Many of them flew like beautiful birds into the distance and were soon lost to sight. My companion beckoned me to follow. We flew toward the East, into the softness and beauty of seeming twilight. Many others joined us, from time to time, some of these being travelers from other spheres, like myself. All were white robed and lovely to look upon, but the angels were lighter of wing and more shining of personality than any of the others.

We hastened to a great auditorium that was without walls or ceiling. Countless millions of radiant beings gathered there. Some sat at ease under the trees; others stood quietly, still others lay on the soft grasses. But all had the seemingly breathless expectancy that made their faces so lovely and tender that I felt my eyes misted as with tears. Silence fell about us like a veil. The air was sweet with the blended aromas of countless flowers. The fountain's song was subdued, almost like a faint echo of itself; and the spray was like dew everywhere, soft and fragrant and bright.

Guided by the Angel, I floated to the very center of the auditorium, to the foot of a great throne that was so shining that I shaded my eyes with my hands. Its jeweled beauty gleamed with living glory, and I fell on my knees and prayed. The very air seemed to be still as in prayer.

In the rose-tinted twilight, the kneeling angels were like Easter lilies. The holy beauty of heaven lay upon them. I think my soul held its breath, waiting, and waiting, and waiting. And then, lifting my eyes, I knew that before me in all its white splendor was the shining Throne of God!

Down the long winding golden stairs, from the very top of the throne, came hundreds of radiant angels, harbingers of glad tidings, all of them with golden trumpets in their hands. As they descended, they formed in line, twelve abreast, with their beautiful, shining robes floating about them and their graceful feet gliding amid the rose-lit glow, as if the stairway were not needed to support their weight. A golden light, tinged with purple, proceeded from their radiance, which poured out its fullness upon all who beheld the glorious sight.

As they descended, the angels made of themselves the form of a double triangle; then the square; and then they formed into a circle around the throne. High above the throne, other angels were pattering themselves into seven-pointed stars, until there were twelve glorious stars. Each point of the star represented a different color; the first was red, then came orange, then yellow, green, blue, indigo, and violet. As we stood in awe watching these radiant beings fashioning themselves into living stars, it seemed to me that the twelve stars covered a radius of at least one hundred miles in circumference. The Angel communicated to me silently that the overshadowing of Infinite Love was thus represented as a glorious canopy, and that all this beautiful ceremony was taking place around the throne in preparation for the arrival of the Lord.

Suddenly, there came harmony as from a thousand harps, blending with the melody of musical instruments of every tone. The holy angels sounded their trumpets in joy and triumph. The living stars shone softly in unimaginable radiance. All faces were upturned. And then ... The Lord approached His throne!

Around Him shone the rainbow of promise, with all the glorious colors blended, until the whole of Heaven became suffused with the Holy Spectrum, full of the Life and power which each color was to impart. These colors represented the perfection of His nature and the fullness of the Divine Love and Wisdom which dwells in Him, the Lord of Life and Light. On either side of Him were two heavenly messengers who serve Him in the inmost sanctuary of Heaven. Their faces glowed in holiness and love, and their raiment was purest white.

At last, I lifted up my eyes and looked upon the face of my Lord, his countenance radiant with the Light that comes from the Glory of the Christ. As I looked upon Him, there before me came the vision of the many times he had revealed Himself to me on the earth, as my Redeemer and Friend, assuring me that he would never leave me nor forsake me. Gazing upon the Son of God in all his Glory, my soul was filled with a great awe. My heart overflowed with adoration for Him, the Lord of Hosts, King of Glory, the gentle Christ. I kept my eyes focused on His face as He stood between His Angels. The light about us grew softer and lovelier still. The time was now at hand for services in the Divine Temple not made with hands.

The reverberating music became a soft refrain. The paeans of praise were changed into murmuring rhythm like far away echoes of song. The radiant face of my Lord was turned toward me, and His beautiful, tender eyes gazed into mine. I knelt at His feet and lifted a fold of His robe to my lips. He smiled upon me, and I knew that my tears were falling, and I was also smiling. His Presence enfolded me like a garment, and I have felt it about me ever since.

His voice! How can I describe it? That exquisitely lovely, gentle voice! Every word could be heard by all the millions gathered there. With rapt faces and softly shining eyes, they listened with their Souls.

He spoke as naturally as He must have talked to His disciples when on earth. There were no lowly ones and no exalted ones in that vast audience; all were equal. The mantle of His love lay upon all alike. His smile was for each and for all. Truth flowed from his lips. Peace lived in His Presence. Forgetting all else, the great throng listened as one being--listened until His voice died away. And then, there arose once more the lifting loveliness of angel voices, and the music of the fountain could once again be heard.

I did not know when our Lord left His throne. I only knew that I had been drinking from the fountain of Divine Knowledge, and that I must take its waters back to earth in the brimming cup of my soul. No longer was I afraid of forgetting, for I knew that I could tap the source of memory at will. I had lost all count of time. So much had been said, and so much had happened.

Once more the angels assembled in groups, but it was plainly to be seen that His words had stirred them so deeply that they sought quiet meditation instead of companionship.

The Angel led me to a seat under the trees, and then others joined us there. In the following pages, I will try to recount the wisdom unfolded to me in that fair garden. Many of the Great Ones of heaven came quietly and sat with us, talking and teaching. These teachers were not inclined to have me repeat their words, giving them credit. Their only desire was for the message to reach humanity. So I shall give it as closely as possible in the form in which it was given to me.

I was told that the earth was about to put on immortality, and that the Lord would return to claim and rule His Kingdom. Many who talked to me were former inhabitants of the earth; philosophers, musicians, poets, statesmen, as well as many great souls of the world who had never received recognition there.

Always, my guardian Angel remained at my side, seeming pleased that so many others came to us with their offered wealth of wisdom: and he appeared to be gratified that I so eagerly gathered it all into my consciousness.

I looked at the panorama of living beauty unrolled before me. Lifting my hands full of jeweled pebbles and then letting them fall back in glittering beauty upon the terrace, I said: "Many will say that I have only dreamed. Others will declare that psychic visions came to me. Only a blessed few will say: 'I, too have seen the Holy City, and it is just as you have said." One of the teachers answered: "Give your message without thought of how it may be received. Sow the seeds of Truth. Even though some may fall on stony ground, others will find rich soil in human consciousness, and eventually will bear the ripened fruit of Truth."

After a short period of silence, he continued: "A new era is dawning on earth. Humanity is evolving in spirituality as never before. When man was compelled to struggle against the elements and unknown dangers, ever fighting for bare physical existence, he was unable to turn his full attention to needs of the Spirit. But now he is being freed from the bonds of fear, and his soul will call to him for its heritage of development and joy, and he will answer that call by lifting his eyes from the dust and seeking to read God's Word as written by Him on the eternal pages of His Book of Creation. As the soul develops, it must be released from the time consuming routine of physical existence, so that it may have leisure and accumulate its store of power for the greater purpose of spiritual unfoldment. In this new day, that it be accomplished, and Man will be born anew. It is your task to hasten this new birth of mankind, together with all other earthly teachers who have found God through Love and Service to His children on earth."

As I listened to voices of those who so freely and gladly poured forth the riches of their wisdom, the music of the fountain was as an accompaniment, rising and falling in harmony such as we have never dreamed on earth. There was rhythmic movement everywhere in this glorious City, whose living beauty seemed to breathe. The leaves of the trees and plants swayed gently. The flowers seemed to whisper to one another. In the distance, millions of angelic beings were busy in work or study or play. But even when the leaves and grasses and flowers showed no movement at all, they were strangely vital, as if filled with unlimited power of feeling and expression in growth.

At last, I found myself alone once more with my angel guide. There seemed to be no need of haste, but I sensed that much more awaited me, and so focused my attention on the glorious scene before me, that I might paint it in my mind in glowing colors that would never fade. Lying still and relaxing on the velvety grass, that was not crushed by my weight, and with the fountain's gentle spray playing upon my face, I recalled much of what I had learned on earth. I knew that my task would be to unlearn many of those things mistakenly taught me as Truth. I thanked God for His wisdom in leading me to a great and wise teacher on earth, and I thanked him that my soul had found its way from the lowlands of consciousness to the heights of spiritual understandings, had entered the Holy of Holies and heard the voice of my Lord.

I remembered how I had thrilled when "Science" proclaimed new findings, how tirelessly I had sought knowledge from earthly sources, and how tragically my weary soul had faced the fact that all those beautiful pictures were but mirages in a desert of despair. And then I remembered those rare times when the closed doors of the Spirit had opened wide, and I was led forth into the dazzling light of understanding, seeing life not as a little span of time but as an eternal flow of precious essence from God Himself.

Looking into the quiet face of the Angel, I noticed that he was seemingly lost in thought. But soon he turned his eyes toward me as if trying to read my inmost heart. At last he smiled and said: "Yes, it is true that the great scientists of the earth and of other planets are ofttimes misled through their own limitations, and so teach wrongly even though sincerely. However, it is far better for them to do research that later must be corrected, than that they fall into mental apathy through idleness of mind. Only those who rise high enough spiritually to secure knowledge from the unpolluted "Source" may lead humanity aright. Such leaders are few."

The little children of your world look up to and feeling and revere ignorance, clothed in the tinsel robes of make-believe, Bigotry and intolerance walk proudly over the earth and smite all who would say unto them "nay". While simple unassuming wisdom, seeking no adulation, waits quietly for heart-weary suppliants to find their way to her, and seek her sparkling waters of pure knowledge from the hidden Spring of the Spirit.

"It is true that the dark ages have not yet passed from the earth. Humanity stumbles and strays and suffers, ever seeking and finding not. And all the while there is the shining path that leads from grief to gladness, from pain to peace, from ignorance to knowledge; and the path lies before each Soul, waiting for his straying feet to find its haven at last. Into this path your Soul found its way long ago - but none may travel it with you save he who seeks and finds the path through his own desire and endeavor."

"Are there imminent changes for the better?" I asked. He said: "Humanity is rising in consciousness daily. New leaders will come forward as needed and be used as instruments for man's upliftment, inventing marvelous things, making new laws, blazing new ways.

"Electricity will be known as the Cosmic Force used by the Divine Creator for the making of all things and the governing of them in their relations to one another. It will be used by man with such wisdom and intelligence and knowledge, eventually, that he will find himself possessed of a power unlimited in scope.

And as his spiritual horizon broadens, he will find the hand of Divinity consciously in his, guiding him to undreamed of accomplishments. So long as man walks in the narrow pathways of the flesh and materiality, he limits himself; but when he steps forth unafraid into the broad highways of the Spirit, he lets fall from his shoulders the dragging yoke of physical imperfections and weakness, and walks unhampered in his newly found power and perfection."

At a signal from the Angel, I arose and followed him, once more flying through the air as if to a definite goal. My attention was called to the River of Life ever flowing between flower bordered banks, and into branches and springs in the gardens of those lovely mansions. I marveled at the beauty and glory of it all, and knew that John and those others who had preceded me never could have expressed in words what it must have been in their hearts to say, even as I would strive in vain to picture the City of Heaven as it really is.

Because I was thinking so intently of John at this time, he appeared at my side and began talking with me. Among the things he said, I especially remember these:

"The teachings of Jesus were governed by love. It ran through all of his sayings like a golden thread through pearls, binding them together into one shining strand. Love thy God with all thy heart... Love thy neighbor as thyself... Love thine enemies.

The Lord is the ruling Deity of the universe. Man's development and destiny are in His care. He gave the world a perfect example of life in the fullest and highest, which was his mission of Love... and now humanity is rising into that spiritual consciousness."

He impressed upon me the importance of earth's schooling, saying that we should apply our selves diligently to our lessons of self-control and patience and tolerance, ever striving to see beyond the lesson itself into the reason for the task set before us. And he said that earthly teachers should not fail to remember themselves as students also. I agreed with him, and he smiled upon me and passed from sight again.

Seemingly without limit, the Holy City lay before me in its unimaginable splendor. Great and wise souls came, from time to time, as the Angel and I traveled from place to place, and they seemed anxious to pour forth their riches of knowledge. Always, when my mind dwelt on a thought or a question, there was immediate response from them. In like manner, I could define the thoughts of the Great Ones near me and answer without words. In answer to an unspoken question from one of these, regarding the effect my journey to the Celestial City was having upon me personally, I replied, mentally:

"I know that all I am witnessing is the Eternal Truth. I know that God reigns over all His creation; that this glorious City of Heaven is His abiding place; that man is His beloved son, created in the Father's true image and likeness, with the power to rise in consciousness until he can live forever in his ultimate home. I know that eye hath not seen, nor ear heard, nor hath it entered into the heart of man to conceive the marvelous things that God hath prepared for all who love Him and obey His Laws. And I know that my beloved Lord reveals Himself to all who truly love and serve and follow Him, and that He will return to earth and claim His Kingdom there, even as has been prophesied. My soul is quickened to hear and see and feel as never before. Realizing that my work on earth is a sacred task yet unfinished, I am reconciled to return and be about my Father's business. In the name of my Lord 1 faithfully promise to transmit to others all knowledge and wisdom from all channels that shall be opened unto me".

He who had questioned me, smiled as I finished and I knew that he was pleased with my answer. My ministering Angel continued with his dis course, which had been interrupted when other joined us. He said: "It will be unnecessary for you to give scientific data, when you return to earth. Others will be used for that purpose. You are an inspirational teacher and writer, and your work will be to gain the interest and attention of humanity, describing the Holy City and its location, revealing much of its philosophy, and yet avoiding controversy.

The great Sun's electro-magnetic energy creates this delightful climate, never too warm nor too cold, where flowers of tropical beauty may bloom constantly. On earth, in the near future, many wonders will be demonstrated through the use of electricity, the magical force of which humanity knows so little today. And when this time comes, it will be easier for man to comprehend that the Sun is not hot, as has been taught in the past."

As the Angel ceased speaking, an unuttered desire entered my mind. I wanted to see myself, separated from my physical body, and I wanted to know if my Soul in its state of new freedom and power could vision that inert body, without returning to earth. Immediately, I saw a vision of my Higher Self standing about three feet above my physical body, which was still lying on the couch and seemed fast asleep. The Angel said:

"This body is your personality, the earthly instrument of your Soul. It represents the cross of matter, which the Soul must take up each day and carry wherever it goes; for without the cross of flesh the Soul could not manifest on earth. The Soul builds its own cross and must carry it alone, and take care of it until it is needed no longer During the night the Soul rebuilds the worn-out cells and tissues and bones, so that its house may be kept in repair."

Then I said: "But what is this part of me that is so shining and bright?" The answer was: "It is your Soul, or Sun, that is created in the image and likeness of God and which is birthless, changeless and deathless.

The earthly vision faded. I heard again the music of the fountain and felt its spray on my face. The Angel continued speaking of the Soul. He said:

"The physical robe changes continually from embodiment to embodiment, but the Soul never changes. It ever develops, but it is always the same Soul, a divine atom of Almighty God. When man becomes conscious of his own true divinity, he will arise from his groveling in the dust and lift himself to the glowing heights of the Spirit, forever free from the prison of the flesh even though still on earth and functioning in physical body.

His destiny is glorious beyond human conception. But only by graduating from the lower states of consciousness into the higher, the Christ consciousness, can he become attuned to Deity, and find himself indeed one with the Father. The materialists of earth cannot remain materialists, for they must gain spiritual knowledge. Cults and creeds should not be condemned. They are needed by many as temporary guides; but when the soul receives its greater sight, it walks alone without need of such guidance.

The most important thing for man to know is that he is an immortal being, that the loss of a physical body does not deter the soul in its schooling, for the Great Teacher gives His lessons everywhere, according to His will and the student's need. When a great genius dwells no more in his visible raiment, the flame is not extinguished, but burns more brightly within another form. For nothing great nor beautiful nor pure is ever lost in all eternity."

I thought of the wonderful earth as a great school, where the Father's beloved children were given their tasks in order for them to learn wisdom according to their ability to learn. If only all humanity could vision themselves in this way How futile would seem the strivings to satisfy ambition, the heart breaking efforts to accumulate wealth. How beautiful would be the tasks of every day, how sacred would be the heart's dreams of Love and Faith and Truth. Our churches of earth would open wide their doors and never close them again. They would become the busiest centers of the cities and towns, where the problems of souls would be solved in the ever shining Light of Truth.

Lovers would build their love on the foundation of purity and joy, and they would walk together under the stars of heaven with no fear in their hearts. There would be no mourning for those who only go ahead for a little while.

The Angel said: "There will be many changes on earth in the near future, in both business and religious life. As originally given by the founders, the teachings of the majority of the religious movements on earth were purely and beautifully spiritual. For all who were ready to receive such sacred knowledge they contained the Divine Wisdom as interpreted from the higher sphere; but man in his limited understanding and visions of Truth, caused the true teachings to be crystallized into lifeless ceremonies.

Those who were chosen to reveal the truth were exalted by man to high places, yet the inner meaning of the spiritual message was lost in the personal worship of the message bearers. For example, so much of the personal has entered into the teachings of Jesus, that the Christ has been lost in the objective manifestation. The true Christ has been dethroned within the religious systems, through exaltation of the person of "Jesus of Nazareth".

"In the spiritual mysteries of the Egyptians and the early Greeks and the ancient Hebrews, and in the revelations given through Jesus of Nazareth, the misled and mistaken followers took the sign for the thing signified, burying the inner meaning in the outer symbol. In this manner, they took the personality of Jesus to be the Christ, thus they failed to perceive the truth for which Jesus strove.

"This is the great danger of the present time, which must be guarded against. This can be accomplished only through understanding of the true nature of the coming of the Lord. Christ is not a man, nor is the Logos or Adonai a man, though in reality He has part in every human soul system. He is ever like the Unmanifest One, of whom He is the manifest. He overshadows the soul, but He is never the man. He is always transcendentally greater than the one filled with the Christ Consciousness."

"When a human being attains the Christed Consciousness, as did Jesus at his baptism, he is filled and illumined from the Eternal Christ, the Adonai or Logos. It is not the Man who is the Christ, but the soul or sun of God, who has attained to the state of consciousness of the indwelling Divine Presence within him. When one reaches that state of consciousness all things personal, national, and racial, are transcended in the Christ or Universal Consciousness. It is the state of consciousness that connects the soul knowingly to the Kingdom of Heaven, when they awaken to their true Oneness with the Father... for then it is the Father within that speaks, and it is also He who doeth the works."

"The soul must never worship a man, it must worship God alone. It is not the personality of Jesus which was the Christ and the Lord, but the soul or sun within the glorious states of consciousness. The teachings of Jesus were brought down from the highest spiritual plane to which they belonged, to the lower earthly plane."

"The teachings of Jesus of Nazareth must again be given to the world by those willing to be as Jesus was. Their mission must be to heal the sick, to lift souls up into a life of purity and love. On earth there are many great souls, illumined from the Divine Presence within, whose work will be to lead all who are able to follow the path of Christhood, the path to Regeneration.

Some are with you now, and there will be many more. Some of may appear to be higher than others because of the nature of their ministry, but there are neither high nor low in the Kingdom. All teachers sent forth from God are one in spirit and in love, one in heart and in service. They are but the vehicles of manifestation given through them. He who is the greatest, even the Eternal One, is servant of all souls, and all teachers are only His servants."

The voice of the Angel ceased, but my soul still drank from the brimming cup of his wisdom. I thought of the earth and wanted to cradle it in my arms, yearning over its griefs as a mother holding a hurt child to her breast. So simply could all the problems be solved, so quickly could all the wounds be healed! The sick world cries out in its troubled dreams, yet will not awaken and walk in the Light of the Spirit.

"Tell me," I said to the Angel, "tell me about the coming of the Lord. The distress of the world lies upon my heart, even while here in heaven. Give me some definite word to take to the suffering ones of earth. Give me hope to take to take to them. I will return and give my whole life to service, as I have done in the past. But I know that the clouds of war are lowering everywhere. Men, made in the image of God, are marking themselves with the brand of Cain.

Little children are being robbed of their childhood, made to labor beyond their strength that greedy ones may profit. Hate and despair are filling the world with madness. Oh, let me do my part to lead it back to sanity and peace. Give me wisdom! Give me strength! Send me back with something so substantial to give that the world must heed my voice. Mankind is stumbling in the dark. Only the Christ can lead them unto the light. When will He return?"

And the Angel answered: "The second coming of the Lord has already taken place on earth, coming even as a thief in the night, as the Master said. It came when no man was aware, in a manner wholly unlooked for. For behold, I say unto you that it has already come to the planet, in the approach of the angelic world to the earth planes to communicate with every soul able to arise in spiritual consciousness and receive the very life-stream of the Father-Mother God that is being poured out from heaven upon all the planes of earth, *(Note: notice that they said earth planes, in plural, as spoken of in the last newsletter)*.

Only the older souls upon the earth, unto whom it has been given to understand these events, are able to receive this truth at present. The great change which is now taking place in the social, national and religious life of the nations, is not only a preparation for the coming of the Lord, it is the first result of that coming, in the manifestation of the earth's being overshadowed by the angelic world which encompasses it."

Into the glorified face of the Angel came such beauty that I could not turn my eyes away. I saw what humanity should be, what it can be, what it is to be. And I knew that a ministering Angel was eager to guard and guide every soul on earth, as I was guarded and guided by the Angel at my side. A great weight seemed to fall from me. Taking my hand in his, the Angel said, 'Come!" Once again, we flew through seemingly unlimited space, until at last we came to rest at the very crest of a great mountain. I could not speak for the rapture that possessed me. From the very heart of heaven, down through all the heavenly planes, the mental planes, the astral planes, even to the earth, throngs of glorious beings made a great white way.

"See," said the Angel, "the path is before you that leads from earth to heaven, and from heaven to earth. It is ever thronged with angels, preparing for the return of the rightful King, who is to rule the earth! Herald his truth to all who will hear. The time is at hand when the old order of things shall be no more. But first there must be the shaking of the earth to its foundation, and breaking of all the hard and cruel conditions of man's nature, even as though some spiritual earthquake were taking place.

Man must awaken to the realization of his oneness with his Creator. He must find his place in the Father's house, that he may be counted worthy to be called a Sun of God when the manifestation of the Divine Presence takes place. Behold, I say unto you, that the Christ hath once more appeared unto all who have eyes to see and ears to hear. Many cannot yet realize the changed spiritual conditions coming upon men and women, the opening of the heavens unto so many souls, and the illumination given to those who are ready.

"It was the Lord who overshadowed the Soul of Jesus, and it is that same Divine Father over shadowing the earth planet. It is His Presence within the soul's sanctuary that constitutes the Christed Consciousness, or the return of Christ to His Temple. The music of the heavens is penetrating all souls, attuning them that all may find Harmony Divine.

"This is taking place in heaven and on earth now, for all who have eyes to see and ears to hear. Your work is planned for you. You have been shown the Celestial City of God, that you may return to earth and teach humanity Truth. The way will be hard and many difficulties will beset you, but you will take your message to all parts of the earth; and when your sacred task is finished, you will find your shining palace awaiting you here.

"Look once more at the Blessed City, my child, for this hour must you return to earth. To all the world you must tell what you have seen and heard. You will be upheld and guided every step of the way. The blessings of the Father, and of our Lord and all the angels of Heaven will follow you... forever!

The scene faded. The voice of the Angel was stilled. The music died away...

Once more imprisoned in a body of flesh, I arose from my couch and gazed upon the familiar surroundings of my earthly home. I do not know exactly how long I was away, but it must have been at least nine hours. In my household, orders are given that I must not be disturbed until I give the word, so no one had come to my door during the morning. It was almost noon when I went downstairs. I felt unusually refreshed, as though I could never feel weariness again. And, strange as it may seem, this actually has been the case. I have never felt a touch of weariness since that time!

* * *

PART III: THE SECOND COMING OF THE LORD

While my body lay in sleep, I was suddenly caught up in spirit, away above the earth plane. I realized that an angel was by my side, and I was told that I was to behold the great catastrophe that is to occur on this earth, that I might warn the people and to help them to get ready to meet their Lord.

Then I saw this earth planet rock from one side to the other three times like you would rock a cradle. I saw the buildings crumble as though they were made of paper, until not one building was left standing except the Great Pyramid. People thought that the end of the world had come.

Those who had not been caught in the buildings or killed outright were running to and fro, not knowing which way to turn. There was wild panic everywhere, and such fear and anguish as no one in the world had ever dreamed could be.

Volcanoes all over the world began to erupt, and great volumes of smoke and fire and sulfur fumes poured out to such an extent that the atmosphere of the entire globe became so filled with deadly fumes and smoke that it seemed impossible for any living thing to breathe.

And then a great quake occurred and the mountains were split open, and the ocean was split as you would spill water out of a basin, and I saw people running to and fro, frantically screaming and tearing their hair, for they thought the end of the world had come.

But it was really the judgment day that had come upon them and everyone was being judged according to their own deeds that were recorded upon the great Book of Life, for the seals had been opened and the names and the record of their lives were all recorded upon that great book. Then the angle led me back to the earth that I might console these people.

One man was going through such agony of mind that my heart went out in compassion. I tried to console him, assuring him that he would be all right. He answered, moaning and crying: "But you don't understand, oh, you don't understand. Look at them! Look at them!" I asked him what he wanted me to see, and he answered: "They are haunting me. They are haunting me! I cannot get away from them!" I asked him: "Who are they?" And he replied, wringing his hands and moaning: "I was a surgeon.

All whom I have caused to lose their bodies by operating upon them are here, condemning me, for I did it for money! They would have gotten well, but I murdered them, I destroyed their bodies for money.

I did not know that the human body was the living temple of God, so for love of money I caused hundreds of human beings to lose their temples. They are haunting me, and their eyes follow me everywhere I turn. Can't you see them? Oh, can't you see them? They are everywhere around me, and they will not leave me alone.

Oh, what shall I do? What shall I do?" So great was his despair that no words of comfort could penetrate his consciousness. I had to leave him to his sorrow and turn to someone else. Lying prostrate on the ground a man was weeping and praying for mercy.

He too was reading the terrible pages of his Book of Life. I bent above him and asked if I could do something to help him, but he only continued moaning and praying. Then be said to me: "I was a real estate dealer, and I foreclosed on the properties of others to gain them for myself.

I put the defenseless poor out of their homes to face suffering and despair, when I should have helped them to save their possessions. They had so little, and I had so much, but I persecuted them.

I was a very rich man, and now I am left desolate, for all my property is destroyed, and I have nothing left in the world but the memory of a misspent life. Oh, what did it profit me to gain all that wealth? In the twinkling of an eye it has all been destroyed. I have nothing left, yet I cannot forget the ones I wronged. I cannot forget...."

Then my attention was called to another poor Soul, who seemed to be in such torment that he was striking himself and pulling his hair in anguish. I tried to tell him that God was merciful and that he should be glad he was still alive, but he cried pitifully: "What is the use of living, now that I am weighed in the balance and found wanting? I was a minister of the Gospel, but how did I minister to my flock? I was supposed to be their shepherd.

I was told to preach the Gospel of Jesus Christ, to open the eyes of the blind, to heal the sick, but all I did was to preach! I did not comfort those that mourned; I did not look after the widows and the fatherless; and when the members of my fold came to me for healing, I sent them to physicians and surgeons, instead of ministering to them myself, And now I realize that it was through our lack of faith to heal these sick that hospitals had to be built, asylums had to be filled, and penitentiaries had to be provided for all those who had lost their way through our failure to be true shepherds to our sheep.

Oh, if I had only known! Had I only understood and realized what I know now, how differently I would have lived! But now it is too late...too late! I have betrayed my Lord!"

I tried to comfort this poor Soul, to assure him that it was never too late. I tried to tell him that God, in His infinite love, would forgive to the uttermost. But his remorse was so great that no words of mine could have any effect, for he felt that he had committed the unpardonable sin. I left him in the care of the Father and turn my attention to another Soul, a woman who was crying as though her heart would break.

It seemed that this woman had hardened her heart to the sacred duty of caring for her sister's son. He was motherless and fatherless, and was frail of body. She was rich, but had refused to help him.

He tried to work his way through college but it was beyond his strength, and he passed out of the body, because she had hoarded her wealth instead of using it to help one of the "little ones." Now all the wealth was gone, and there was nothing left but the memory of the great wrong that she had done. She too could not be comforted.

I turned to another suffering one. He was a banker who, through misappropriation of the funds of his bank, had caused many hundreds of people to lose all their earnings. Many of these were aged people, who put all they had in the world in his care and trusted him, and he had betrayed their trust. He was a pitiful object to behold, so great was his remorse. I passed on to another. This man was a capitalist whom the world had held very high, both socially and financially, but oh what a poor thing he felt now, in Spirit.

Gone was all the wealth that had been secured for him through the grinding labor of poorly paid employees. Gone was the prestige of the world. Now, when it was too late, he realized how many he could have blessed and made happy, had he lived according to the Brotherhood of Man.

He remembered one of his employees, an old women who should have been in her prime. She had worked for him for many years, and had not received enough from him to keep body and soul together, and had died in poverty. And he knew that he could not say, "Lord, Lord!" and enter into the kingdom of heaven. Bowed down with regret and remorse, he dared not even pray.

Here and there a few radios were on, and from all parts of the earth came reports of the catastrophe that had spared no country on the globe. But at last, the radios were unable to work because of the increasing denseness of the atmosphere. Country was cut off from country by the unbreakable wall of silence. Cities and towns became isolated, unable to communicate in any way.

Chaos reigned everywhere. Parents and children became separated, human beings no longer ruled the earth, but were only helpless things scattered over the ground, or crawling about in the dimness, feeling their way as if ill and blind.

The living and the dead huddled together, not knowing the one from the other. Always, the moaning and crying of those who faced the judgment of their own Souls, mingled with the noises of crashing walls... for even in the darkness, the Book of Life was before them, every page being read in the light of memory.

And there was no redress! The records stood as they were. The law of sowing and reaping was being fulfilled. The poor unwise judges of the earth had given wrong verdicts because they could see only a part of the Truth, but these who judged themselves could not dissemble. The verdict of "guilty" blazed about them on every side. Wherever they turned, the results of their wrongdoings were pictured on their own Souls. And they could only cry and moan for mercy.

Everywhere that I looked there was the same anguish stamped upon the features of those who had survived the great day of judgment. And all this time the volcanoes were active and the atmosphere became more and more stifling. Darkness fell upon the world, for the Sun had ceased to give its light, and now the stars were falling from the heavens, until at last there was such pitch darkness that not a living soul dared stir.

I had no way of telling how long this lasted. I seemed only a moment, and yet it seemed forever. But finally the intense blackness began to lift from the earth like the slow dissipation of a heavy fog until human forms could be distinguished among the unimaginable wreckage. The whole earth resembled a battlefield, for there was nothing but devastation, north and south, and east and west.

And then I began to hear the music of the spheres. It was as if a million trumpets and voice blended with the sound of harps of a thousand strings, echoing and re-echoing. Then, once again the whole planet began to rock, to the right and then to the left.

Instead of turning clear over it righted itself. And in the twinkling of an eye it was as if two angels had been holding a curtain, and all at once that curtain parted and the veil of materiality was rent from top to bottom; and lots millions and millions of angelic beings filled the heavens, and they sang Praises to God in the Highest. And then, Jesus the Christ appeared, although He had come out of the Sun, with a halo of glorious light 'round His head. And he was attired in white, while above Him spread the rainbow then formed a complete circle around the earth.

His beautiful form seemed to float in space, and on His face there was a smile of the mother bending above a baby on her breast. His hands were outstretched on either side, and He said: "Behold!" The vibrations of His voice penetrated to every part of the world, like a thousand radios.

When the vibrations subsided again He said: "Behold!" And He turned his compassionate eyes from the north to the south and from the east to the west, saying: "Behold, you have passed from death into life, and you shall inherit the earth, for this is to be your heritage, the New Paradise.

All who have survived this great catastrophe will remain on the earth as immortals, for this planet now has put on immortality, and there shall be no more birth and no more death. And every government shall be upon my shoulders, and I shall rule with love and forgiveness and mercy. And all of the resources of this earth shall be used for the good of all, for all shall share equally in the bounty of the One Father. But all must work together in harmony in the rebuilding of this glorious Paradise."

When those who had survived heard His words, they were filled with joy and new courage, and they rose to their feet and freely offered their services, saying: "Lord, what can we do? Put us to work so that each may do his share." There seemed to be no thought of pay in any form. So great was their happiness in having passed from death unto life, that they were concerned only with giving of themselves, each one to the fullest extent of his capacity to serve. Many had never lost their physical bodies at all... these were the ones who had possessed and used their knowledge of God's laws.

Others were in their etheric bodies, yet all were rejoicing. I shall never forget the happiness of that gathering of beautiful Souls. It seemed that heaven and earth had blended into one. Those of the earth who had put on immortality recognized their loved ones that had passed to the great beyond, for they too were functioning in their immortal bodies. It was the greatest reunion of Souls that the planet had ever experienced since the stars had sung together in the long ago.

Mothers found their children; husbands found their wives; parted lovers were drawn together by the immutable law of attraction; friends found their way to friends. All the sorrow and heartache had passed forever, all the unforgiveness was forgotten; all the bitter feelings and words of the past had melted into rejoicings and words of praise. The Kingdom of Heaven had come on earth, and the Will of the Father was to be done by His once prodigal children who had once again returned to the Father's house, never to wander again.

I asked, "But what has become of the 'wicked,' those who continually made war with God's children, those who would not believe in the Christ whom He had sent to save the world?" The answer was that they had been deported to another planet. I said, "Another planet? What planet?" The answer came, "To the moon planet." I said, "I thought the moon was a dead planet." The answer was, "At one time it was, but it too has been resurrected.

For many centuries it has been in preparation to receive the stragglers of the earth, all who had not arrived in consciousness to the state where they could put on immortality." I was told that these had to be deported, for the time had come when only those who awakened to the Fatherhood of God and the Brotherhood of Man, and who had washed their robes in the tears of tribulation and sorrow could remain on this planet.

Then I asked, "Will these people who have been deported to the moon remember that they have come from the earth?" The answer was: "No, they will not remember, even as the people of the earth do not remember that they have come from other planets.

And I asked, "What kind of bodies will they have?" I was told that they would gradually put on bodies of the same substance as the moon planet, bodies suitable to the climatic conditions and atmosphere of the moon, just as the inhabitants of this earth once lived in their etheric bodies, before they were clothed with flesh.

I asked many more questions and always received a reply. The last of the clouds disappeared. The radiance of the sun enveloped the earth once more. The day of judgement had passed. Song and beauty and service and love took the place of discord, ugliness, greed and hate. The Lord had received his own unto Himself.

The Celestial City Of The Sun
- end excerpt –

CLOSING NOTES

As a continuation of the last newsletter, this one gives us a glimpse into the highest of the spirit planes associated with the earth. To those of us trying to see above the limitations of flesh, such ac. counts begin to awaken our memory of what Life was intended to be. We might wonder why such understanding was not given to mankind sooner, yet we have only to look a little deeper to see that it has. For those who think that all such experiences are part of the current "New Age Movement", you might be surprised to know that this account of THE CELESTIAL CITY OF THE SUN was first published almost 65 years ago. Even though it was probably read by many thousands of people back then, it has long since been forgotten upon the dusty bookshelves of time.

In 1954, when the one then known as Jesus healed Sister Thedra of cancer, he asked her to feed his sheep, and he also gave her his true name "Sananda", which she was asked to give out to the world. For those who are inclined to think that this is his "New Age Name", you might be surprised to know that the name "Sananda" was spoken of long before the time of Jesus, within the Ancient Sanskrit writings of the Hindu's. The following excerpt is from the translated text of the Bagavad Gita, an ancient text derived from the Sanskrit writings of the Rishi's and Yogi's of India, whose writings reach back several thousands of years. It is called the Path of Divine Knowledge, and it reads:

.... I am the first and the last, the center of All that Is, Was, or ever will Be. That mortal who knows that I am the "Source" of gods and sages, the Lord Supreme, is least deluded of all mortals, and is freed from bondage.

... I am the God indwelling. All of the Ancients, Sananda-na, Sanatana, Sanat Kumara... these were born by the merest operation of my Thought, and each partakes of all my Power by Divine Right.

- end excerpt -

Now compare that to an excerpt from the work given to Sister Thedra in 1989, which was printed in newsletter 70, which reads:

... From the thought of Solen Aum Solen was made lesser light yet of the same and only Source, for there is but one "Source of life. From this step in creation, was created by thought, one which went forth into the ethers as a conscious Being (the Son). This one divided and became two, yet this one remained of mind and spirit, yet two. This pair was endowed with the power to create in the Fathers likeness. These are now known unto thee, mine beloved, as Sananda and Sanat Kumara. These are known as the "First Born" of the Father...

- end excerpt -

We like to think that these are "New Age Teachings", but in fact the only thing that it new is that we are finally awakening our hearts and spirits to the Truth that has always been.

Within part III of THE CELESTIAL CITY OF THE SUN we are told of the rocking and the shaking of the earth as she flips from side to side during a great upheaval. It speaks of those who will inherit the earth, and also of those whose destructive natures have made them incapable of putting on immortality, who will be removed from the earth to begin again upon the Moon. Although this account was printed in 1933, compare it to the following excerpts from the last two books given to Sister Thedra, entitled "Mine Intercom Messages and "The White Star of The East". They read:

... Do ye understand that which is meant by "birthing process"? There shall be born from the womb of the Earth Mother a Son, which shall rip, tear, and be painful unto her body. As she is yet in the throes of the birth pains, this shall cause or result in the lurching, tossing, and convulsing of Mother Earth.

... The Mother Earth shall be placed within another port, a place within the firmaments wherein she shall be as new born, wherein she shall be as mother unto a new generation. This generation shall be as

the Sons of God. These shall honor her and I as ones worthy of her, for in her glory they shall rejoice with her in her new freedom.

.... Too, they shall be as guardians of the son which was sent forth from Mother Earth's womb as she took flight through the firmaments. This son shall be as the new moon spoken of aforehand. He shall be as a mature moon within the place (orbit) which the Mother had occupied, for this shall be as the great part of change which shall be brought about within the heavenly spheres.

... She shall nurse her offspring and bring it to maturity, and then it shall too be populated with a new generation. A new people shall be planted upon it, even as the present "hu-man" was upon the Mother Earth, for this shall be the fortune of the ones which have betrayed themself. They shall begin anew from the beginning.

... The Laggards shall be removed, for the time is come when the Earth shall give unto them no footing, no comfort. So be it, as they are prepared so shall they receive. Each shall take with them that which hast tormented them, and be as their own judge, their own tormentor. They shall have no memory of the past; no science shall they have; no knowledge of their former existence within the places of earth, wherein they went their willful way in self-betrayal and denial of their true heritage.

Their memory shall be blanked from them and they shall begin at the beginning. While we of the Host shall await their time of maturity, we shall be prepared to give unto them of our love and strength, even as we have done with ye which have prepared thine self for to be brought out.

- end excerpts -

In light of what has been said, I would like to add one more excerpt from the BAGAVAD GITA, the Ancient Sanskrit text. In light of the information within this newsletter it might not seem as far out as it once may have. It reads:

... There are two paths, the first leads to the eternal Heaven. It is the path chosen by him who under stands the full meaning of God and worship. It is said to deal with fire, daytime, and the light of the Sun, and is the pathway unto Heaven.

... There is also another path. It is said to deal with smoke, night, the dark of the moon. The one who follows this path is said to go upon the moonpath, only to the moon, and must return to birth within cells of flesh.

... These two paths, one bright, one dark, are the Sun-path and the Moon-path. He who treads the pathway of the Sun does not need to return (to flesh) ... but he who treads the Moon-path must.

-end excerpt -

In reading these ancient writings, we begin to realize that there is really nothing new under the sun. It should make us a little less puffed-up when we speak of "New Age Teachings, for they are not new... they have always been with us, but only now are we beginning to understand the fullness of the great plan for Man's upliftment. It might help us to understand it all if we look at one more thing. I'm sure you have all read the words: "And the meek shall inherit the earth", but who are the meek?

In the closing excerpt from THE CELESTIAL CITY OF THE SUN we read of those who were to inherit the earth? From what was said they were NOT those who are seeking for greater light and understanding, nor were they those who truly seek to awaken to their true oneness with the Father.

They were the sleepers who had not awakened the greater light within themselves, those who felt remorse only when confronted with their own record within the Book of Life, and who then felt shame that they had never had the courage to seek for greater spiritual truth within their own lives. They were the meek of spirit, yet through God's grace they were to inherit the earth in all its purity, that they might continue their spiritual development in an upward direction.

So what of those who seek to incorporate greater Light and Love into their lives, those who seek understanding of the spiritual teachings being given for our upliftment, who sincerely seek to remember their true oneness with The Father.

Sananda has said: *"They shall be free from the gravitation of the earth, and free from the attraction of the moon"... "they shall have the privilege of going and coming between worlds, and as one of these, they shall be without limitation of any sort".*

- end excerpt -

These shall be freed from the limitations of earth, or of any other planet for that matter. They shall step forward to claim their birthright, to return unto their rightful place within the Father's creation. They shall have awakened to their true identity, beyond flesh. This is spoken of in the following excerpt from Sananda:

... And this is the last time I shall lower my light to accommodate the sleepers and the laggards. It is Finished! It is Done! I shall return unto my Father, and those who so choose to follow me shall return to the Father with me. These shall go where I go, and they shall be as I - free and without guilt or blemish, for they shall be as ones prepared to enter into the place wherein I AM.

- end excerpt -

We have all read of the "Golden Age" upon the earth, which shall come about after the sifting and the sorting. But the earth will first be cleansed, and we are told: *"And the time is at hand when all shall be removed from the Earth for a period, for she shall be made new, and she shall rest. For every atom of the Earth shall be cleansed and made new, even as ye children of the Earth.*

- end excerpt -

When the earth has been purified and cleansed, and when those who are to inherit the earth are prepared, the earth shall be re-populated to begin that golden Age so often spoken of. This will be a time when those who inherit the earth will bring forth the Father's will upon the earth. They will continue their spiritual development, yet man will create Heaven upon the earth, even as he was in tended to do in the beginning. While this, in and of itself, is a glorious vision... take the time to lift your eyes just a little higher. Remember the excerpt in newsletter 71, from the book entitled "The Third Millennium":

... The coming turn of the millennium will begin the final decade of My awakening into the field of collective human consciousness. It will be the last decade of a process that has taken many centuries. It will be a time of great change, during which a large percentage of humankind will choose to enter this stream of consciousness, leaving forever the realms of history...

... Those few who may choose to remain behind will not be un-cared for. They will experience an age of further history... as they gradually wind their way through the same learning process that now find the majority of you ready to migrate beyond the shadows of illusion, to the conscious shores...

- end excerpt -

Although we might hold glorious visions of the coming Golden Age of Man upon the earth, the underlying message throughout the highest of spiritual teachings, is to see beyond all illusions and limitations. Remember Sananda's words saying: *"I shall return unto my Father, and those who so choose to follow me shall return to the Father with me.*

Those who choose to follow him will, this day, return to their Oneness with the Father, will once again claim their birthright which was forfeited when we went down into flesh. While the Golden Age upon the earth may be unlike anything the earth has ever known, it will still be a continuation of man's history, a continuation of the development for those who have chosen not to fully awaken at the close of this present cycle.

Set your vision only upon the Father, who is the very Source of the life that we now know. Seek to awaken to your living oneness with that Source... *"Enter this stream of consciousness, leaving forever the realms of history... beyond the shadows of illusion, to the conscious shores of a fully awakened life...*

* * *

SANANDA

"The Sifting and the Sorting"

Sori Sori: I am come with a host that there be a gathering in. The season is come when the harvest shall be brought in, for there are great changes within the wind. There shall be great shock waves, great unrest, and much confusion within the populace.

The ones which have given heed unto mine call shall be as ones which have been up and about their preparation for this day. These, which shall find their way as ones prepared to walk with the lighted Ones, shall be as ones which have given of themself that there be peace and Light within them. They shall be clean of hands, pure of heart. They shall be filled with love and right action, and peace shall abide within them. These shall be the chosen ones, for none other shall enter into mine place of abode.

I have called unto them for long, "Be ye up and about thine preparation, for the day of sifting and sorting is upon thee". Now it is come when the sifting and sorting shall be done with swift dispatch... and the traitors shall cry and lament their plight. When the waves roll over the land and they find no footing, they shall remember mine call and be as ones filled with remorse. Many shall remember that which they have said of me and mine word which is designed to awaken them.

This is a simple reminder for one and all which hast a mind to comprehend. Let thine hands be clean, thine heart be pure from all hatred, all judgement and deceit. Let no foul and impure thoughts find a hiding place within thee, for that should be unto thee thine own downfall. It is written that nothing unclean may enter into mine place of abode.

Hear me well, ye man of Earth. The time is now upon thee when ye shall be called to account for thine self. Ye shall be as ones to read thine record as ye have created it, recorded it. None shall be thine judge, for ye shall be thine own judge. This is the time of accounting which hast been foretold many times, in many ways. Have ye heard? Have ye listened? Or, have ye made mock of mine words?

Be ye as ones which have been at the business of cleansing thine self, and thine abiding place shall be cleansed in like manner. For this am I now speaking, for the time brings great stress and pressure upon all and sundry.

It is for our love for thee that we, the Host of Light, have drawn nigh unto thee, that ye be as one alert and brought out before the day of sorrow.

The Day of Decision

Sori Sori: Mine beloved, I speak unto thee at this hour for the good of all. Mine word shall be as healing balm unto the souls of the ones seeking relief from bondage - a light to their feet to guide them on their sojourn into everlasting freedom. Let each one which has a will to learn of me, mine plan, find me as one sent to deliver them up.

I am he which is sent to bring them which have the will to come out, no more to cry from oppression and bondage. The ones which are prepared shall be caught up with me, as One with me. These shall be as new born - and their memory shall be restored.

No more shall they cry in darkness and ignorance, for I shall reveal unto them that which they really are - their inheritance willed unto them of the "Source". These which arise with me shall be as the "Prodigal Son" returned. There shall be great rejoicing, and love shall abound.

I am come that all mankind awaken and be as One with me. I am the light, sent to rescue thee from the darkness which is ready to swallow thee up. Now I say unto all, that ye shall have thine memory restored, and with this ye shall cry for joy and praise the eternal "Source" for His grace and mercy. Yet ye shall be as ones willing to come, as One with me, for none are brought against their will. I have called long and loud: Learn of thine self! Know thine self as one of free will. Ask with a contrite heart, sincerely, for deliverance.

Prepare thine own self to come out of the darkness which hast bound thee in suffering and sorrow.

I am not a traitor. I make no idle speeches or false promises. I speak in simple terms that all might understand mine meaning.

"I Shall Pass This Way No More!"

Beloved of Mine Being: I am come this day to give unto thee this word, that all men might profit thereby. I am the one which hast revealed unto thee the name Sananda, and I proclaimed it unto thee that they might come to know me. So be it I am he which is known by many names, yet they which are mine flock shall come to know me as thou knowest me. And for this shall I touch them, even as I have touched thee... then they shall know and they shall no more turn their face from me.

Now it is come when many shall proclaim the name, yet they shall not be as ones prepared to receive that which I have kept for them. I say, to proclaim mine name is not sufficient, for they must be as ones prepared to enter into the place of mine abode.

I have said, I shall come as a thief in the night, and it is so. I AM COME, yet I find them sleeping. I speak out that they awaken, yet they but stir themself and then return unto their dreaming. So let them stir themself and arise and follow me, for I pass this way no more. I shall move on and return unto them NO MORE, for another shall come after me, and the laggards shall await another day. And the book shall be closed, for I shall be as one finished, as one which hast done mine part and taken mine leave. Then another shall fill mine place, mine "office", and he shall do his part (of guiding the on-going progression of those upon the earth), even as I did mine part.

Let this be given unto them which seek the Light. Let them read that which thou (Thedra) hast heard, and let thine name be written upon it that they might know for a surety that I have given it unto thee.

I am Sananda, the Lord thy God.

- - -

Never Again

I say unto thee, behold the work which I shall do, for I shall keep valid mine word, and I shall be unto mine people that which the Father has willed that I be. I come that it be done, finished, for never again shall I dim mine Light that I might walk amongst them that it be accomplished.

I say it shall be accomplished this day! I shall be no more responsible for them (the laggards and sleepers) for they shall be given another place, another day. And the ones which come forth as mine own I shall take with me as part of mine host, and I shall not fail. I shall do mine part, yet I ask of them, arise, ye which have a mind to follow me, and come follow me that ye might go where I go. So let it suffice that I have come to gather mine own unto mineself.

So be it, I am the Lord thy God, Sananda

- - -

The Seventh Day

Sori Sori: This is mine word unto them which have followed me unto this point: There is a time and a place, a season for all things. It is now the time for this mine word to become manifest in the world of man.

This is the time for such as I shall do, for man is now in his "seventh day", and the time is at hand when he shall come into his own. He shall be as one responsible for his own part, and for his inheritance which he hast forfeited so long ago. Now he shall see and know that which he hast forfeited.

I am He which is sent that ye return unto the Father's House in this thy time, for thy time hast come when the door stands unbarred. Ye have but to turn the Key and enter in, all ye which are prepared.

I stand at the door and I say: "Pass ye in, all which are prepared"...

The above are excerpts from the Scripts Recorded by Sister Thedra

Sananda

And it is indeed wise to ask of The Father that ye might receive me, for in no wise shall I intrude upon thy free will. Yet it is the will of the Father that I bring thee out of darkness, and for that do I wait, that ye may come of thy own free will.

This is for the ones which have as yet not learned the wisdom of saying - "Father, Thy Will Be Done In Me, Thru Me, By Me, And For Me" - for therein is the KEY unto thy legirons which have bound thee. I shall be unto thee bondsman, and I stand ready to loose thee of thy bondage at thy request. Ye have but to seek the Light which is of the Father.

* * *

For over 40 years Sister Thedra recorded Sananda's words that we might become aware of the one Great Truth which he would have us know. But the foundation of his message is not that we just remember what he has said to us, but that we AWAKEN to the Living Truth of what he has said. He is not just telling that we are part of a Greater

Reality beyond our lives in flesh... he is trying to AWAKEN US TO THAT REALITY.

As greater light begins to flood the earth, many things are written about the spiritual awakening process. Much information is touted as being of a spiritual nature, yet all too often it focuses our attention back upon the manifestation of flesh instead of awakening the greater Light within our own Living spirits.

The intent within these newsletters is to try and "Empty Out The Cup", so to speak... to empty out the waters muddied by trivial information, and to begin to fill it with the sparkling pure waters of the very Source. It is about looking at the very foundation and Source of life itself, and awakening to the Living Truth of all that we ARE.

The Living Truth

The Living Truth is not a belief or a concept, nor is it the information which we believe to be spiritual. We begin to see the Living Truth only when we begin to awaken to that which we truly ARE and that which we are a part of. We begin to BECOME that Truth when we begin to awaken to our Living Oneness with the Source of life itself, when we allow the Light behind our own spirit to replace our limited awareness of "self".

We have all read through countless books trying to understand greater light, but when we begin to see the Living manifestation of that Light within our own Living spirit, we begin to realize that we already ARE that which we are seeking. We begin awakening to the One Great Truth which is at the very center of our own lives... Our Living Oneness with the very Source of life itself.

The First Cause

... "Seek ye the light and it shall not be hidden. Knowest thou the meaning of this? I say seek ye that which is behind the manifestation, *the "Cause" of the manifestation... that which is the "Cause" of ALL manifestation, the "FIRST CAUSE".*

- end excerpt -

Light of the First Cause is the first great mystery. When we hear the term "First Cause", it means just that... the First Cause of life itself, the One and only "Source" of Life itself. All beings who know Life, including each and every one of us, including each and every being on all of the planes of Spirit, including the various Angelic and other Orders, including Sananda and the Order of the First Born Sons, and including the Father Himself, all know life because there Is and ever SHALL BE the Mystery of Mysteries... the Living Source at the center of ALL that IS. It is not an individual spirit, it is the Source OF Spirit.. the Source of the Light which all Beings know as Life...the Living Light which flows to each one of us with total unconditional Love. It is not something separate from you, for within the One Eternal Reality you ARE a living expression of the One and only Source. *form which can tell this unspeakable story of The Beginning.*

- end excerpt -

The above excerpts speak of the two First Born Sons, who were brought forth within those high dimensions of Light and Spirit long before the universe of matter existed. They went through vast periods within their own spiritual development, and it was only after long aeons that these two awakened to their true Oneness with the Source, wherein they received the power of creation. In seeking to bring forth the Father's will it was they who brought forth the universe of matter as we know it, for matter was to play an important part in the Father's plan for Creation.. Too often we view the universe of matter as being separate from the things of Light and Spirit, but the only place where Light and Spirit are absent is in our own thinking. !

While the universe of matter (of worlds, suns, and star-systems) is a relatively recent unfoldment within the fullness of the Father's Creation, it was brought forth for a far greater purpose than we can presently imagine. Because of our limited understanding, we do not yet realize the reasons or the true importance of our lessons here in flesh. We do not remember our true origins within the high planes of Light and Spirit, and we have not remembered that long ago we chose to come into the universe of dense matter to play a very important role in the future unfoldment of this biological creation.

Consider the following excerpt from 'The Third Millennium":

... Twenty billion years of unfoldment leave this universe yet in its early stages. It is still a realm of vast extremes, of frozen worlds of rigid matter, contrasting the awesome heat of the stars. What biology there is appears only as a slight film on the surface of but a few worlds, yet in that biological film lies the future.

... It is a relatively new substance, biology... its day has only now begun to dawn.

- end excerpt -

Brothers & Sisters of Light

While the First Born Sons existed long before the Order of Man, we are ALL of one parent, all of one Source. While the Order of the First Born Sons were brought forth by the Father long before the Order of Man, that simply make of them our "Elder Brothers" who have grown to maturity and now seek to guide us in our awakening.

Yet there are also ones which are of the same Order as we, our Brothers and Sisters who still dwell within those high planes of Light and Spirit. While we chose to leave those planes of Light and Spirit to descend into these planes of matter which encompass this biological creation, they remained within those high planes of Light and Spirit wherein we all had our true origins.

Consider the following excerpt from the book "The Third Millennium":

... To you it must seem long ago, the time before your embarkation, before you journeyed through the fields of matter to surface upon this world. But to us the hour is still early, and much will change before "Our" morning has passed. You left us with instructions to bring you this record when the dawn was full. Come gather around our conscious fire, peoples of the earth, and listen to the spirits of the stars.

... Aeons ago, before there was physical matter, you were one of us. Your essence remains, even now, indistinguishable from the unified field of Spirit out of which we all flow. In oneness with the Eternal Source, in realms of Light and Love, we lived together in the early age of the morning. Together we shared a common "I" within the ONE.

... The majority of human beings have not yet thought of Reality in a broad enough terms to see what is truly happening. The possibility that human history may be reaching a climax, a completion, a moment of final fulfillment has occurred to only a few. That all which has gone before might have been merely a gestation cycle for a planetary awakening is too large a concept, too broad a vision for those who choose to remain cloaked in cultural bias.

... These transmissions are designed to give you conceptual tools for those times when you may need them, tools that will reduce the likelihood of your sliding again into the sleep that has characterized this recent age on earth... yet to understand your fall into these troubled times of your history, you must first recall the context in which it occurred.

- end excerpt -

The Fall of Man

While man of earth has forgotten his true beginnings within the eternal fields of Light and Spirit, he never-the-less remains to this day the essence of that which he was brought forth to be. While man has not remembered his past or his true origin, he is, in truth, the highest expression of divinity incarnate within this universe of matter. His spirit is a Living expression of the Father, brought forth as Living Sons of the Father. While it was understood that man would go through a period of development in which he would expand his identity to include his individuality within the planes of matter, it was never intended that he forget his true identity within the Light. While it was intended that he take on individual form within the planes of matter, it was never intended that he come to inhabit or identify himself completely with the mortality of flesh and bone. This was brought about by the fall of man, wherein he forgot his true identity within the Father, wherein he lost his living memory and came to identify himself only with the animal form of flesh and bone.

The following excerpts are taken from the book "The Third Millennium":

... Your fall into fearful thought and non-fluid patterns of identity was not mere happenstance. An influence encouraged you in this direction, encouraged you to identify with a sense of separate self. With the exception of those angels who were the first to incarnate humanly, virtually all members of your race fell under the spell of this influence at some point during their journeys into biological form. We call this influence the materializing influence, or the forces of materialization.

... This influence is personified, as are all qualities and influences in this potent universe. Yet your stereotypical images of Satan have prevented many people from understanding the real nature of the materializing principle....

- end excerpt -

While the above speaks of the Forces of Materialization, within the Scripts recorded by Sister Thedra we are told that man was turned from the Father's plan by one named Lucifer. While we are told that Sananda and Sanat Kumara were the First Born Sons of the Father, there later came forth an entire Order of First Born Sons, one of which was called Lucifer, At one time Lucifer was a bright and shining Son of the Father who had received his inheritance in full and therefore received the power of Creation, yet he misused that power, as spoken of in the following excerpt from Script #10, recorded by Sister Thedra:

Excerpt

..."For he had the power invested within him of God the Father to create worlds, yea to create and to populate them. He was of the Father born, and he had received his inheritance in full, yet he had the audacity to call himself Father of all that is and was. He used the Law for his own end, and gave no heed unto the warnings of the Father.

... And when he, which is called Lucifer, was given an ultimatum, he called together his followers and said unto them: *"Ye have seen my work... have I not created these things, have I not given unto these things life, and have I not been with you these days? If ye follow me I shall make of thee great and wondrous beings"*... And when they gazed upon his handiwork they fell down and did worship him. I say great was and is their sorrow, for unto this day do they pay the price"...

- end excerpt -

Lucifer had received his inheritance in full, yet he became puffed up with his own power, and he came to believe that since he too had the power of creation that he was the Father's equal. He turned from the Father's plan for Creation and sought to bring forth his own plan for creation. He convinced many who had not yet fully awakened to their true Oneness, that he was a Creator in his own right, and he offered to make of them "Great and glorious spiritual Beings" if they would but fol. low him.

Thus man was hoodwinked into turning from the Father, wherein he forfeited both his living memory and his inheritance as Sons of the Father. Man eventually forgot his once high estate as Sons of God, and without the Father's Light to guide him he eventually became lost within his identity as creatures of flesh and bone, wherein he came to believe his flesh to be himself.

Through Sananda, the First Born Son of the Father, a plan was formulated for man's return unto his rightful estate. It honored man's free will, yet it called for man to enter into a long cycle in which he would be bound within a progression of embodiments within the mortality of flesh. His living memory would be sealed up, and he would begin the cycle within the primitive forms of early man. Over millions of years he would slowly progress upward, ever seeking within his mortality for his true identity, until he was once again able to know and accept the Truth, wherein he might once again choose to become that which he was brought forth to BE.

Now, whether or not you might believe that Man's fall came about through a Son called Lucifer, or that it was the influence of the forces of materialization as we descended into matter... it is really not important. If we were to awaken in a deep dark pit without any memory of how we got there, it would matter little whether or not we were pushed or fell into the pit. The only thing that is of real importance is that we focus our attention on getting ourselves out of the darkness and into the bright sunshine once again... and that sunshine is the Light which we are now seeking.

Consider the following excerpt from the book "Starseed, The Third Millennium":

... The Fall of which you have heard is not an irreversible tumble, but rather a momentary lowering of your sights. In my eyes it is but the first stumbling steps of a child. No great matter. You face no angry God. I have seen too much to be overly concerned. It is natural when a knee is bruised to focus upon the damaged skin, but do not loose sight of the rest of your body which remains healthy and robust.

- end excerpt -

While man has searched for his identity within the passing forms of his mortality, in his essence he has never ceased to be that which he truly IS... Living Sons of the Father, and Living expressions of the One Source. As this long cycle now reaches its fullness the way is now being opened that man might once again rise above his mortality, wherein he might re-claim his Living memory and his inheritance which he forfeited long ago. Man might now choose to re-awaken to that which he truly is, to free himself forever from the mortality of flesh and bone, and to once again become that which he was brought forth to BE... the hands and feet of the Father, WITHIN the universe of matter. Remember the excerpts from The Third Millennium, printed in a previous newsletter:

... I assure you who may feel trapped in historical situations, that there is no human force, no agency, no influence what-so-ever that can keep you from discovering the current of My consciousness within you, once you are aware of its existence and choose to look for it. My thoughts flow into your consciousness in each and every moment, within each breath. On the current of your awareness they enter. Lift your eyes from the conditioned interpretations. Look up... and see clearly again.

... You are already living in the dawning hours of the Age of Planetary Awakening. Though there will be much awakening of individuals prior to the final unified movement of the awakening... this final movement, like a first breath, will occur in but a single moment.

It is then that the Starmaker will consciously awaken within all (individual) systems of human bio-circuitry capable of sustaining universal awareness. Though there have been many centuries leading up to this movement, when that movement comes it will be decisive. There will be a great shift... a single moment of quantum awakening. This is the event that is central to all of human history...

- end excerpt -

The Passing Cycle of Darkness

This passing cycle of darkness upon the earth has been but the preparation for man's re-awakening, a period in which man has had to learn the results of his separation from the Father's will. He has had to learn by experiencing the direct results of his own "self-will" acting independent of Source of Creation. Throughout this cycle man has not used his Life to give thanks to the Father or to uplift His creation... he has looked upon the earth, its resources and its people, and he has plundered and exploited them for his own selfish gain. He has now experienced firs-hand the results of his own actions, the destruction, the fear, the hatred, the pain and the chaos he has created by going his own willful way.

But man has now reached the end of this cycle. He has collectively reached the point where he is now capable of re-awakening to the greater Light, and the growing light of a new day now calls man to awaken from his long sleep of forgetfulness. This is the day in which man might come forth of his own free will and re-claim his living memory, to reclaim his true inheritance as a living Son of the Father, and once again return to his Oneness with the Eternal Creation.

Darkness is Ignorance

While man has ever been sustained within the Living Light, he has not embraced that Light. He has not "enlightened" himself, therefore he has dwelled within the darkness of his own unknowing. Yet darkness in and of itself is not evil, it is simply the absence of Light. For the most part man's darkness is simply his ignorance, the absence of Light within his thinking. It is his ignorance, through forgetfulness, of the One true Source and purpose of life itself.

All Life, as it comes from the "Source," knows no darkness, for Life IS the Living Light which sets itself apart from the eternal void of non-existence. That same Light goes forth from the Father unto each and every Soul within His Creation, and it too knows no darkness, for each and every Soul is born of the Living Substance of Life... it is Living Light.

It is only when we use that Light (which is called Life) wrongly do we bring forth darkness. This is the great lesson we have had to learn in flesh, for that which we create becomes our own, and the darkness which we bring forth returns to torment those who created it.

Free Will

Darkness and light are never compatible, for light always dispels darkness. While Light is the benevolent expression of the One Great

Purpose of Life itself, darkness is the wrongful use of that Light by a spirit who has forgotten the Living Light within their own Soul.

A man cannot be both enlightened and ignorant at the same time, he must choose one or the other. While Bright spirits are those who allow the Living Light within their own Soul to shine through their developing spirit... dark Spirits are those who have turned from that Light, and they continue to cling to their unknowing as the only true reality. While those of Light comprehend both the light and the darkness, those in darkness do not comprehend the light, therefore they dwell in darkness.

The Awakening

We have all had dreams in which we found ourself in joyful, or fearful, or even absurd situations, and within the dream we actually believed the image we saw to be ourself. We may even have feared for our own life, for we did not perceive it was only a passing dream, an illusion which existed only within our own minds. We had forgotten completely about the reality of our lives on earth, and for that moment we perceived the dream to be the only true reality. Yet when we awakened, the illusions of the dream fell away, for in truth it had no lasting substance, for it existed only within our own thinking.

So too, our spiritual awakening is the process in which we begin to awaken from our dreams within the mortality of flesh, believing we are flesh. It is awakening our own living spirit to our true identity beyond flesh, our true identity as a Living spirit within the fullness of the Eternal Creation.

If we are to begin to awaken to this greater truth, we need only take a look at the meaning of the words "spiritual awakening". While trying to understand the spiritual awakening process we are often confused by the amount of information being touted as "spiritual". Too often we fail to see the difference between lifeless information and the Living Truth.

We do not awaken from a dream by gathering information about the dream, but by awakening to reality. So too, the spiritual awakening is not about gathering external information about ley lines, pyramids, photon belts, crystals, vortexes, etc, etc, etc... it is about awakening our own Living spirit to that which we ARE. When we begin to realize that our own Living spirit is a manifestation of Living Light, we begin to see that trivial information has little to do with awakening our spirit, and has little or no importance at all to an "awakened spirit".

The Living Truth

So what are we truly seeking? What is the Living Truth? Is it words? Is it the concepts describing God or Light? Is it information about the "things" which are so often touted as spiritual?

The "Living" Truth is present within each "Living" spirit which KNOWS itself to exist. It is that which awakens within the consciousness of each and every spirit which comes to KNOW itself to be ONE with the Source of all Life. It is fully manifest within the spirit we refer to as the Father... it is fully manifest within the First Born Sons, who are ONE with the Father and with the Source... and that same "Living Truth" is manifest within the Living soul and spirit of each and every one of us. While we, as man, have come to identify ourselves with the mortality of flesh and bone, our Living memory of this One Great Truth has ever remained vibrant and alive within the fullness of our own Soul. Therein is the "spiritual awakening"... the awakening of our Living spirit to its One-ness with our own Living Soul, which IS the Living Light of the Source.

When we continue to fill our thinking with a lot of "information" and call that "spirituality", we are overlooking the very thing which we are seeking. If we truly seek to understand the Light which IS Life, we need only awaken to the Living Light which we ourselves ARE, for we ARE Life itself.

Co-Creators of This Creation

We usually think of Light in visual terms, but Light in its First Magnitude is far more than incandescence, it is the Living Substance of Life itself... it is the "Living Light" which shines within and through the consciousness of each and every being in existence. As each spirit continues to awaken to their true Oneness with the "Source" of that Light, the greater the Light that is able to manifest through their own spirit.

Realize that we, as man, are not just expressions 'within" the creation. We were not brought forth simply to be "things" within the Father's creation. We were brought forth through and by the Father's Love, as Sons of the Father and Living Expressions of the Source within the Creation. We were brought forth to become co-creators with Him of this on-going creation, yet our first creation must be ourselves. We must first bring forth the Living spirit which we ourselves are to BE, a spirit which is a reflection of the Living Light within its own Soul.

While man has repeatedly gone in and out of embodiments throughout this long cycle, he has not remembered his true origins, nor has he understood the great lessons he was learning throughout his many embodiments in flesh. Yet the time has now come for man to step forth from the mortality of flesh and bone, to awaken his Living Memory of his true origins and his true nature.

The New Day is now dawning wherein man might once again come to know the great Love, Joy, and Freedom which are the inheritance of ALL Sons of God. Man, as a being of both spirit and matter, might now take his rightful place within the Creation, as the hands and feet of the Father WITHIN the Creation, to oversee and guide this biological creation towards its infinite potential in greater Light.

Even as we have been guided and helped throughout this cycle by those of the higher planes of life, so too will those who now awaken reach back within the next cycle to guide those who choose to cling to their unknowing and close their hearts to this great light. While some might need further experiences in flesh before the longing within their own hearts cause them to seek for greater light, yet it is the will of the Father that ALL eventually awaken.

The Father's will for His creation is not a great mystery. The Father's will is simply that we each awaken to our true Oneness with Him, that we awaken to greater Light and to greater understanding of the great plan for Creation, and that we express our individuality in an uplifting and loving way towards the whole of Creation.

Self vs Individuality

Man of earth has long associated his own life and individuality with "self". He has not under stood that to go beyond "self" is not to lose his identity or individuality, for "self" is identity wrongly placed... it is ignoring the fullness of that which we truly ARE.

We have historically disregarded the Living Light of our own Soul, and we have come to identify only with the shadow it casts within the world of matter. We have not under- stood the true nature of our own Living spirit, for we have empowered its temporary reflection of "self".

The great ones throughout our history who have manifested great Light through selfless service to humanity (Jesus - Gandhi - Mother Teresa - etc.) are those who had freed their identity from the smallness of "self". They were "self-less", yet their individuality was not lost nor diminished. To the contrary, their individuality manifested in far greater light and strength, for it was no longer misdirected through the smallness of "self".

Nothing which is attained for "self" is lasting or permanent, for "self" exists only in the passing form of our own mortality. When we ask of the Father: *"Thy Will Be Done, In Me, Through Me, and By Me,"* - we are simply turning from the smallness of "self" and asking that awaken to that which we truly ARE.

We are reaching beyond the smallness of "self", and asking that we might awaken to our Oneness with Him. We are saying that we trust in his great plan for His Creation, that we trust in his great Love and Wisdom, and that "will" to awaken to that which we were created to BE.

The Sifting and Sorting

Throughout this long cycle the whole of mankind has moved towards this present day. While many have moved steadily forward, some have moved more slowly in their spiritual growth, and still others have lagged far behind in their spiritual development. Before we can move forward into the new cycle there must first be a sifting and sorting of mankind into his varying natures, each as he has chosen for himself.

Those of you who are reading this newsletter have sensed this great change, yet the vast majority of those upon the earth are yet asleep to this greater Light which is beginning to flood the earth. They are still content to sleep on within their unknowing, for they do not yet realize that the GREATER REALITY is beckoning them to awaken, calling them to raise up from their dreams in mortality, to awaken their Living spirits into a fully awakened life.

In the same way that a mother must shake a child who refuses to awaken for school, so too, many in flesh will have to be shaken from their lethargy and their desire to sleep on. The upheavals upon the earth and within the affairs of man (which have so often been spoken of) are not meant as punishment, but to upset our comfort and cause us to look beyond our mortality. While fear has played a destructive part within man's past, it is also the great motivator that will cause many to open their hearts to the Greater Reality in which we ALL exist.

As this cycle draws to a close many are preparing themselves to step beyond the mortality of flesh, to re-claim their living memory and inheritance as Sons of the Father. Many who are yet asleep will soon begin to awaken and will eagerly embrace their new found awareness. Some may need to be shaken before they are willing to let go of their unknowing, but eventually many of them will rise up from their lethargy and seek for greater Light.

While a few who have devolved backwards to the point of being just plain vicious, those who have repeatedly used their progression of embodiments to bring about hatred, oppression, crime, destruction, and war upon their fellow man... having brought forth nothing that is of any worth within the Greater Light of the True Creation... will begin once again at the very beginning, in primitive forms, upon another planet.

The following is an excerpt from the book "Return of The Bird Tribes":

... The potentials of this universe are infinite beyond number. But there are no star wars or advanced fearsome civilizations beyond your own... because if civilizations are fearsome they do not advance beyond your own. They become extinct, to rise up in another world, until they finally learn.

... There does come a time when those who would deprive others of their right to biological expression cannot in rightness, in justice, and in harmony with the sacred way, be protected any longer. They need to continue their lessons in another ecological nitch where they affect no one but themselves.

... The Great Day of Purification has begun, a short but essential cycle of division and separation that will gather those who promote fear and violence and separate them from this season of the world, just as the chaff is separated from the wheat at thrashing time. During the next two and a half decades (1987. 2011) humankind will experience this separation... for a new era is dawning.

- end excerpt -

Such is the sifting and sorting which is now going on. While the wheat will be gathered up and separated from the chaff, the weeds are also gathered up that they might not contaminate the next garden. For no matter how much light is spread upon the earth, those who continue to harbor seeds of selfishness will at some time revert to what they hold within their hearts. No matter how much light might come upon the earth, those who have not purged the darkness from within their own hearts will sooner or later attempt to use it to their own ends. This is the time of that purification, as described in the following excerpts from the book entitled "The Third Millennium":

.. Five centuries before the dawn of this present cycle, we brought to the awakened ones of that age a timetable which they carefully recorded in stone. The Mayan calendar is now recovered from the moss and ferns. In it are chiseled the dates that correspond to the Great Day of Purification, dates that correspond to your years 1987 to 2011. The winter solstice of the last year will see the purification completed, and the era of human history brought forever to a close.

... This wave has much to yet engulf and utterly change before it has washed fully across the shores of human affairs, yet the greatest effects of this wave will come during the late 1990s and the first decade of the twenty-first century.

... As our present wave of consciousness washes highest upon the shore of this world toward the winter solstice of the year A.D. 2011, a Great Cycle will culminate. The new season that dawns then, as the days of the southern latitudes shorten and the North Pole begins its move towards its months of sunlight, will be more than the closing of a season of a single year.

... A moment is coming, after which nothing will ever again be thought of as it was before... a metahistorical moment, an event that is simultaneously Alpha and Omega to your species and to all your species has ever known...

- end excerpt -

Now consider the following message given by Sananda in the Summer of 1989.

... By the calculations of man, he hast but 3 times three plus 9 years to prepare himself for the ultimate change, in which there is no turning back or reversing all that he hast set in motion. This is the beginning of a New Day when ye shall arise and be about the Fathers business. This is the day of redemption, this is that which has been foretold in the ancient records. The Lord, thy God of Truth and Light, hast given of himself that there be a plan which is now come to its maturity, the fulfilling of the word, the promise made 2000 years ago. It is now

written in the heavens that mankind shall awaken unto his true estate, arise from his slumbers, and return unto his Source.

- end excerpt -

In the above two messages we begin to see a time-table (1989-2011) which denotes the final periods which will bring this cycle to its final conclusion. In the above message Sananda refers to 3 periods of three years each (1989-1997) and one period of 9 years (1998-2007). He tells us that this 9 years period will be the time in which all will make their final choice, either to embrace the Light of their true being, or to cling to the darkness and ignorance of man's past. He is telling us that after that point (2007) there is no turning back or reversing that which each of us has set into motion, for each will have made their final decision as to which way they will go.

But what might transpire within that period (1998-2007) which will cause the sleeping masses to begin to take notice? For those of you who have not read the book recorded by Sister Thedra, entitled 'The White Star Of The East", I will include the following excerpts:

The White Star of the East

... "That which was spoken in the days of the great plagues of the earth are as naught today. The firmaments shall declare a New Order, which shall be given within the Heavens as a promise of thine freedom. This shall be manifest within thine sky as a gleaming white Star. It shall move from east to west at the speed of a star, yet it shall have the appearance of a Sun. It shall cast it's radiance upon all the earth as no other heavenly body".

... There shall be a great light come forth within the radius of mans telescope which shall enable him to see this light. This shall be as a mystery which shall confuse and confound him, for there shall be no accounting for this presence of such a light.

... "There shall be great confusion within the men of science, for they which have thought themself wise shall be at a loss to explain this wonder, for they have not foreseen the coming of such a body of light. This we would have them know... that there is nothing to fear. It is The Star of Deliverance, sent of the Father. This, The White Star of the East, shall go before the host now, as it did of the day so long ago when the child was born in Bethlehem. Wast it not foretold? Or have ye heard!"

... It shall be called "The White Star of the East", and the name shall indicate the abiding place of the Host which hast come as One with me for to fulfill mine plan.

... "By the time of this lights appearance, ye of this knowledge shall be as one prepared to go forth as mine emissary unto them which are of a mind to follow this White Star. These shall be as the ones to learn of the Lighted Ones which are ready to receive them."

... "Give ye heed unto that which is said unto thee, yet be ye not so foolish as to run hither and yon preaching or expounding thine own "opinions", for it is a great responsibility which could be thine downfall. We would have thee prepared by and through us of the light before ye go out as an emissary. For this we have prepared a place (a school) for such learning. It is as a "place", not an imaginary idea of a fiction writer. We are speaking simply in such a way that each and every one come to know that we are of good intent, and that is their deliverance. So let it be".

... There is now a school prepared to receive them for the purpose of enlightening these ones which have the will to awaken unto their heritage. This school will be within the place which is designated to the Earth, yet it is not upon the Earth. It is as a school of light: therein is no darkness. There shall come forth from the new school of revelation, things which are beyond mans imagination. This shall upset all his theories and preconditioned ideas. This shall be the beginning of the "New Day."

... "Ye may ask, where is this place" I say unto one and all. It is not known unto man of Earth, Ye find this place not by man's means. Only thine record, if clear of any darkness, shall be sufficient unto thine entrance".

... Before man shall glimpse the glory of this place which I have referred to as a school, he first has to give unto the Source of his Being recognition that he is a Being brought forth through the Great Creator (The Father), as ONE with Him, made manifest in the material world, and destined to go forth to know himself and his Oneness with his Source. In his experiences man hast forgotten his Source, and for that he has wandered and wondered much from whence he came and wither he shall go. So be it he hast fallen from grace to become a lost being. He is lost, and for his forgetfulness is his bound unto materiality. Knowing not his origin, he hast lost his way back unto his rightful place from which he went forth... forgetting his inheritance, his true birthright.

... For this we offer ourself that there be greater light within the world of man, that all darkness be no more, that there be peace within the place wherein mankind shall be placed when the hour strikes, for Mother Earth shall be evacuated. This hast been referred to... have ye remembered that which hast been said as a warning? Did ye take note? Are thou prepared to go forth as one prepared to enter into the school of which is prepared on behalf of the children of Earth?

... Now that it is so recorded, let them which dis cover this White Star take note that it is so recorded within this day of so-called miracles. I say it is the greatest project which hast been brought into manifestation. Ye cannot even imagine the magnitude of such as is brought forth in love and mercy that there be light in the days of darkness. This shall be as a continual effort until every living creature is removed from the planet upon which ye now have footing.

(added note: Just before Sister Thedra's passing it was hinted that the appearance of the White Star might take place in the year 2000)

- end excerpt -

In reading these excerpts we begin to understand why many who now scoff at such things will soon be shaken from their lethargy, and many will begin to reach out and embrace this greater Light. It also becomes clear that only those who stubbornly and willfully cling to the ignorance and darkness of the past will fail to respond to the Great Light which will flood the earth.

Sananda also goes on to speak about what will occur when this period of choosing comes to an end. Within the book "Complied Communiques" recorded by Sister Thedra we are told:

.... It is our intention that all hear, yet shall they be <u>mindful</u> of that which they hear is the question, for there shall be no slothfulness within the place prepared to receive the ones which arise from their sleep.

... Some shall be removed (from the earth) unto a place of safety to return at a later time... some shall be removed by natural cause... some shall perish and be as ones to return no more.

... I am the one which has provided the way for thee to safety, wherein ye shall be spared the destruction. These shall be as the ones to be brought out before the day of sorrow.

- end excerpt -

While Sananda speaks of the year 2007 as the point at which all will have made their choice as to which way they will go, he tells us that those who chose to embrace the Greater Light will be removed from the earth before the great day of sorrows. In the previous message from "The Third Millennium" it speaks of the year 2011 as the time in which "The era of human history will be brought forever to a close". The three and one half year period from 2008 to 2011 would seem to coincide with the Great Day of Sorrow so often spoken of.

In the last newsletter we printed a portion of the book "The Celestial City of The Sun". In part III of that newsletter we read a vivid account of those final years, a time when the earth would flip its axis, causing world-wide upheavals and eruptions as the forces of nature released the negativity which man has sent forth over the centuries, which has built up within the ethers surrounding the earth. This description seems to coincide with the two previous messages, for it was evident that those who had embraced the Light had already been removed from the earth.

Those who remained were those who would hear none of it, for they continued to cling to the darkness of the past. For them it was truly a Day of Great Sorrows, for not only did they experience the results of the darkness they had chosen, but amid the destruction and chaos they were endlessly haunted by the vision of their own Living Records showing their lives of selfishness and greed.

Yet even then the Father's Great Love and mercy did not fail them, for as this cycle drew to its final conclusion a Great Light filled the earth, and those who had gone through the Day of Sorrow and who had reached out in shame for forgiveness and for Light, were embraced within the Father's Great Love, and they came forth from their time of darkness as Sons of Light. The only ones who were to be seen no more upon the earth were those whose hearts had been so filled with selfishness, with hatred and viciousness, that there was no Light within them. These had been removed from the earth to another planet wherein they would begin again at the very beginning.

***

The following messages from Sananda were recorded by Sister Thedra prior to her passing:

The Time of Awakening

Sananda

... I say unto them that it is now come when there shall be great changes which shall come suddenly. The populace at large shall be in lethargy and they shall be as asleep, yet I have been calling unto them for long years. The days have been shortened and the way hast been made obvious that a time hast been set by a power greater than mankind. Even the stars bear witness of the change, for by the signs set in the heavens shall ye which sleep be awakened. *("The White Star of The East")*

Time is now come that the awakening shall take place. It shall be sudden as far as mankind calculates time. The sleepers shall remember in their awakening that which they have learned in their sleeptime. Many shall come forth as New Born... these shall be as ones which remember the sleeptime no more, while others shall remember and wonder at their slowness. Some shall find they have betrayed themself, and these shall know great remorse and cry out for help. Their suffering shall be great, even though it be for their own progress.

It is the Law of the ONE that there be no stagnation. Forever and forever there is growth, movement forever and for all time to come... forward movement toward the All Light, the Source of All. This progress is not always seen by mankind, as he is bound by flesh and knows not himself to be immortal.

It is now come that he hast been given the choice to arise above the darkness of his own way, for he shall become dissatisfied with his apathy, his lethargy, and he shall seek the Light. These shall be the first to come up higher and see with greater vision. These shall be as the ones which shall be as beacon lights unto the laggards.

* * *

Empty Out Thine Cup

... To learn of the light of the "Source", is to understand the word which I the Lord God give unto mortal man for his well-being. He hast but to listen and follow mine way without any preconditioned opinions. Empty out thine Cup and ask for pure water from the fountain head, the Source, and it shall be filled... yea, to overflowing. I am the one sent from the Source of Being, in which all beings have their existence. I am the Son of the Living God, which has given unto me the power to create even as He.

Now it is come when all knowledge is available unto the creation known unto us as "Mankind". Earth man has now finished the old cycle. He now enters into the new one in which he shall come to know himself to be One with his Source. For this I am come, that the sleepers might awaken unto their rightful inheritance, Eternal life, with freedom from bondage, never more to descend into darkness or the limitation of flesh.

For this I am come, that ye might prepare to enter into this new cycle with me.

I come with a great Host of Light Beings which are free even as I. We are One with the divine plan for man's freedom, man's salvation. Yea, as man is lifted so shall the Earth be made new, and the heavens too, for all the cosmos changes according unto the Father's will, his word made manifest with perfection.

Oh man, what a great awakening it shall be! Let it be! Let it be! Know ye that ye are part of it. Accept it as thine gift divine. Arise and alert thineself. Ask of the Light in all sincerity, and ye shall be heard and answered unto thine intent.

* * *

The Wonders of Heaven

So be it that I say unto them which have ears to hear and a mind to learn, that I am come into the world of dense matter that it might be lifted... that it might bring forth greater light, that all the atomic structure of the Earth be lifted, that each and every being within the physical realm might be quickened and restored unto their original estate,

Now ye which hold within thine hand these mine words shall ponder them well, and ye shall do that which the law requires of thee. Ye shall have no malice within thine heart, no false concept of me, and ye shall be as ones assisted in thine quest for knowledge. There is a mighty host sent forth to assist thee, and they are well prepared, for they have been prepared for many long eons of time. They have waited this day when they might step forth and make known themself, for they have within their hand the power to bring unto thee great light such as thou hast not known. I say unto thee, fear not, for thou art Sons of God, and He hast not forsaken thee. Ask of Him comprehension, knowing that ye shall receive.

It is now come when great shall be the revelation unto man, of man and the wonders of heaven. I say unto thee, the wonders of heaven shall no longer mystify thee, for the Father hast willed that thou taketh upon thineself the whole armor of God and arise above the animal state. And know ye this... that thou art divine in thine origin, and thou art the Sons of God which hast fallen asleep within the world of darkness and gross matter.

I say unto thee, thou shall become alert and ye shall arise from thine sleep and walk upright. No longer shall the Earth hold thee in bondage. No longer shall she give unto the laggards footing. No longer shall the forces of darkness hold the Sons of God bound, for I say unto them, thine time is now come when thou shall be freed from bondage.

While I say unto thee, "First seek ye the kingdom and all things shall be added", I too say that ye shall not run hither and yon seeking after saints, prophets, seers, and the wonders of their making. Ye shall stand steadfast upon the Rock which I AM. Ye shall dispatch thine duties with love and gladness, and ye shall not run away into hiding. Ye shall know that ye are servants of God the Father, and know ye that I am the Lord God sent that ye be found and prepared, for it is so.

The Gift of Free Will

... Now it is come when each and every one shall choose his course. He either chooses the hard and dangerous way of darkness, or the sure and safe way of light, in which I abide. Thus I am prepared to bring everyone which gives unto me his hand willingly. I ask nothing except obedience unto the Law of the One. I have spoken of this Law... simple it is, and often overlooked.

I am sent of the Father, and as the Father hast sent thee forth with the precious gift of Free Will, I pay homage unto each one, for I know ye to be an Eternal Living Soul which hast slept a deep sleep. I am come to awaken thee unto thine true identity, thine true estate. My word I have given freely. My Love is consuming when accepted. In it ye are protected from all harm, and nothing of darkness shall overtake thee.

This is mine word that ye might come to understand mine intent, that all might be prepared to share in the great joy of the New Day. So be it and Selah...

A TIME-TABLE OF CHANGES

Within this newsletter we have tried to take a closer look at the foundation of what Sananda has been trying to get us all to see, through both Sister Thedra's work and through other sources of Light. Within the Scripts we are told that great changes will come about within the world of Man, and are told that when these changes begin they will come about in rapid succession. In this newsletter we have tried to understand the magnitude and the purpose for these events, as well as the "time-table" of their unfoldment, that we all might begin to see that the time is indeed growing short.

Flyers

Many people write to ask about flyers that they can put up on bulletin boards in bookstores, Health Food Stores, Light Centers, etc., to let others know about the work of A.S.S.K. While Sananda has often said that we are not to force this material on anyone, he has also said that it is the responsibility of each one of us to share this information with those around us who might be searching for greater understanding.

The Universe of Matter

This newsletter is the seventh in a series which began with issue #70. Within these newsletters we have tried to look beyond all of the information and concepts, to begin to see the Living Light behind our own existence, the foundation of our lives as living spirits here upon the earth. We have tried to take what has been said through the clearest sources of Light and Truth, and to begin to understand the underlying truth of the spiritual awakening process.

While many people sense that a great change is taking place, most do not yet realize the magnitude of what is truly taking place. While many of us view it within the context of our own lives, if we are to understand the magnitude of this change we need to look beyond our own lives, beyond the context of our own personality, and begin to awaken to the greater reality wherein we ALL exist.

There is an excerpt within 'The Golden Scripts" which says: *The awakening is not for those who simply stir within their beds mumbling "The dawn is come"... it is for those who sit up and begin to open their sleepy eyes.* Our spiritual awakening entails more than just speaking about it while waiting for Sananda to bring it about... it entails looking within our own spirits to the source of our own lives, awakening to the Living Light which we already ARE, and accepting the responsibility for our own awakening. If we truly wish to awaken to greater Light we must first come to realize that our own Living spirits already ARE that Light. Too often when we think of our own divine spirit we image ourselves as a glorified human ego, but we are far, far more than that. To begin awakening our own Divine spirit we must look beyond all wishful thinking, we must look beyond all self-image, and begin awakening to that which we truly ARE.

Too often we think of our embodiment here in flesh as the limitation which keeps us from knowing greater Light, when for the most part it is the contentment of our own sleeping spirit which continues to limit our spiritual perceptions. Consider the following selected excerpts from "The Third Millennium":

... Aeons ago, before there was physical matter, you were one with us. Your essence remains, even now, indistinguishable from the unified field of being out of which we all flow. In Oneness with the Eternal Source of light and love we lived together in the early ages of the morning.

.... The movement of your system now brings this star system into a new region of space. You stationed us here, Angels of the Primal Coherence, to remind you to awaken. "Lest in sleeping, I forget", you said. "Lest in dreaming I become lost in the wonders of time."

... You knew us once, O human ones, for the flicker of a millennium or two when you first left us to dress yourselves in human form and forget your spirit dreams.

... You realized when you initiated this human project that the forces of materialization would play some role in developing the values of

your incarnating spirits, but just how extensive a role was difficult to estimate.

... And so you chose to sleep for a while, allowing the materializing influences to flow freely in and around your developing (human) species. But while your sleep itself was intended, the excessive dominance of materiality during humankind's development was not.

* end excerpt *

We have all experienced the illusions of our own nightly dreams, both joyful and disturbing, wherein our minds and emotions perceived the dream to BE reality. We identified ourselves so completely with our experience within the dream that we never stopped to question the validity of our perceptions. We identified ourselves so completely with our experience within the dream that we completely forgot about the greater reality behind the dream. It was only when we finally awoke that we remembered the greater reality wherein we were dreaming our dreams... and we also came to see that we were never "within" the dream... the dream was "within us", an illusion which existed only within our own mind.

Within that very same context, our own living spirits have slept behind our experiences here in flesh. While the flesh IS real, it is only the form we occupy, it is not who we ARE. Our Living spirits have their true existence within the Living Light of the Eternal Creation, but we have forgotten the greater reality and have come to identify ourselves completely with our experiences here in flesh. We are the LIVING SPIRITS who are asleep behind this experience, and the Greater Reality is now calling us to awaken from our dreams in flesh, to awaken to the greater reality, to the very Source of our eternal spirits.

From the previous excerpts we begin to realize that long ago our Living spirits once dwelled within the Oneness of the Eternal Creation. Within the Scripts recorded by Sister Thedra, Sananda has often said that Man, of his own free will, chose to come into flesh. But while we may have chosen to take embodiment within physical forms, it was never intended that we forget our true identity and come to identify ourselves completely with the forms.

Our spirits chose to sleep for a time while we underwent our human development, wherein we would gain an understanding and first hand knowledge of these planes of matter. It was understood that when the development of the Human species was complete our Living spirit would reawaken to their Oneness within the Eternal Source, and for the first time fully conscious spirits, Living Sons of the Father, would become incarnate within biological form. Man was to be a Living expression of the Father, His hands and feet WITHIN the universe of matter, to oversee and guide this biological creation towards the magnificence of its infinite potential.

The following excerpt is from "Star Guests":

... Man was divine from the beginning, an emanation of the Father, knowing both good and evil yet sustaining from creating that which had no loving purpose. He was to gain knowledge of flesh that he might harken to the cries of flesh on future planets under his care. Man would eventually rule, each in his own right, over planets not yet born. He was to know the Power of Creative Thought, and was to be as the Father in lesser mold.

* end excerpt *

Too often we think of the Universe of Matter as being far removed from the things of Spirit, but it is only the thoughts and actions of Man that are lacking in Spirit. The universe of Matter was brought forth and is sustained by the very same Light which sustains ALL Creation, and it has a far greater purpose than we allow ourselves to realize.

Recently NASA used the Hubble Space Telescope to take the first "deep space" photograph ever taken, which can be viewed on the internet (http://www.nasa.gov/) The idea was to select a specific point within the heavens wherein they believed no known stars or galaxies to exist. The telescope was set to look as far out into deep space as possible over a 10 day period to gather as much distant light as possible.

Within the photograph of this supposed tiny empty region of deep space astronomers were astonished to find over 1500 spiraling Galaxies of every conceivable color and shape. Each of these Galaxies is estimated to contain a hundred billion stars. It is worth the effort to view this photograph, for in seeing it one cannot help but to realize the awesome grandeur of this Universe of matter.

Realize that within the vast Eternal expression of Creation, this Universe of Matter is a relatively new creation in its first 20 billion years. While there are trillions upon trillions of living spirits who know life and who serve the Father's great plan within the vast planes of Light and spirit, yet Man is the only Order to incarnate in biological form. His embodiment here did not come about by accident, nor was it meant to be as a punishment. I think the following selected excerpts from "The Third Millennium" will instill within us a greater appreciation for the earth as well as the whole of this vastly beautiful Universe of Matter:

Excerpts from the Third Millennium

... Twenty billion years of unfoldment leave this universe yet in its early stages. It is still a realm of vast extremes, of frozen worlds of rigid matter contrasting the awesome heat of stars. What biology there is appears only as a slight and nearly indistinguishable film on the surface of but a few worlds, yet in that biological film lies the future. It is a relatively new substance, biology. Its day has only now begun to dawn.

... Each of the fiery stars is a seed, each with inherent designs yet to be released, as distinct from what stars are today as the oak is distinct from the acorn. Through you (incarnate spirits) the potential of this implicit creation will one day dance to life. New beings, new creatures will appear among the fields of what is now still formless space, to share with us the joys of universal exploration.

... The movement of your system now brings this star system into a new region of space. You stationed us here, Angels of the Primal Coherence, to remind you to awaken. "Lest in sleeping I forget", you said. "Lest in dreaming I become lost in the wonders of time." In this quarter century, your dream produces its harvest. The bridge between Creator and Creation appears.

... From the center of each galaxy intelligence flows outward to each star and multiplies again. From the center of your own sun star (see NL#74) it now flows to the earth's nearly activated planetary nervous system.

... But perhaps you sense it now, perhaps you already feel the awakening. We address you now upon the frequencies of your essence, to remind you, to help you recall.

... To you it must seem long ago, the time before your embarkation, before you journeyed through the fields of matter to surface upon this world. But to us the hour is early still, and much will change before our morning has passed. You left us with instructions to bring you this record when the dawn was full.

... Come gather around this conscious fire, peoples of the earth, and listen to the spirits of the stars. We would tell you of the early hours when your thoughts first came to rest upon this world, when your love first illumined this world, days when we were with you yet, back when the world was young.

... Eons ago, before there was physical matter, you were one with us. Your essence remains, even now, indistinguishable from the unified field of Being out of which we all flow. In Oneness with the Eternal Source of light and love we lived together in the early ages of the morning. Together we shared a common "I" within the landscape of our eternal home.

... You and those of your Light Circle long ago chose to spearhead the Eternal One's exploration and development of the material Universe. There are some of you, having now achieved partial memory, who conclude that the descent into biological form would not have occurred had it not been for (the fall), yet this is not the case. Incarnation into biological form was intended from the beginning. Your fall from awareness of your eternal nature into the illusion of separation was not a single event, it was a gradual and a very subtle process.

... Your fall into fearful thought and nonfluid patterns of identity was not mere happenstance. An influence encouraged you in this direction, encouraged you to identify with an exclusive sense of separate self. With the exception of the Luminous Principalities, those angels who were the first to incarnate humanly, virtually all members of your race fell under the spell of this influence during their journeys into biological form. We call this influence the materializing influence, or when speaking in the plural, the forces of materialization.

... You realized when you initiated this human project that the forces of materialization would play some role in developing the values of your incarnating spirits, but just how extensive a role was difficult to estimate.

... And so you chose to sleep for a while, allowing the materializing influences to flow freely in and around the developing species. But while your sleep itself was intended, the excessive dominance of materiality during humankind's development was not.

... This influence is personified, as are all qualities and influences in this potent universe. Yet stereotypical images of Satan have prevented many people from understanding the real nature of the materializing principle.

... Though it can take many forms, in human consciousness the materializing influence appears primarily as a pattern of convoluted logic that encourages fear-centered thought rather than Love, and can lead to self-destructive behavior. This influence is being driven out of human consciousness by the intensifying energy field generated as the collective awakening proceeds.

... Your challenge now is to awaken from the spell of matter while still retaining your identity with the human forms you have gathered about you during your descent into this physical world. Our legions are here to encourage and support you. We remember your instructions from the moment before you scattered into the seeds of humanity. Even as we watched your many individuations drifting downward in the spiral dances of gathering structure, your words rang in our ears; "Wake me", you said, "that I might arise in the forms that emerge at this journey's end, and through them bestow my gifts upon this world... that together we might work to magnify the beauty and the wonder of these physical domains."

* end excerpts *

As we begin to put this all together, we see that aeons ago our spirits once knew the fullness of Life within the high planes of Light and Spirit. We knew our own Oneness as Eternal spirits. We were fully conscious spirits, at ONE with the Eternal Source of Creation. We, as Man, chose to leave that Oneness for a specific purpose. We were to spearhead the exploration and development of the material Universe, to begin to incarnate as Living spirits into this biological creation. Man was to become a uniquely new creature, which was to be at once both Spirit and matter. He was to become a Living spirit incarnate within biological form. Man was to bridge the span between the vast Planes of Spirit and the Universe of dense Matter, wherein he would oversee and guide this biological Creation within its unfoldment. It was here, during Man's development within biological form, that his Fall occurred.

The following are selected excerpts from "Star Guests":

... *"Know that since time was, Man hath been created. That is to say, man hath his existence within Thought Incarnate, or Holy Spirit. Man had no beginning and shall have no ending except that he chooseth it himself. Man hath made his own destiny, aeon unto aeon. He hath had his planetary habitation shown unto him, and verily hath he either ennobled it or defiled it.*

... Know that he did bring with him to earth certain propensities of Spirit towards Godlike manifestation, He was placed upon the earth to witness certain events of creation, and with this knowledge he was to rise higher than angles in systems of creation. He was to be given promise of such induction into honorable godhood. He was conscious

that he had such divinity, but he lacked, most of all, patience. His wisdom became his plaything. He broke his covenant with the Father and tried to be god too soon, before his education was completed.

... Man tried to embrace the opportunity to make himself god of earth-creation without awaiting the proper experience, thus he did fill the earth with Thought-Forms (physical forms brought forth through the Power of Creative Thought).

... While they (Man) were not exactly vicious in what they conceived to be the occupancy of these forms for their own purpose, those changes came gradually in their thought concepts. They saw what could be created by the Power of Thought and experimented to see how far their own experiences in manifesting organisms could carry them. But soon they were plunging into sensuous enjoyments and naught else. Sensuous enjoyments occupied all their "thought time", to the exclusion of spiritual educatings. They "forgot themselves", we might put it. They forgot who they were (Living Spirits) and for what creative and constructive purposes they had first sought the earth.

... "It has been many ages since the spirits that have since become known as men arrived upon this earth plane and engaged in creative mischief with the spirit particles developing here, imbedding qualities into their composition that were never intended to disclose here.

... Long ago it was decreed that man should meet with mishap. That is to say, the forces of ignorance and mischief often called "evil" had gained such ascendancy over the race that Man was losing his identity. Bestialities and abominations, the crossing of immortal man's spirits with gross animal forms were producing a race of hybrids so terrible that something had to be done about it. Thought Forms (created by Man) were crossing with evolutionary form (animal forms): animals and men were becoming interchangeable. The whole sum and substance of life on earth was a colossal abortion, serving no practical purpose, celestial or mundane... and the work of cleansing mankind was well-nigh imponderable of execution.

* End Excerpt *

In reading the above excerpts to begin to see that Man, as divine spirits, once possessed the Power of Thought Creation, the ability to create by Thought. As a conscious spirit Man chose to begin incarnating into physical form. His spirit chose to descend downward into matter, ever lowering his vibration to conform with that of the ever denser planes of Matter, until his own vibration was the same as that of the primordial earth. As Man descended downward into matter he made a conscious choice to allow his divine spirit to sleep for a time, "*allowing the materializing influence to flow freely in and around the developing (human) species*", allowing his human nature time to develop a sense of individuality in its relationship with Matter. It was apparently here that the fall Occurred... yet it was not so much a fall from his true nature, as a fall into human forgetfulness of his true nature.

It would seem that during Man's development his human nature took on a mind and a will of its own. Man became so over-identified with his experiences within physical forms that he forgot about his own divine spirit. Instead of awaiting the awakening of his own Divine spirit, instead of becoming as a species prepared to embody his divine spirit, his human nature became impatient and tried to claim his godhood without awaiting his awakening.

As Man experimented with his own creation he not only brought forth forms for his own occupation, but he crossed them with the animal forms indigenous to the earth, creating abominations both human and animal, "*serving no practical purpose, celestial or mundane*". To bring a stop to his abomination and to bring order out of this chaos a new cycle was begun, wherein Man was to lose all memory of his former knowledge. The earth would be cleansed of all the abominations (both human and animal), and man would begin this new cycle clean within the Ape form, the forms of early Man as Neanderthal (see NL#71). Though Man had no memory of his past, the darkness and selfishness which now filled his heart continued to motivate his thoughts and actions... and these once-divine spirits who had come to over-see and to uplift the whole of the Father's biological Creation, instead became its destroyers. These once conscious spirits who once dwelled within the Oneness of the Eternal Creation had reduced themselves to beasts who fought and killed each other over scraps of gold and dusty tracts of land called kingdoms, embodiment after embodiment, century upon century, millennia upon millennia.

While many have used this long cycle to slowly reawaken their true nature, slowly incorporating it into their lives, embodiment after embodiment... there are also those who have continued to embrace the darkness for their own ends... therefore, with the closing of this cycle there must now be a sifting and sorting, each as they have chosen for themselves. With the closing of this cycle it would seem that the spiritual awakening which was intended for Man aeons ago is only now coming about, yet it can only come about within those spirits who chose to look up and once again embrace the Greater Light of their true Being. Yet remember too: *The awakening is not for those who simply stir within their beds mumbling "The dawn is come"... it is for those who sit up and begin to open their sleepy eyes.*

The following excerpt is from the book "Star Guests", given by the Christ spirit:

... I am come to you in that I want you to know that I am He who instructeth you for reasons of Loving consideration for your identities. I am He who was sent unto man for a purpose. I am He who was instrumental in saving man from extinction as men (hu-man), causing them to return unto the Father in ways of thought.

Know ye that thousands upon thousands of years ago came two vast catastrophes... one was the flooding of all abominate parts of the earth, the other was the fiery: destruction of those parts of the earth not affected by that flood. The species that thus survived Here purified. By flood and fire were the abominable forms destroyed, and man was left clean in the Ape form, which he has since pursued (see newsletter # 71 concerning the forms of early Man).

Know that I did make representations unto the Heavenly Host that I would come to the earth to aid man to regain his lost angelic status over tremendous periods of time. Know that I offered my life as mortal, not once but many times. Know that in form on for have I come and gone in matter since the days of the Great Purification. As Spirit made manifest for the purposes of divine instruction have I come and gone in the races of the ape man. See je thus how the Plan came about.

Men (before the cleansing) were practitioners of whoredoms, they were consorts of beasts, they had filled the earth with abominations being neither man nor beasts. The cleansing time came, the species were made sterile unto all but themselves, and the knowledge of "Thought-Creation" was taken from man. Man as man was never brutish by divine intent. Man was created angel in potential power and privilege. His sojourn on this solar planet was meant in the beginning to be brief. He was to know the ordeal of pain and endurance that he might return to the Host wise because of his experience.

Know that he did bring with him to earth certain propensities of spirit towards Godlike manifestation. He did know of those attributes and was glad to be thus conscious. He was placed upon the earth as a volatile spirit to witness certain events of creation, and with his knowledge of pleasure-pain he was to rise higher than angles in systems of creation. He was to be given promise of such induction into honorable godhood. He was conscious that he had such divinity, but he lacked, most of all, patience. His wisdom became his plaything. He broke his covenant with the Father and tried to be god too soon, before his education was completed.

While the Father was not vengeance-given, in His heart He was grieved for He had planned much good for man. He did not war on impatient man for making mischief with his premature powers of wisdom, He only rebuked man with colossal catastrophe, and handicapped him from making further mischiefs by taking away his former knowledge.

... Man as "Man" had deteriorated so far that only through untold millennia and much instruction could lie win back his former standard of intelligence. He began reincarnating in the form which the Host itself had employed (created)... a sort of sublimated Ape, or physical man as you know him today... slowly working his way up through the aeons...

... the essential part of the plan was this: Man has inherent in his spiritual nature much of his lost heritage, but is forbidden by Thought Forces superior to him to use it until he has reached that time when he is so spiritually balanced that he will never again employ his knowledge selfishly or malevolently.

- end excerpt –

This long cycle which is now drawing to a close has given each of the spirit who have fallen the opportunity to once again reclaim their own birthright. This great plan for Man's redemption was brought forth by and through the unconditional Love of the First Born Son of the Father, who we have come to know as the Christ Spirit. This one who took embodiment 2000 years ago as Jesus, and who we now know as Sananda, has watched and guided Man throughout his long ordeal from darkness into Light. The following communique by the Christ Spirit is taken from "Star Guests":

... "We gather as agreed; the day is well. spent. Now my dear ones, let me make lengthy speech with you. Ye have come far with me... I have come further with you. Know that I so loved the world that I gave it my life. My life was the price paid for man's redemption.

Man was doomed to extinction as "Man" many ages ago. His thoughts were of darkness; he loved the darkness; his animal perversions had blotted out his divinity. The plan had not been successful for him as a Creation of method and order. He had despoiled his own house; the evil which he had done was an abomination. He made antics of the Father's beneficence. He had made riot in holy places. His (man's) whole creation was a misanthropy.

Know that I did pity him for his dumbness and impatience. Know that I did give up residence on Higher and Farther Planes to be close to the material earth to try and bring order from his chaos. Know that I so loved suffering mankind that I did enter into a compact: I OFFERED THE FATHER MY OWN LIFE IN EXCHANGE FOR THE LIVES OF THE WORLD. My life was not desired of the Father, but He was so touched by my sacrifice of higher, greater, and vaster joys of eternity, that He gave me the earth-plane upon a condition; I was to come into the world as a humble unknown. I was to live as one of those whose ordeal was an abomination. I was to know pain and suffering and physical death, but I was likewise to know Resurrection for a purpose... that the world might thereby take to heart the example of my life and have it ever before it an ideal of permanent divinity.

I came into the world to save it from literal, physical extinction. There would have been a heavenly holocaust. Stars would have fused. Mankind would have perished as a created Order. There would have been no world as men know the world.

Man was not to know that I had bought them thus for the price of an ideal. They were to think me human, and they were to be shown what human creation could accomplish. I gave them example until my thirtieth year, then came the Father's angles to me and we did sit upon à mountain top and discuss mankind. I did come down from that mountain with the determination within me to save humankind even at the cost of physical death, hoping to show man thereby that even death of the body can be conquered by faith.

So they killed me. They did spit upon me and revile me. They did make mock of heaven and of orderly Love. Well knew I that they might do such things. Well knew I that I was as a sheep among wolves. Well knew I that I had volunteered for a mission of ignominy that I might hoist a banner of hope amongst the ranks of the doomed. Appraise ye the sad results...

I came into this world and it received me not. I did open the eyes of those who were blind, and lo they saw me not. Gave I the Water of Life to the perishing, and they did make sport of my generosity. The beast lingered within them. They stayed unclean, yet did I persevere, for I knew there was a spark of divinity in the hearts of beastial man, and I would save it. I knew that sooner or later men might come to see that their Order of Creation (Man as Hu-Man) might be brought back to the Father, whom I serve as Son.

Waxed I industrious in my ministrations. Gave I freely of time and effort, persevering in compassion though they stoned me and reviled me and made mock of me. Yet did I triumph over death and come back as Witness of the lost idealism. The world was slow to acknowledge me, yet acknowledge me it did. In that acknowledgement were the hands of my devoted disciples, the people of the Goodly Company who have returned with me to the earth again and again, times beyond count, seeking to turn men's hearts and faces in the upward way.

Yea, and even ye were on earth time and time again. Yea, did ye work and preach and reveal. Yea, did ye die even as I died that men might know the Love that I brought them from far, far planes. Yea, did ye preach me in scores of guises, generation upon generation, until ye be yourselves in the present, seeking and working in My world to turn men's hearts to the Higher Way. Verily I honor you for such service.

The world maketh progress towards the Father, yet it is ever retarded by the sons of darkness (those spirits who have embraced the darkness for their own ends). They are workers of iniquity in that they love iniquity. The beast hath left its mark upon them, and generation unto generation it showeth its fangs.

They who have been of good report have suffered cruelly because of those who have clung to the darkness. They who grew to love me and keep my commandments of loving service were reviled and slain by these workers of iniquity. Sorely, sorely, hath my patience been tried. Sorely have I doubted if my work and sacrifice were worthy of the time and pain. Sorely have I been tempted to let the holocaust appear and go unto my Father in the apex of Spirit Creation and there abide. Yet ever have I been touched by the sight of the cowering, they who would walk upright if they but had no fear. Ever have I beheld the humble lift up their hearts to enlightenment. These have made me rejoice. These have caused me to be of faith that down far generations the world might be entirely cleansed of the mark of the beast. So was it thus... so it will be.

Man has shown willingness unto redemption. He hath shown less and less of the brute in his heart. Verily hath he made progress up from the darkness, yet still have we seen the Beast stalking. With the Angelic in man it conflicteth continually. Today have I been with Thought Incarnate, the Principle behind Created Matter. There have I seen mysteries too great for mortal mind to grasp. There ye were once, my greatly beloved, but ye now have earthly brains intervening in the exposition thereof. I tell you I have given account to the Father of the work I have done upon this planet. His word is: "Well done beloved, continue thou in grace".

The world little suspects how slender is the thread on which hangeth its perpetuation. If I but gave the word, lo the heavens would shower down fire, the continents would tremble, and a night of inky blackness would fall upon the cinder of a once-world that would eventually fuse with other nomad planets and form a flashing nebula far out into empty space.

BUT I GAVE NOT SUCH WORD! I keep within the hollow of my pierced hand the safety of this planet. I tend and watch it.

Daily I see the life of the nations. I watch pranking statesman make mock of our labors over many generations and I rebuke them not, knowing that if there be but a spark of Light within them it will one day redeem them. I too watch the humble rise to affluence and give a good accounting of their talents, and I am encouraged. So be it.

We are of one substance (Light). We are of one flesh to save the humble seekers of Truth from the mark of the beast. We come to save the humble and the worthy, to take them upward to the Father. Our work goeth in progressive stages. One by one do we eliminate social cancers. One by one do we despoil the idols of Mammon and tear apart the al- tars of convenience for nefarious ends. One by one do we eliminate the princes of evil from their petty thrones, raising up potentates under us who are of the Goodly Company. Now mark this beloved:

I AM COMING BACK TO THE EARTH PLANE IN PERSON! I have said it before, I say it again. Sufficient do I consider the number of progressing ones to encourage them by demonstration of power and personal appearance. They will hear of my living presence and leap for joy. Others (spirits who have become dark and vicious) who are doomed to the Great Extinction, will be angered and vindictive and revengeful, crying: "What have we to do with thee, thou Son of Light?"

Take heart my beloved, be bright of countenance. This day have I communed with the Spirit behind All Creation and heard the pronouncement: "So Be It". The world is redeemed I tell you, by the sacrifice of your own spirits. Blessed be your names!

Spirit Divine am I... Spirit Divine are Ye! Spirit Divine we manifest in flesh. Spirits ennobled do we go before the Host and give accounting of our trust. Lo, the world is made to see the Father's works manifest in us, and we shall be its saviors.

* end excerpt *

In reading the above message we begin to glimpse the magnitude of the drama being played out here upon the earth. Each of us are playing a part within this great drama, and we are now within the closing act upon the earth.

Too often we assume that the spiritual awakening process simply means freeing our spirits from the bondage of flesh to go into the planes of spirit, but where do you think you were before you took this present embodiment? If our highest good was to dwell within the ease of the planes of spirit we would not have left the planes to come into embodiment. We have each taken embodiment at this time for a very good reason, and it was more than just to read a few spiritual books and then proclaim ourselves "Ready to make our ascension". We are here to PARTICIPATE. We are here to awaken our own living spirits to our Oneness within the Greater Reality, and then to anchor and spread that Light here upon the earth. We often speak of selfless service, yet selfless service entails more than just catching the fastest train out of town and leaving the work for others to do.

As this long cycle now draws to a close, tremendous effort is being put forth to try and awaken a world, who for the most part, would rather sleep on within the ignorance and darkness of the past than to awaken to the bright new dawn. Those who profess to be Light "workers" need to be willing to put forth the effort where it is needed the most... and nowhere in all of Creation is there a greater need for Light and selfless service than here upon the earth during the time of this great transition.

Each one of us within embodiment are playing a part within this great drama, and when all is said and done each will have written their own page within this chapter of the Book of Life. If we profess to be light "workers" then we must be willing to do more than just focus upon self-centered spiritualism... we must be willing to awaken that Light within our own spirits, and to hold that Light for those who are still struggling within the dark. Light workers are known, not by what they claim they are, but by their selfless actions... and it is by and through such selfless service that each one EARNS their eternal freedom and passport into the higher dimensions of Life.

The following excerpt is from "Star Guests":

... Be consoled in this: You live in a world of profit and purpose, and whosoever tells you otherwise is an enemy of your spirits. You are alive upon earth to work out a program, and you each know profit as you live it.

... Came I into this world to restore the dignity and wisdom which was lost. Came we to restore man to the consciousness of their true relationship with us. Thus hath the plan worked out. Over and over have I visited the world in physical manifestation, and over and over have I been helped and interpreted by you, my servants. Over and over have we raised up patterns for men to live by and profit by in their ideals, that they might one day regain their surrendered godhood.

Know that ye have been my disciples and servants since time was. Over and over have we conspired together to lift man up from his bestiality and return him once again to clean spirit, fit to ascend to form reunion with the Father. I am Spirit manifest by Love, seeking my lost spiritual sheep to herd them back into the fold of my Father, making man to regain his lost estate... as spirits fit to reign over a hundred thousand million worlds that have not yet taken form...

Know that I have seen our work progress faintly though steadily. Know that I have guarded well my trust. And now we make the last assault on the final vestiges of the beast in man, making him to lay aside his combativity towards his own species. We are a company, in loving conspiracy to help men be as gods, without the admixture of abomination or change in physical species. We are making the plan succeed by eternal effort, by Love and patience, yet always remembering that man born of woman is prone to darkness, stemming from the uncountable aeons when he suffered himself to abominate.

Know ye that it maketh you as spirits of Christs yourselves that je do aid me in achieving this last redemption within the present. I tell you that it calleth for Christs to live among men in blindness and in darkness, yet always awakening in each life experience to their true identities, making it of moment. Ye have done it before, ye will do it again. Ye are immortal of Soul and spirit, and of loving mission.

Whence think ye cometh your love for humankind? Humankind hath not this love each for the other. Only Christ and his servants have such love. Mankind findeth joy in bargaining and taking profit from his brother... he findeth joy in quarreling for quarreling's sake, for the mark of the beast is still upon him.

... My servants, I say, have ever been sorely tried, as I too have known trials. They have clung to their ideals of Me though great forces have waged unhallowed war against them. Yet have they seen the future from trend of events.

Know that I have heard the cries of my servants' hearts upon a thousand nights as I stood without the doors of spirit awaiting the word of admittance. Know that I have seen the blunders of their childhood with a smile. Know that I have witnessed their errors of young manhood and womanhood with a sigh. Know that I have seen them defenseless early and have thrown about them the blanket of My protection. I have beheld their goodly works from day to day and knew them as my *beloved of old, struggling through the mists to reach my side. Know that even today they are so struggling, but the mists are now but a web of gossamer that shall presently be burned away before the Sun of righteousness.*

Know that I have kept my pact. Know that I have told my Father that we are ready for the mission presently, when we are come into full knowledge and cognizance each of the other. From many lands I call those who are mine. We do journey into sunrise with all Souls of goodly works.

... There is no disposition on the part of the Christ Forces to come unto men and yet not come unto them... to acclaim themselves for that which they ARE and yet do nothing to affect it (mankind) positively. Do you acclaim yourselves as of that wondrous company? If you feel the impulses of the Christ personality bestirring in your breasts, it is the identification of your own divinity. No one is excluded as belonging to that company if you but feel its impulse.

Know that I have drawn strength from my Father, which I sent unto you that your awakening may progress and be presently complete. Ye have been honest in wanting the veil rent asunder, but there have been reasons for it to hang between us for yet a little while. Knowledge cometh swiftly - wisdom groweth hourly. Men are not made to see the Light too quickly lest damage result to that which they call vision.

Ye, my servants, wherever my words find you, have been coming from the darkness of many earthly sojourns. Ye are blinded by the light, yet it the blinding from such Light that amazeth you, not the fact that Light blazeth. We are approaching an era of brilliance when the world shall shine with the Fathers' Glory, and mankind shall be ennobled. We are coming to eternal magnificence I tell you, manifest in physical triumph over the darkness of spirit. Accustom your eyes to the Light, my beloved... I Am its matter and its core.

* end excerpt *

It is often perplexing to understand why, with so much light being focused upon the earth, that there is so much confusion and falsehoods clouding the truth of this awakening. This following excerpt might help us to understand why this outpouring of Light and Truth attracts more than just those who are searching for greater Light. Remember too the many varied spirit planes spoken of within newsletter #73.

The following excerpt from "Star Guests" is given by the Christ spirit:

... I say unto all of you who do my work, no matter where earthly residence findeth you, there cometh a time in your revelations of identity when you know yourselves for the essences je are. Cometh also with such knowledge within your subconscious mind, is a series of vibrations which disclose you (as Light workers) unto the myriads of discarnate, disgruntled, half-developed, or partially dead spirits who do hate the light for that which Light discloseth them to be. They do make tremendous mischiefs, hoping thereby to thwart the missions ye have undertaken. By such a process of thwarting they hope to hold back the development of mankind until they can catch up, or even to reduce man back to the errors of abomination that they may have company in their dilemma.

Ye are not as yet wholly aware of your own powers to counteract such activities. Become aware of your own powers (as Living Spirits) and use them, and the enemy retreateth. But you can also become wearied from much vigilance... these are the times when the enemy plagueth you most, being aware of your mortal weakness.

Your defenselessness in these times, I instruct you, is not dangerous. They are but annoying, for ye do rise above them and stand strong within the consciousness that your revelations are real and that your identities are true as ye perceive. The enemy whispereth that ye are hoaxed, yet in your heart of hearts ye know that ye are not hoaxed. Take no thought of these whisperings I tell you. Know that always the mood doth pass. Know that such revelations are godlike and God-given until that moment when ye do recall our pact by your own memories. I say unto you beloved, that moment cometh swiftly.

Earthly men and woman ye were when the spiritual revelation started... spirit-men and spirit-woman ye became when the revelations had begun. These revelations cometh day unto day and night unto night. Think ye no more of yourselves as earthly, but recall yourselves as angels and ministers treating with, by; and in earthly flesh, within this world which needeth us.

Rest peacefully my dear ones, and think ye of these mysteries that I have expounded...

* end excerpt *

While many of us read spiritual books and follow our own spiritual practices, how many of us look beyond ourselves and allow our hearts to speak directly to the Source of our own existence. How many actually go within their heart of hearts and speak directly to the Father. How many are truly willing to let go of all that we have imaged ourselves to be, and ask that we awaken to that which we ARE.

Consider the following excerpt by Sananda, which was recorded by Sister Thedra:

... "And now it is given unto them which seek Truth to be given these things which shall be unto them their Shield and Buckler within the days ahead. For now I say unto thee, "*Unless ye ask, it shall remain hidden*". And therein is wisdom, for it is the Law that when ye are ready ye ask, and the Father stands ready to supply thy needs.

And so shall ye seek within thine own self for the Light, for light is like unto itself, it attracts more light - and for that have I made myself manifest unto them which have sought me. And as they have sought me their light has expanded, and it has been added unto mine that the whole Earth might become a Sun.

And therein is great revelation, for as Man of Earth is lifted so is the Earth that she might fulfill her mission. And be ye fruitful unto the Father, for He has given thee permission to be within the Earth for the fulfilling of this age... and that is a privilege given unto thee of God the Father.

And it is given unto me to speak unto thee as I have not for the past years of the "Silent period". And the silence shall be broken in all the lands of the Earth, and again I shall walk the byways and the hiways and be as ye. And as ye come into the age of comprehension I shall sit and counsel thee, and I shall teach thee the Precepts of the Father which has sent me unto thee that ye might awaken unto thy own "Sonship" and be as the wayfarer of Satan no more.

And it is indeed wise to ask of The Father that ye might receive me, for in no wise shall I intrude upon thy free will. And yet it is the will of the Father that I bring thee out of darkness; and for that do I wait, that ye may come as ye are called. and by thy own free will. This is for the ones which have as yet not learned the wisdom of saying *"Father, Thy Will be done in me, thru me, by me, and for me"* - for therein is the KEY unto thy leg-irons which have bound thee. Be ye as one which knows wherein ye are bound, and wherein is thy freedom. I shall be unto thee bondsman, and I stand ready to loose thee of thy bondage at thy request. Ye have but to seek the Light which is of the Father.

* end excerpt *

In looking at all that has been said within this newsletter, it might seem that Man has put himself through a great deal of pain and sorrow for no other reason than to learn the lessons of his own willfulness... but nothing within creation is without a greater purpose. The following are selected excerpts from the book "Return of the Bird Tribes":

... Do not be surprised when we, who have roamed among these stars, tell you that you are special, that you are precious, that you are so incredibly loved by the Source of All that IS. Your earth and your Sun are conception points for the new life of worlds yet to come. The attention of the Universe is focused on this earth. The Universal Mother herself is conscious within this very world. The Father of every star now looks through the eyes of this one Sun (remember "Celestial City of The Sun" in newsletter 74). *Your race is about to awaken as the*

circuitry of consciousness, the global intelligence system that will be half star, half material world.

... I will tell you, I who am an Angel of the winged tribes, I have been consciously creating beauty for twenty billion years, and I have never seen at any moment of that time the potential that I see at the close of the 20th Century upon this fair earth. I have seen many spirit beings throughout the stars, intelligent societies on the higher planes of many worlds, but none of these were biologically incarnate. None of these had entered into material dress or come to such intelligent terns with matter. Nowhere have I seen such exquisite sensitive creatures of biology who exhibit your capacity.

You are the first species upon material worlds where the necessary balance is appearing to support this new blend of consciousness, the consciousness that is at once both spiritual and material. No biological species has ever before looked up of its own free will and taken charge of itself as an individual spiritual being.

... O humans of this yet sleeping age, there is so much more. So much more. It is hard to place this awareness within your words, for your words are of only one dimension, of only one meaning at a time, and the Living Reality behind this universe and the things of which we speak are multidimensional.

There are many reasons why your world holds the attention of the universe... your initiative, your capacity, your potential for what you have demonstrated in your hours of vision and nobility are some of them. But your fall, your rebellion is yet another... for you see, when the egos of your warring tribes first ran off into the jungle we knew that we were confronting certain fundamental issues that would have to be faced again and again throughout the far-flung stars. On earth we were confronting these issues on a miniature level, and if we could work it out on this micro level of this earth, if we could use the very value systems of the rebellious one to convince them that every interest that they held vital would be served more effectively through their voluntary cooperation with the spirits of God; and if that lesson could be recorded and imprinted indelibly within the genetic structure of all existing and yet to be created organisms of this new type... well then, do you see? Do you see? The suffering of your human history would be turned to advantage, for it would never have to happen again.

... The angels of conception who are guiding biological development seek ever to minimize suffering, not only your suffering but that of races yet to come. So you see that when your race fell our attention gravitated here. Why allow future worlds to experience warfare, starvation, suffering and depravation born from the human egos' rejection of their own spirits, when one world would do. And if that one world were the source world, the point of conception for all similar future physical forms to come, there would, after the lesson was learned, be a built in genetic immunity to such rebellion in the future.

... You knew us once, O human ones, for the flicker of a millennium or two when you first left us to dress yourselves in human form and forget your spirit dreams. We saw the sparkle in eyes that we recognized. We were patient when your ego-ruled ancestors ran off into the jungle night. We knew that someday your own intelligence and light would lead you to seek contact with us once again. We held the earth carefully and assigned to her the brightest spirits. In this present age our patience is rewarded. There are those of you who at last are looking up to see beyond the microscopic interpretations of your egos.

... Within your lifetime you will witness revelations that will show the foolishness of much of what was once deemed wise. Behaviors that once made sense to creatures who imagined that they were islands of individuality is abandoned by those who experience the interconnectivity of all of life.

... We are the Pattern beings, the Winged Ones, the Light Bearers. We are the Reality of your own perfect spirits, coming now to consciously incarnate in your own human fields. During the long millennia of your unconsciousness we obeyed your instructions. We maintained the precise temperature range that would produce a species, a mingling of both star and planet, an autonomous biological-being of a new and blended kind. The requisite human life forms now cover the earth; their physical forms are completed.

... A three and one-half billion year creative process culminates now in your awakening. The human information Age now explodes in unprecedented comprehension waves. Pulsing comprehension waves flowing into a Solar Age. A Starchild once again rides the crest of Light, once again bathes in Light... is born again in Love.

* end excerpt *

These above excerpts should begin to give us a far greater appreciation not only for the Universe of Matter but for these physical forms which we are presently embodied within. While physical embodiment does impose a great deal of limitation upon our spirits, yet our greatest limitation stems from the contentment of our own spirits to sleep on within the identity of our human nature.

These closing excerpts are taken from both "The Return of The Bird Tribes" and "The Third Millennium":

... This (awakening) has much to yet engulf and utterly change before it has washed fully across the shores of human affairs, yet the greatest effects of this wave will come during the late 1990s and the first decade of the twenty-first century.

... As our present wave of consciousness washes highest upon the shore of this world toward the winter solstice of the year A.D. 2011, a Great Cycle will culminate. The winter solstice of the last year will see the purification completed, and the era of human history brought forever to a close.

... A moment is coming, after which nothing will ever again be thought of as it was before... a metahistorical moment, an event that is simultaneously Alpha and Omega to your species and to all your species has ever known.

... At the moment of quantum awakening, changes will occur rapidly, rippling across the terrestrial surface like a wave. Everything in the earth's gravitational field will be affected in some way. The consciousness that will ultimately emerge will be the consciousness of

the Eternal One, the Creator, the Being of Life, awake and aware for the first time inside the material universe.

... The ultimate purpose of human form is for spirits to share with me in the enjoyment of these dimensional realms, and to assist me in the creation of future life forms, entities both spiritual and biological who will then join us in the ongoing exploration and development of matter.

... Do not think you are unworthy or unprepared for so great a step. In some ways you have always been prepared... in other ways there is not, nor could there be, any preparation. ... Long have I observed you from within, from behind your thoughts and feelings. I know the moment when the odds are in your favor, when the likelihood of your making the choice of eternal life is greatest.

... Now is such a time. You are ready to make the vital decision. You now have all that you need to release the conditioning of history and to ride the ascending wave of consciousness beyond the spell of matter, into an awakened life.

... It may be that we will wrestle together with your past, yet there is no need to examine what you have been, no need to overly analyze that which must change and fall away. I am content to let it go if you are... but the choice must be yours.

... I have waited for you yesterday, I will wait for you again tomorrow if there is need. But the wave of which I speak rides upon a tide that spans only a few circlings of your world around this star, and some of those circlings have already passed.

... The coming turn of the millennium will begin the final decade of my awakening into the collective human consciousness. It will be the last decade of a process that has taken many centuries. It will be a time of great change, during which a large percentage of humankind will choose to enter this stream of consciousness, leaving forever the realms of history.

... The stream of consciousness of which I speak is the river of my Eternal Life. It is the dividing line between the subconscious realms where creatures know not their origins in God, and the conscious realms wherein all creatures know that they are projections of one unified field of Being, co-creators individually focusing a shared field of awareness.

... For those who choose to remain within the subconscious realms this choosing will not be final, but for most of them much time will pass before they choose again. They will experience an age of further history, (within another place) much like the history that humans have experienced in the past... as they gradually wind their way through the same learning process that now find the majority of you ready to migrate beyond the shadows of illusion to the conscious shores...

www.ingramcontent.com/pod-product-compliance
Lightning Source LLC
LaVergne TN
LVHW051515070426
835507LV00023B/3126